All of Baba's Children

"For a work of non-fiction to become a classic means that it has made a significant contribution to a particular culture by creating a breakthrough in its consciousness and by heralding a new stage in its evolution. *All of Baba's Children* achieved this by its vibrant, radical, and revisionist perspective on multiculturalism.... *All of Baba's Children* has become a manifesto that has yet to be surpassed." — George Melnyk

———

The Doomed Bridegroom

"Kostash has invented a rich literary genre: the erotic-political memoir. With grace, intelligence, knowledge and humour, Kostash leads us through her romantic odyssey, a voyage that records her own sentimental education, but also major events of this waning century's political history." — Alberto Manguel, *The Globe and Mail*

———

No Kidding: Inside the Life of Teenage Girls

"Kostash writes with a poetic grace that vividly captures the look, feel, and smell of her subjects... the book goes beyond the numbers to bring its young women to life. *No Kidding* should join Dr Spock on every parent's bookshelf." — *Maclean's*

GHOSTS IN A PHOTOGRAPH

Ghosts in a Photo graph

A CHRONICLE

Myrna Kostash

NeWest Press

Library and Archives Canada Cataloguing in Publication
Title: Ghosts in a photograph : a chronicle / Myrna Kostash.
Names: Kostash, Myrna, author.
Identifiers: Canadiana (print) 20220131473 | Canadiana (ebook) 20220131538 | ISBN 9781774390573 (softcover) | ISBN 9781774390580 (EPUB)
Subjects: LCSH: Kostash, Myrna. | LCSH: Kostash, Myrna—Family. | LCSH: Ukrainians—Alberta—Biography. | LCSH: Authors, Canadian—20th century—Biography. | LCSH: Alberta—Biography. | CSH: Authors, Canadian (English)—20th century—Biography.
Classification: LCC FC3700.U5 K67 2022 | DDC 971.23/00491791—dc23

NeWest Press wishes to acknowledge that the land on which we operate is Treaty 6 territory and a traditional meeting ground and home for many Indigenous Peoples, including Cree, Saulteaux, Niitsitapi (Blackfoot), Métis, and Nakota Sioux.

Excerpt from "A Treaty is a Gift" reproduced with the permission of Niigaanwewidam James Sinclair ❡ Excerpt from *Burning in This Midnight Dream* by Louise Bernice Halfe - Sky Dancer, published by Brick Books, reprinted with permission of the author.

Editor for the Press: Smaro Kamboureli
Cover and interior design: Natalie Olsen
Author photo: Markian Lozowchuk, www.itsmarkian.com

NeWest Press acknowledges the support of the Canada Council for the Arts, the Alberta Foundation for the Arts, and the Edmonton Arts Council for support of our publishing program. We acknowledge the financial support of the Government of Canada through the Canada Book Fund for our publishing activities.

#201, 8540-109 Street
Edmonton, Alberta   T6G 1E6
www.newestpress.com

NeWest Press

No bison were harmed in the making of this book.
Printed and bound in Canada   22 23 24 25   5 4 3 2 1

In memory of cherished friend and writer of distinction,
Erna Paris (1938–2022), and writer Brian Fawcett,
brave heart and loyal friend (1944–2022)

CONTENTS

FOREWORD

Eventually we inherit the family photographs. In shoeboxes, frames, pasted, taped or affixed in albums, on cardboard backing or slotted into plastic sleeves. Mine go back as far as maternal Baba Palahna's wedding in Edmonton in 1911 and to early threshing scenes on the paternal Kostash homestead in 1915, then move on through funerals — strangers-to-me in a Galician village, a widow leaning into the coffin for a last kiss, Dido Fred Kostash in his open coffin — and Mum and Dad's courtship and wedding, other weddings, my baby pictures, reunions, again funerals, and so on, until I began to make photo albums of my own.

But it was an incomplete record. My parents each had grandparents, aunts and uncles and cousins of their own, back there in the Old Country. I never asked about them and they never told. They never took out the photographs that may have represented their forebears, and by the time such photographs came into my possession at my parents' deaths, it was too late. I had no idea who those people were. Within a generation the two branches of the family had become strangers to each other, or at least *strange*.

————

At the point of emigration or immigration, a family history splits in two. *Ghosts in a Photograph* is a Canadian granddaughter's account of her grandparents' lives in Canada and the mystery and strangeness of the lives left behind in Galicia, now Ukraine.

Each narrative of my grandparents is assigned a kind of *vita*. There are five of them, the fifth being my mother's stepfather. They all emigrated from villages within shouting distance of each other in Galicia and immigrated into Canada between 1900 and 1910. Their stories, as I received them, began on day one of their settling in Canada.

When I had first thought of the project that has become *Ghosts in a Photograph*, it had been a century since all my grandparents had arrived in Canada. It was also some forty years since the publication in 1978 of my first book, *All of Baba's Children*. That book had been written from the intense curiosity I felt — in the era of official and popular multiculturalism, so enthusiastically embraced by Ukrainian Canadians — about the life experiences of my parents' generation, the first born in Canada. As for the immigrant settler generation represented by my grandparents, they had been reduced to the stultifying pieties of stories of "pioneers" as assembled by grateful descendants in Canada, and dismissed by me as of little interest.

Now, however, informed by my own history, literary and personal, that ranged over issues of feminism, the New Left in Canada and Eastern Europe, the dissident movement of artists and intellectuals in Soviet Ukraine, Slavic roots in Byzantium, narratives of violent Indigenous and settler conflict in Western Canada, I was eager to look again from multiple perspectives at the lives of my grandparents, be they farmers or child-bearers, members of a local intelligentsia or working-class menials, socialists or the pious unlettered.

It all began with a photograph and the revelation (better late than never) that my grandparents, who had all emigrated as adults, had had a life in the villages of Galicia before their momentous leave-taking for Canada. And in those villages their lives had intertwined with family members and relatives of whom I had little or no inkling. An exception was the small family of my maternal Baba with whom she had been corresponding since the early 1960s, but even so there were gaps, sensationally so.

As all these lives in Alberta and in Galicia came into greater focus in the course of my research and I learned of the particular circumstances of each life, I became aware of the feelings they evoked in me, indignation and disbelief as well as empathy and pride. And I was struck by the vastly different outcomes of the two sets of families: my maternal grandparents, who lived in Edmonton, were unskilled, often poor, and sympathizers of the Soviet Union, while my paternal grandparents were well educated (grandfather) and deeply religious (grandmother), and eventually materially secure thanks to their base on a homestead in the Ukrainian bloc settlement area east of Edmonton. I could see that these outcomes had been prefigured well before emigration, in their very different circumstances in Galicia. By marrying, my parents brought both streams into the life of their children, my sister and me, and so I grew up with an appreciation of both ethnic and class solidarity (not that I framed it in such terms as a kid).

The scope of my published work (essays, reviews, anthology contributions, books) has engaged, almost alternately, current social issues of Canada and historical issues arising from those parts of Europe in which I discerned a prior identity to that of the hyphenated ethnic in Alberta. I sense my restlessness as I moved from one project to another, seeking first here at home in Canada and then over there, in what our families always called the Old Country, the stories in which I located myself as a woman writer of Ukrainian heritage in western Canada.

As a nonfiction writer, I was always loathe to make things up, so each of my books involved tremendous amounts of reading, travelling, interviewing, and note-taking, the entire apparatus of nonfiction writing methods before I had written a word of my own.

However, when I began organizing my thoughts about how to tell the life stories of long-dead grandparents, I immediately saw that I had a problem. From the very first indecipherable photograph from the Old Country to the very last reminiscence of my now dead mother Mary, I was left with no living informants except for a sibling and a handful of cousins, all of my generation, for whom the details of our grandparents' lives proved often to be as patchy and unreliable as mine.

I have been forced as a result to make use of a variety of methods and materials to help me understand and tell of lives beyond the writ of fact-checking. These include memorabilia such as newspaper clippings, letters and a hand-drawn map, official documents such as a marriage certificate and immigration cards, photographs from family albums, excerpts from my own published work, a researcher's taped interview with my mother as well as my own memory bank. Invaluable as sources of particulars that relate to my forebears have been my father's unpublished memoir, *A Gift to Last*, and his translation, posthumously published, of the memoir of his uncle, Peter Svarich, *Memoirs 1877–1904*.

Given the fragmentary nature of these source materials, I have also made use of secondary sources such as scholarly publications by archivists, historians, and ethnographers, biographies and autobiographies, reports, conference papers, even novels and poems as well as what I call ephemera — postcards, song lyrics, the memorial book from a funeral — to fill in the gaps where other testimony is missing. (Unless otherwise noted in the Works Cited, all translations from the Ukrainian are my own.) In the narrative that follows, then, my voice echoes different sources and takes different forms — straightforward narration, storytelling, intervention in other people's texts, speculation, second-guessing, and argumentation, often with my own previously published texts. These interventions are signalled in the text often in italicized or indented blocks of narrative, and/or by change of tense. This range of voices has produced what Ben Highmore calls "a new genre of non-fiction: public family history," a hybrid form of nonfiction that is "not history from below so much as history from inside." A public social or historical or political "landscape" is constructed in which figures are "embedded" (Highmore), their particular lives never lost sight of but filled out with details suggestive of a possible, if not probable, life. It is still a family history but one which expands imaginatively to include what is happening around them — a Great Depression, a school system, a labourers' strike, the production of a play, a World War — in order, in the language of photography, to open the lens so that "social groups" larger than the family are brought into view (Edwards 124).

In my family's case, these "social groups" include the Galician relatives of murky identity and the groups — political, pedagogical, military, cultural, and artistic — to which they and their descendants belonged. They assemble as a kind of parallel family history of members left behind by the Kostashes, Svariches, Maksymiuks, and Kosovans in the villages of Tulova and Dzhuriv. In the course of researching family history in Canada, I stumbled upon intriguing, even mystifying, items — several photographs, a packet of letters, and a book — that led me to evidence of the lives of relatives in Ukraine gradually opening up to my scrutiny. The reconstruction of their identities as shoots from the family trees involved a considerable amount of sleuthing, and I think of my pursuit of them as Myrna-on-the-case.

These Galician life stories protected or hidden within family and community in Ukraine and Canada function as illustrations of the chasm that splits open family histories at the point of emigration. I have looked and looked and looked again at family photographs — some a hundred years old — and there are faces of relatives, in Canada and in Ukraine, that I cannot identify.

I am reminded of the necessary evolution of family storytelling across generations and locations (continents!). Members have dispersed from the villages to larger towns in Ukraine or abroad; not only time and distance but also historical events, especially in Eastern Europe and the Soviet Union in the twentieth century, which were beyond the control or desire of my relatives, have severed connections irrevocably. This is where I step in, with the self-assigned creative task of their recovery.

I pick up a photograph, lay an imaginary grid over it, and, starting at the little square in the top left corner, describe what I see, square by square — it could be a wave of a hairdo, a moustache, a string of pearls, the brim of a hat casting a shadow across a face, a hand resting lightly on a vintage carbine — until I pull away and look at the whole photo again. I am now provided "some illusion of continuity over time and space" (Hirsch 1997, xi) that connects me to them and so I can begin to tell their story.

—————

In 1973, while I still lived in Toronto working as a freelance journalist (I would return to Alberta in 1975), the editor of *Saturday Night* magazine, Robert Fulford, asked me to write a review of a new novel by Edmonton-based writer and English professor, Rudy Wiebe, *The Temptation of Big Bear*. I was unfamiliar with Wiebe's work, but by the time I had finished reading *Big Bear* and had begun writing the review, my perspective on the era of the "clearing of the plains" in western Canada had changed utterly.

I recall that reading the novel had moved and even disturbed me, and now, when I reread my review, almost fifty years later, I am struck by the force with which I expressed my disturbance, and the foreshadowing of what I would come to understand and write about myself decades later.

In my review I wrote of the People (Wiebe's name for the Plains Cree of the 1870s and 1880s), of the past we white people shared with them, of "the inglorious advance of our technology across the bony bleached prairie, while they were pressed back into the corners we did not want for ourselves." I wrote of Wiebe's description of the arrival of the railway across the plains, as seen from a Cree point of view, that haunted me for a very long time. Cree hunters on horseback watch from a hill the slow but inexorable progress of the Iron Road. "For the first time," I wrote, "I began to understand how it *felt* to grow homeless, to face the buffalo across the border of the CPR and know they were dying along with you, to watch Medicine Hat go up on the sacred hills, to live cramped and immobile, told to be a farmer on one, small, designated piece of land" (Kostash 1974, 32). And, for the first time, my own heroic antecedents — the "illiterate peasant refugees arriving in the middle of their nowhere and making a go of it — assumed a double edge. I could see the People watching their arrival, sick with their own banishment" (Kostash 1974, 33).

It had never occurred to me that this nation-building, transcontinental event, so celebrated by settler mythologists such as Pierre Berton and Gordon Lightfoot, represented the eventual devastation of an entire culture. For the train would bring the settlers. It would bring *us*. And we would plow the so-called *vil'ni zemli* (free lands) of another people's ancestral homeland and call it ours. As for the terms of Treaty Six, signed in 1876, by which traditional Indigenous territories were ceded to the Crown in exchange for areas known as "reserves" (i.e., protected from encroachment by white settlers), they were never mentioned. As far as we settlers were concerned, the land was a gift of the Crown and her Minister of the Interior, Sir Clifford Sifton. It was received as such, and with a gratitude that swelled in following generations to the proportions of settler mythology.

Galicia and Surrounding Territories, 1900

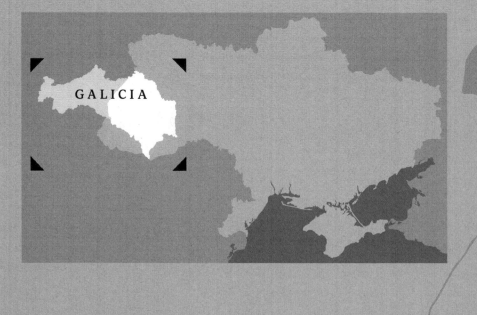

RUSSIAN EMPIRE
(NOW POLAND)

• CRACOW

AUSTRO-HUNGARIAN
EMPIRE

GALICIA

RUSSIAN EMPIRE
(NOW UKRAINE)

now in Poland   now in Ukraine

LVIV •

TERNOPIL •

GALICIA

• IVANO-FRANKIVSK

Eastern Carpathian Mountains

• HORODENKA

KOLOMYIA •   • RUSIV
                    TULOVA
ZABOLOTIV   • • • SNIATYN
ILLINTSI •   VYDYNIV
DZHURIV

IAVORIV •

ROMANIA

NOTES ON DATES
AND PLACE NAMES

1795–1918: Eastern Galicia was the eastern part of Austria-Hungary (also often referred to as the Austro-Hungarian Empire or the Dual Monarchy) in which Ukrainians formed the majority of the population. Bukovyna was the easternmost Crown land of the Austro-Hungarian Empire from 1775 to 1918; it became part of Romania after World War I. Eastern Galicia and Bukovyna were the territories from which emigrants left for western Canada circa 1900. Today's Galicia comprises the *oblasts* (regions) of Ivano-Frankivsk, Lviv, and Ternopil. Bukovyna is currently split between Romania and Ukraine; northern Bukovyna comprises the Chernivtsi Oblast.

Depending on the context, I use Western Ukraine interchangeably with Eastern Galicia. During the German occupation of Ukraine (1941–1944) Western Ukraine comprised Galicia and Volhynia, the region just north of Galicia. I use eastern Galicia and western Ukraine when referring to a location rather than a geopolitical territory.

1872: The Canadian Homestead Act, commonly called the Dominion Lands Act, passed, and remained in use until 1918. It aimed to encourage the settlement of Canada's prairie provinces of Alberta, Saskatchewan, and Manitoba, especially by European, American, and Eastern Canadian settlers. The act also launched the Dominion Lands Survey, which laid the framework for the division of the prairie provinces into one-square-mile sections for agricultural purposes.

1876: Treaty Six was negotiated and signed by Crown represent-atives and Cree, Assiniboine, and Ojibwa leaders at Fort Carlton and Fort Pitt, Saskatchewan. Its boundaries stretch across central portions of present-day Alberta and Saskatchewan, and set aside reserve lands held by the Crown "for the use and benefit of the respective bands for which they were set apart" under treaties or other agreements (McCue).

1885: Completion of the transcontinental Canadian Pacific Railway.

1885: North-West Rebellion, also known as North-West Resistance, an armed insurgency fought March 1885 to November 1885 mainly by Métis militants and their First Nations allies, was the culmina-tion of unsatisfied grievances against the Dominion Lands Survey and broken Treaty agreements. "They sought assurances from Ottawa that the titles to their river-lot homesteads and farms would be guaranteed in advance of any large-scale influx of set-tlers" ("North-West Rebellion").

1896: The first group of settler immigrants from Galicia arrived in Canada, the majority of them settling in Edna, District of Alberta, northeast of Edmonton.

1914–1918: The Great War.

1917: Proclamation of the (Bolshevik) Soviet Republic in Petrograd, Russia.

1917: Central Rada, the revolutionary parliament of Ukraine directed the Ukrainian national movement, 17–21 April.

1919: The collapse of Austria-Hungary, formalized in the Treaty of Saint-Germain-en-Laye, which also acted as a peace treaty.

1921: The Peace of Riga gave all of Galicia to the Polish Republic.

1922–1992: The Ukrainian Soviet Socialist Republic (Ukrainian SSR, UkrSSR) was one of the constituent republics of the USSR until its breakup in 1991; Eastern Galicia/Western Ukraine was annexed in 1945.

1929: Founding of the Organization of Ukrainian Nationalists in Vienna, a radical far-right and ultranationalist Ukrainian political organization.

1932–1933: A man-made famine, also known as the Holodomor ("to kill by starvation") resulted in 2.2 million to 3.5 million deaths in Soviet Ukraine.

1939: By a secret non-aggression treaty between Nazi Germany and the Soviet Union, the two powers partitioned Poland between them. On September 17, 1939, the Soviet Union invaded Poland (Eastern Galicia) from the east, sixteen days after Germany invaded Poland from the west.

1939–1941: On November 15, 1939 the Supreme Soviet in Moscow passed a law making the former eastern Polish territories (Eastern Galicia) a part of the Ukrainian SSR.

June 22, 1941: Germany's Operation Barbarossa began with the invasion of the German Army into the Ukrainian SSR, the Western Ukrainian lands that had been annexed by the Soviets into the Ukrainian SSR. They were now overrun by Germany.

1941–1944: Galicia became incorporated into the General Government, governed by General Governor Hans Frank. The rest of Ukraine was occupied and governed as the Reichskommissariat Ukraine — including Volhynia — by Reichskommissar Erich Koch; or under direct German military occupation; or in parts occupied by Romania and Hungary.

1944: Western Ukraine was reoccupied by the Soviet Union until 1991.

August 1944: Retreat of German army from Western Ukraine.

1942–1956: Ukrainian Insurgent Army, a Ukrainian nationalist paramilitary formation, fought mostly in Eastern Galicia/Western Ukraine. It was under the political leadership of the Organization of Ukrainian Nationalists and military Supreme Commander, Roman Shukhevych (1943–1950).

1948–1949: Collectivization of Western Ukraine, the consolidation of individual land and labour into collective farms called *kolkhoz* (Russian) and *kolhosp* (Ukrainian).

1985–1991: Perestroika (restructuring) and Glasnost (openness), a political movement for reformation within the Communist Party of the Soviet Union.

1988: Canadian Multiculturalism Act was enacted by the Parliament of Canada.

1991: The Act of Declaration of Independence of Ukraine was adopted by the Ukrainian parliament, reestablishing Ukraine's state independence.

2015: Canada's Truth and Reconciliation Commission final report is released.

ABBREVIATIONS

AUAS All-Ukrainian Academy of Science

AUUC Association of United Ukrainian Canadians

BWIU Beet Workers Industrial Union

CPWU Communist Party Western Ukraine

NKVD People's Commissariat for Internal Affairs
(renamed in 1946 MVD Ministry of Internal Affairs)

OUN Organization of Ukrainian Nationalists

ukrSSR Ukrainian Soviet Socialist Republic

ULFTA Ukrainian Labour-Farmer Temple Association

UPA Ukrainian Insurgent Army

VUSPP All-Ukrainian Union of Proletarian Writers

Fedor/Fred Kostash(chuk)
1871–1938

The reluctant homesteader

1992: My father and I are trying to find the farm. They've straightened out the highway, taken down the grain elevators and removed the gas station at Royal Park to make way for highway twinning. With the old landmarks gone, we have lost our way. Eventually a farmer points us in the right direction, and we find the road in. The homestead is now a ruin, the house having burned down long ago (local teenagers, beer cans, firepit) and the pig sheds collapsed into a tumbled heap. The path from the house site to the

barn is thick and treacherous with weeds and the hedge-
row gone wild. The barn, though, is still magnificent. High
and sturdy, faintly red, with the date of its construction —
1917 — still legible under the eaves, and inside, above the
stalls, the names of the horses: Prince, Blackie, Brownie,
the family's early attempt at Anglo-Saxon nomenclature
for beasts. The interior is soundless except for the drone
of flies cruising above the fermented straw.

It is as though I have stumbled upon some archaeological
site and stubbed my toe on the shards of an earlier civiliza-
tion. All is humbled, unregarded, fallen out of significance.
In two generations, this farm has been established, then
mutated and disintegrated. In one generation the materials
of everyday life have become obsolete and unrecognizable.
I am the first in the long descent of generations not to
recognize a spindle, a flail.

ADAPTED FROM MY BOOK,
ALL OF BABA'S CHILDREN (1992, X)

It had never occurred to me that the farm had not always been
there nor that someone had come along from some other place to
build it. And so to be told, as I was, that Baba and Dido had emigrated from the Old Country to Royal Park, that they had broken
sod and harnessed themselves to the plow, that Uncle Harry had
lived in a dugout, that my own father had walked miles to school,
kicking buffalo skulls out of his path, and that after many hardships the family had prospered and produced all the aunts and
uncles, cousins and second cousins of the family reunions on the
farm, was like the recitation of a well-loved folk tale. It was marvel-
lous. But it had all happened in some other, primordial time, having
come to its satisfactory conclusion in our family's secured settlement well before my arrival.

The founding father

Fedor was the Dido I never knew and about whom I remember no stories told. He died before my parents married. I grew up with only two photographs that revealed his features and countenance. One showed him as the already-aged *pater familias* whose six sons' portraits, and a cameo of their one daughter already long married, encircle Fedor's and Baba Anna's own portraits. The second photograph was taken of his open coffin as it was being carried out of the house on the farm on the shoulders of his sons. Much to my chagrin, I have misplaced this photograph, but I remember the impression it left of a man who, as he lay cushioned in funerary satin, looked remarkably similar to his photograph.

––––––––––

I may have never heard him speak, but others speak of and for him.

After my father retired from teaching at age sixty-five, he took up several literary labours the nature of which I was only dimly aware of. He had a study in the basement where he typed industriously at a portable Remington, the desktop littered with bits of correction tape, shredded carbon paper, and lead pencil shavings. Years later, I was tasked with clearing out the cupboards in his study, left undisturbed since his death, and learned, at last, what had preoccupied him: essays on current world politics, especially in the Soviet Union, philosophies of education, the history of the Orthodox Church (this was a surprise), and distillations of the arguments in John Milton's *Paradise Lost*. With a little whispered prayer begging forgiveness, I trashed the lot.

However, for my own shelves I kept the three-volume *An Intellectual and Cultural History of the Western World* by Harry Elmer Barnes, already in 1965 in its third and revised edition. Judging from the underlinings and marginalia, Dad only got through Volume One, *From Earliest Times through the Middle Ages*. He seems to have been greatly taken (as I would be twenty-five years later from other sources) by "Byzantine Learning."

I knew at the time that my father had carried to completion a literary project of another order of magnitude: the translation of the *Spomyny* (*Memoirs*) of Peter Svarich (1877–1966), his uncle and the brother of his mother Anna née Svarich. Svarich had written his memoirs in a smooth and legible Cyrillic script in Ukrainian and handed the manuscript over to the editors of *Ukrainskyi Holos* (*Ukrainian Voice*) newspaper in Winnipeg where they were serialized after his death in 1974 or 1975. In 1976 the entire Ukrainian-language text was published as a book. Intermittently in the 1970s and early 1980s, Dad worked, from the *Voice*'s newspaper pages, filling 276 handwritten sheets of notepaper of what would be his uncle's memoirs translated into English for the first time. I picture him, zippered file folder tucked under his arm, on his way to the nearby cafeteria on the university campus, where he took over one of the tables, spread out papers and dictionaries, and drank cups of coffee filled and refilled by a clutch of solicitous wait staff, mainly middle-aged women, who by all accounts thought he was a "real pet."

His handwritten translation, cross-outs included, begins: "Peter Svarich's memoirs. #1 July 10/74. I was born in March 1877 in the village of Tulova ... Sometime in my fifth year, I began to accompany my father to church. He always made me stand in front of the ~~Heavenly Gate~~ Royal Door. ~~Here I was fascinated by the play of various colors on~~ where I was happy because I had ample opportunity to look around me. I was fascinated by the play ..." and so on.

Dad's translation with notes was published in 1999, five years after his death. Given his intention — to "preserve the [autobiographical] spirit" of a "readable account of his [Peter's] involvement in many events.... A man of great parts ... one we could all brag about and tell to our children" (Svarich xvi) — my mother and I were very grateful to have it published precisely so that "grand-children and great-grandchildren" and beyond would read the narrative of a forebear whose life in Canada from 1900 spanned work on railways and in mines, in the Klondike gold rush, as postmaster, school organizer, commissioner of oaths, founder of a Ukrainian agricultural co-operative in Vegreville (it failed), an early member of the Ukrainian Orthodox Church of Canada, and contributor to *Ukrainskyi Holos*. Peter Svarich was also the translator of the *Alexandra Primer* (the first textbook for the teaching of language) into Ukrainian for use in Alberta and Saskatchewan schools in the early 1900s.

Of *this* "Uncle Peter" (as he was called by all generations) I knew nothing as a child. I knew him only as a much-feted if unloved personality in the Ukrainian Canadian community in Alberta and as an occasional visitor to my parents' home, a skinny, glowering, white-mustachioed old man thumping his way on a wooden cane and addressing us all rather imperiously in Ukrainian, rendering me speechless.

It is too late to thank my father for the work he did in translating the memoir of his uncle and Fedor's brother-in-law, Peter Svarich, so I gratefully acknowledge that labour now. For it is in Peter's chronicle of the first two years of homesteading in Alberta that I watch Fedor working at hard labour alongside his father-in-law, Ivan Svarich, and Peter. He does not speak for himself but is folded into Peter's "my family and I" as the lone brother-in-law — and only the third male in an emigrating party of nine — who is assumed to have shared in the general confidence that "life in Canada is better than it is here," than it ever was in Tulova. As soon as Peter leaves the homestead for greener pastures, Fedor disappears from the memoir, for Peter's overweening interest is in himself.

My father also wrote a memoir, *A Gift to Last*, distributed among immediate family members, and here Fedor makes more frequent appearances. He was already thirty-five years old and six years in Canada when my Dad was born the fifth of seven children. (Dad would leave the farm when nine years old for schooling in Vegreville.) Looking back at that period of his childhood, Dad conjures up his father in scenes of brief but startling clarity, scenes that I read as eruptions of masculinity into the domestic scene lovingly created by Fedor's wife, my Baba Anna, and lovingly recalled by my father.

But then Dad goes to live and study in town and his parents recede, waving goodbye at the gateposts.

Taken together, these memoirs may be said to construct a settler narrative from the perspective of two generations, to which I add a third, my own. Of all my grandparents' lives, Fedor's life best lays out for me a chronicle of the process by which they all became settlers, for he is the forebear who, unlike the immemorial custom in a Galician village, did not inherit land. Rail ticket and passport in hand, he struck out from the village and rode the deep blue sea to lay claim to a plot of soil and bush that, he assumed, no one owned. In short enough order, Fedor Kostashchuk owned it.

In the succinct phrasing of political scientist Roger Epp in *We are All Treaty People: Prairie Essays,* this is a narrative of how "'vast tracts'" of Canada had never truly been inhabited but only "'roamed over'" (128) by peoples who had been relocated from their traditional territory by some process never closely scrutinized by those who had newly taken possession of it. Told and retold, the narrative becomes a story, first within and down through families, and then outward to entire communities. And there, especially if the community is an ethnocultural or ethnoreligious minority, say, Ukrainian or Mennonite, it becomes a history-from-below. Epp calls this storytelling the "lifeblood and the glue" that holds together communities that had been "vanquished to the margins of modern nation-states." That would be ethnic Ukrainians at the margins of

Russian, Polish, and Austro-Hungarian empires. In this instance, Epp goes on, a "history" is being written not at all by "victors" (99) but by the internal coherence of a community of underdogs.

There is a truth to this among Ukrainian Canadians. Publicly and officially we have nurtured a (hi)story of how, by the concrete act of settling and farming, we overcame enormous disadvantages as barefoot peasants fleeing oppression in Galicia and Bukovyna — strangers at Canadian gates — to become the heroes of our own stories. But are these "retold" stories-from-below any truer than the master narratives of the dominant Anglo-Celtic classes who we are pleased to think of as the colonial powers par excellence?

Beware "the colonizer who lurks within" the settler, writes Paulette Regan in *Unsettling the Settler Within* (11). Our very stories unmask us as "not-knowers," as colonizers who have taken "space": geographic, historical, narrative, cultural, political, legal, intellectual, and pedagogical (Regan 28). Rather than acknowledge our history in Canada as one in which we settlers encounter Indigenous Peoples, we tell the story almost exclusively as though we sprang from the territory self-made — Look what we've made of "nothing" (Epp 129)!

But there is a parallel kind of storytelling within Ukrainian Canadian families. From the Kostash forebears I learned virtually nothing nor heard tell of anything that was rooted in the village-whence-they-had-come, Tulova. Nor was I curious about this Old Country family pre-history. This was its own kind of not-knowing-ness, a willful obliviousness that masked the cultural, historical, and political "spaces" held by ancestral memory, that lurked within my immediate forebears in Canada. And so, with neither the ancestral nor Indigenous Peoples visible or legible to me, the Ukrainian Canadian imaginary was a set of symbols and activities rooted entirely in locations made-in-Canada such as historical sites, community and church halls, summer camps, weddings, dance festivals. I took no umbrage at the time.

Fedor comes from somewhere

I don't recall when I first became curious about Dido's life "before": before me and my parents, before the farm, the barn, and the portraits. After all, dead six years already when I was born, he was utterly insubstantial. It never occurred to me to dig under the Kostash family tree to see what lay at the root of it. Certainly, I had never pressed for a genealogy. But I know better now. He has a backstory, in the village he grew up in, in his family, his education, youth, and marriage. Of all his siblings, he would be the one to uproot himself and his wife and two children from Tulova, to resettle in a Promised Land of "free land" in an apparent "wilderness" that had nevertheless been mapped since 1871 by the Dominion Land Survey of Western Canada.

He is not a *tabula rasa* upon which Canada will imprint itself willy-nilly. It's true that within a generation the homestead in Alberta where the *Kostashes* begin in 1900 will be abandoned a generation later. But the *Kostashchuks* can be said to belong to recorded history, dating back to 1564, in the records of Tulova. As a Kostash I will be the first Canadian to try to leap the gap to the Kostashchuks, whose (hi)story has been unwinding for centuries. In ancestral Tulova I will be Fedor's granddaughter.

My Dido came from peasant stock in Galicia, at the time a province of Austria-Hungary. "The typical Galician peasant farmed in a primitive manner, even in the late nineteenth century. He used a light plow, either completely or mostly of wood. Only the wealthy used factory-made implements. They might also own a chaff-cutter but only the landlord's estate could afford a threshing machine. Most peasants threshed with flails and winnowed with sieves. They used little artificial fertilizer, and crop rotation replaced the three-field system only at the turn of the century.... Most peasant families owned less than 5 hectares

[12.3 acres], the minimum required to support a family" (Himka 1982, 14–15).

The Kostashchuks were not enserfed (as chattel) in the Russian Empire, but even so, after the abolition in 1848 of corvée (compulsory unpaid labour on the landlord's fields), they were saddled with the compensation they now owed him for loss of free labour: millions of dollars in taxes and interest (Martynowych 5). And still the landowners held more than half the arable land as well as all forests and pastures (Fodchuk 1).

It had fallen upon earlier generations of Tulovians to settle a wasteland ravaged by the flooding of the Prut River and to foreshadow the same cycle of labour in the Albertan bush: to uproot tree stumps and thorny bush, plow up virgin soil, build shelters, and strengthen the village's defences in the event of repeated Tatar raids. According to a local chronicler, "Names of fields and boundary-lines still allude to these events in the village's history" (Kharyton and Biiovskyi 6).

And I will read these names again on Peter's maps. *Khobza* (dwarf elder tree), *zholob* (narrow and deep ravine), *terniachko* (thorny), *seredni* (middle), *zadni* (rear). "History is not just unearthed monuments of material culture, ancient adornments, well-known events and wars, beautiful old buildings," the sages of Tulova argue, "it is also the names of settlements, fields and hills, streets and crossroads. The biography of generations is in them. That's why it is so important to recognize these names, bring them to light, look deeply into the past" (Kharyton and Biiovskyi 7). It is a considerable irony that the Galician settlers, looking deeply into their past when they chose names for places and things in Western Canada, in this New Eden, overlaid the biography of Indigenous generations, creating a topographical palimpsest on the land.

In 1880, when Fedor was nine years old, Tulova comprised 142 houses and 730 inhabitants, 648 of them Greek Catholics,

34 Jews, 37 Poles, and 11 Germans. The village boasted a church (for the Greek Catholic Ukrainians) and a one-room schoolhouse (instruction given in the Ukrainian language) but its most active organization was its *chytalnia* (reading club), founded by the *Prosvita* (Enlightenment) Society when Fedor was seventeen. This is of first importance. Although Fedor would continue his education in Sniatyn (historically a crossing point for trade goods and ideas from German lands to the Ottoman Empire) and in Kolomyia (another trading centre and the centre of Ukrainian publishing, journalism, and political radicalism), eventually he returned to Tulova, and its *chytalnia*.

The reading club opened in 1880 and, in the midst of Peter Svarich's exuberant recollection of the "magnificent day" in May that celebrated the occasion, I place Fedor. He helps to erect the triumphal arch — sheaves of grain, flowering foliage, floral wreaths — and waits with the others for the co-celebrants to arrive — clergy, "lay intelligentsia," and a choir from Sniatyn. Fedor's own father, Hrytsko (Hryhoryi), the village mayor, steps forward in greeting, bearing the traditional bread and salt (Svarich 8–10).

The Master of Ceremonies was a member of the Radical Party, the son of a priest who was a law student and village organizer for the Party, which advocated socialism and rights for Ukrainian peasants. In his memoirs, Peter, in a laconic observation about immigrant farmers from Galicia, wrote that they were "inclined toward radicalism." More sensationally, from my point of view as the know-nothing third generation in Canada, Peter's father and thus my great-grandfather, Ivan Svarich, was a "loyal Radical in Tulova." Naturally, nothing was made of this in Canada (Svarich 48).

Now Svarich's claim that the opening of the *chytalnia* signified "a favourable transition to a better life" (9) right there in a radicalized Tulova. For here's the thing. According to historian

John-Paul Himka, in Galicia in 1880, when Fedor was at school, only 17.3% of men and 10.3% of women could read and write. Teachers' incomes were lower even than those of priests (Himka 1988, 60). These dismal statistics may have spurred the opening of the reading room on that joyous May Day in Tulova: the proverbial intellectual murk of village life was gradually being lifted. On the eve of Fedor's departure for the intellectually deficient settlements in western Canada, Tulova's reading room — I am citing from the local history, *There Where the Hunting is Good* — had accumulated 140 books and pamphlets by subscription. "By 1900, sixteen members of the Enlightenment Society were literate, and forty-seven by 1908–1909 of a total membership of fifty [all men]. Such were the results of the activity of the amateur groups around the reading rooms" (Kharyton and Biiovskyi 18). My father was three years old in 1909 and in his memoir will recall no books in the farmhouse in Royal Park, Alberta.

Fedor, having contracted measles, lost a year of schooling and never returned to Kolomyia to complete his education. He was then drafted into the Austrian army for three years. At this point, apparently, he was multilingual: Old Church Slavonic (for liturgical purposes), Polish, German, and Latin. Then at age twenty-five, he is married, and four years and two children later, he is an immigrant in Canada together with his wife's family, chopping logs and scything reeds for a two-room log house with a thatched roof, perhaps repeating Latin verb conjugations as he whacked at weeds so as not to go completely mad. It was a feat that impressed my father. When at the dinner table, "Father proved [his linguistic prowess] by declining some Latin nouns in the 'Nominativus,' 'Genitivus,' 'Ablativus' cases and conjugated some verbs in the 'Pluscum Perfectum' tense." He also read aloud from Ukrainian newspapers to his illiterate neighbours who congregated at the Kostash house on Sundays for just this purpose.

I conjure up an image and it haunts me: while Baba Anna is toiling at the stove, catching phrases of her husband's discourse at the dinner table, Fedor is surrounded by a circle of gape-jawed boys, giggling at his solemn recitation of the Old Church Slavonic alphabet: *Az, Buky, Vidy, Hlahol....* It's what passes for the intelligentsia on a Ukrainian Canadian homestead.

Fedor is an emigrant

Ever industrious and peremptory, Peter had sent for maps and brochures from the Immigration Bureau in Lviv. And had read aloud to the family reports from the pioneering efforts of Dr. Joseph Oleskiw and his two pamphlets in Ukrainian, "On Free Lands" and "On Emigration." The Svarich home became a "hotbed of emigration fever" (Svarich 69). In Tulova's reading room, prospective emigrants pored over the Ukrainian American newspaper, *Svoboda* (*Liberty*), and German newspapers from Canada, and there read the tale: their countrymen had found good hay and forest, and no landlords. No taxes either, nor compulsory military service, and no gendarmes. You want to pick mushrooms? Go right ahead. Nobody owns them.

Not that the Svarich and Kostashchuk families of Tulova had ever felt the need to speak up and curse the *Pan*, the landlord. If you own enough land, you work for yourself, or even hire labour from the poorest of the village's poor. "In this respect," writes historian Stella Hryniuk, "what was important for the peasant's social status and self-image was that he owned land and wanted to own more" (215). Land in Canada was "free."

Fellow villager, Jacob Porayko, already farming in the Edna district east of Edmonton, settled the matter (to go, to stay?) when he wrote of his "good fortune and well-being," and sent back to Tulova a sample of black soil from his farm and another of fat kernels of wheat (Svarich 133). And so, after due deliberation by the patriarch, Ivan Svarich, the decision is made: sell land and implements, pocket a couple of thousand dollars, and be productive almost immediately in Canada. The news of Ivan's decision aroused a torrent of excitement and envy in Tulova. Old man Svarich, "the rich man of Tulova, was preparing to leave," Peter wrote, noting that the excitement was tempered for those "poor viilagers ... who could barely scrape or borrow enough money together" for their passage (70).

Emigration! One hundred and thirty million acres — 800,000 homesteads of 160 acres each — were waiting for the picking in Manitoba and the Northwest Territory (Saskatchewan and Alberta). Yet there is a poignancy to this vision of plenty — oxen! wagon! — on a Canadian homestead. The fact was that the Svariches already had all this in Tulova. Before they left, Peter made drawings, meticulous and fantastically detailed, of the thirty-five parts of a wagon (sideview) and wagon gear, harnesses and horse collars, twelve parts of a plow, oxen yoke in seven parts, harrows, four parts of a silage cutter, tools for preparing skeins of thread for weaving, and plans for a loom (scale 1:20). In the spirit of an archivist Peter documented the tools with extreme fidelity, as though anticipating the nostalgia of the third generation: who of them would grind grain, press oil, assemble and work a loom, forge iron, shape a barrel, and erect a cupola?

Peter and Fedor buy a suit

The two men go to the tailor's in Kolomyia and each orders a bespoke suit to be made from "the best Czech cloth," apparel they unabashedly wear as "members of the intelligentsia."

Desiring to be better informed of this "Canada" that their neighbour Peter Svarich was intent on moving to ("They were all amazed and thought I had truly gone insane"), a steady stream of visitors expressed their apprehensions: that in Canada there lived only English people "whose language was difficult to learn and where only buffalo, Indians and Eskimos inhabited the land of ice and snow." Peter ony laughed "kind-heartedly" (Svarich 74).

The Svarich family apply for their passports. They order and pay for religious services in the church to commemorate deceased family members whose graves they leave to the care of generations to come. They visit the doctor. The women bake rusks for the journey. There is anticipatory mourning as kinfolk recognize these are their last weeks together on this earth. Peter tells us that the community gathers to sing patriotic, that is radical, songs, then the "national anthem," to pump up their courage, belting out a last line, revised from the original — "in our own land" — for the occasion: "We shall be masters in the *foreign* land" (Svarich 77).

Finally, they are ready: suitcases packed, food distributed in small sacks, money sewn into belts and underclothes. Horses snort and whisk their tails, impatient between the laden wagons' shafts. Neighbours mill about the common, restless, shaking their limbs as if they don't know whether to dance or to weep. Fedor moves among them with a large stone jug, pouring out the *horilka* (homebrew) into their wooden mugs. The women do not drink. They wail: "Darling little pigeons [the departing men]! Dear little cuckoos [the departing women]! Do not abandon us, your poor ones, your kith and kin" (Svarich 78). They are joined by a pair of blind musicians who have been singing for their supper up and down the King's Highway. A scythe rests against a tree stump. A goose waddles among the reeds of the pond. Church bells toll but Peter makes no mention of a priest.

The wagons move on, across the Prut River, and on to the regional train station in Vydyniv, the doleful tolling of the village's bells finally extinguished. At the station they meet up with other emigrating groups, and an anonymous reporter from *Hromadskyi Holos* (*Community Voice*) is there to witness the leave-taking.

> This story comes to us from Sniatyn district: 29 March 1900 at 3 o'clock in the afternoon, twenty families from the village of Tulova left for Canada under the leadership of Mr. Svarich (reserve cadet). It was a very sombre image — of being buried alive in the next world. Baggage and wagons were piled up next to the railway station in Vydyniv, just like in wartime. It was a sad sight, one's heart pounded just to look at it. Our long-time friend, radical and fearless fighter, the aged and illiterate Vasyl Chernyvskyi from Volchkivets, said his farewell.
>
> "Dear brothers and sisters, I do not abandon this country because of what it lacks. My family and I had what we needed. I could feed seven other families. You all know and remember how hard I fought your enemies and for the truth. But you so little valued this that you did not want to help me, you were lazy, and I could not fight on by myself. So, farewell!"
>
> Tears prevented him from saying more, tears streamed from the eyes [of his listeners]. (*Hromadskyi Holos*)

Holos makes no further mention of Peter Svarich but in his own memoir he clambers up on a wagon to address the well-wishers. To the unexceptionable sentiments — "Farewell, our humble homes and our village" — he adds a disingenuous note of self-sacrifice, given his monetary interest in the "free lands" of Canada: "We leave to make more room for you — more land so you have an easier life." By his own account, he weeps copiously, "like an old woman."

The crowd wails, and "some were beside themselves and tore their hair in genuine grief." Men pounded their heads against the sides of the Svarich wagon and Ivan Sanduliak, "the parliamentarian," is reduced to stammering, having banged his head so fervently against the wagon wheel that blood gushed forth from his forehead and words stuck in his throat (Svarich 79–80).

Peter writes that Sanduliak made no speech. But *Holos* heard him. Ivan Sanduliak, the parliamentarian from Karlov, was clearly the man to be called on, on just such an occasion, to address across an entire spectrum of emotion all those "dying on this side of the earth, in the old world," now preparing to save themselves in Canada. They have experienced sorrow and disappointment in their motherland, but once they have reached the farther shore in the new world, they will be as though "resurrected" on the other side.

Their native soil is awash with the blood of their ancestors, in vain they fought for their rights, "for freedom of the word and truth," as befits, I am thinking, a radical peasant. "But you did not achieve your goal and you have to abandon your homeland to set off for a faraway land across the sea, in a wilderness, where you will sow your crops in peace, without anger or dispute with others. You, brothers and sisters, will plant in a new world that is untrampled by human footprints.... Over there you will live harmoniously among yourselves and with others, in an orderly manner, much better than is possible in this old world. O woe, woe ... I cannot say anything more to you now, time is getting short, and we must now live forever apart" (*Hromadskyi Holos*).

Even as I translate this text, I am brought up sharp: at the very moment of my forebears' leave-taking from a luckless homeland, their future is already invoked in tropes that will become familiar in Canada. Ukrainian Canadians will tell the story over and over again, of the fabled misery that drove families from their

Galician villages to their Canadian homesteads, of the purported will to secure freedom in a "new" world, a world that was "untrampled" but would soon become productive from their labours, of a utopia in which they would sow and reap in peace and harmony, not just with each other but also with "others." That among these "others" were the people indigenous to the "wilderness" was still unimaginable.

The *Holos* reporter concludes: "Then the locomotive pulled in and, whistling, devoured our emigrants."

It not only devoured "emigrants," it devoured entire families. In a footnote in his translation of Svarich's memoirs, my father writes, "'Relatives' is the nearest equivalent of *rodyna* but lacks the connotation of a tight, loving family group which includes aunts, uncles, grandparents, nieces, nephews, etc. Good fortune for one is good fortune for all; catastrophe for one throws all into throes of grief and lamentation" (Svarich 97).

Fedor is a homesteader

What was he thinking?

Fedor had come for the land, the iconic 160-acre homestead, which, with its ten cleared acres, rudimentary buildings, and a cow, became the foundation of the family's fortune in Canada. Earlier settlers were already reaping modest crops from the rich flatland in the Beaverhill Creek area just east of Edmonton. Further east, in a wide stretch between Mundare and Vegreville, immigrants could still file claim on equally rich soil, and this is where the Svarich-Kostashchuk clan agreed they would settle. Peter had a map. He had produced it for an agent of the Immigration Department in Winnipeg, and, nailing it with one finger, he had showed the agent exactly where on this rectangular grid the group's village was to be located. It would be called Kolomyia. In the middle of the township, on Section 16, thirty-two parcels of land of ten acres each would be set aside for a farmyard and garden for each settler-family. There would be a church, a school, a post office, a store, a wind- and later steam-operated mill at the centre of the village, and nearby a reading room. Not to mention plans for a blacksmith, a cooper, a carpenter, and a shoemaker — everything that would make the community self-supporting (Svarich 102). In other words, a recreation of what they had abandoned in Tulova.

At the notion of such an Old Country arrangement, the agent of the Immigration Department had a good laugh. Every settler must take a whole quarter section and must live on and cultivate it. "You'll live a half a mile from each other. Even this in time will be too close." There would be no village.

The families arrived on Thomas Sunday, April 14, 1900, in Strathcona (across the river from Edmonton), and went directly to the Immigration Hall where the women made use of stoves and washing tubs and Peter and Fedor went window shopping.

As the only youthful Kostashchuk male (Fedor was twenty-nine in 1900) to have left Tulova with the Svarich family, by luck having married into it, Fedor is constituted within Peter's "we." So the "we" who are "most impressed" by Canadian farmers' use of "modern agricultural implements" are Peter and Fedor in Edmonton, even before they've set out to break sod. Hands in their pockets, caps shoved to the back of their heads, they contemplate what's on view in the dealers' shops: harrows, strong harnesses, well-built wagons, hay-cutting machines, steam threshers, and machines for seeding, binding, raking, manufactured in some industrial wonderland. Discs are "awe-inspiring," binders are "remarkable," plows are "efficient." Peter thinks of the wagon shafts in Tulova that bang against the horses' flanks (Svarich 139).

They marvel at the "purebreds" on Canadian farms. "Why, that was power; something to work with," for Canadian horses reminded Peter of the Belgian workhorses in Austria and Germany. The men are not envious, nor are they disheartened. "Someday things would be good for us, we only had to endure the hardships of the first few years and live to a ripe old age" (Svarich 139).

The Kostashchuk/Svariches had not arrived penniless, shoeless, or unprovisioned. Word had already got around that they had arrived with "thousands" of dollars, and two hundred of those had bought the family two starter cows with calves, two piglets, "some" chickens, seed wheat and oats for horse feed. In Edmonton, patriarch Ivan Svarich had spent a thousand on purchases that included two horses and wagons, a plow, three sections of a harrow, a stove, clothing, and some household items (basins, cheap cutlery, bedclothes). Off they all trundled, baggage in one wagon, families in the other.

Wagon trails that twisted around sloughs or wormed their way up and over hillsides led from one newly cleared patch of bush to another — through poplar, willow, spruce, birches, tamarack — and eventually brought the Svarich-Kostashchuk group, on their way to stake out their own homesteads, to the site of pioneering countrymen. Their first sight of an established Ukrainian farmstead in the "promised land" produced severe culture shock. Had they really travelled thousands of miles from home only to be met by their probable future: the house was like a little pigsty, the stable but a crude shelter, both covered with sod; a second well was being dug, and still there was no water. The farmland was rock-hard with alkaline and stones, elsewhere soaked in swamps. "In the Old Country," Peter wrote, "this wretch had a fine home with an orchard, a half-*morg* garden and a beautiful, productive field. And here he had become a beggar" (Svarich 136).

Fedor comes into view

Leaving their exhausted horses with neighbours and borrowing others, Peter and Fedor strike south to pick out their homestead quarters: the landscape was heart-lifting. Chernozem on a raised elevation, thus, not much swamp or bog; poplars and willows for shelter; meadows for grazing the dreamed-of fatted cattle. No sign of human passage through the tall grasses, only the deep treads now overgrown of migrating buffalo herds — or could these have also been Indian trails, as they then called them? Lowlands are thick with wild hay.

The surveyor's line cut straight through the bush and four holes indicated the corners of four sections — the CPR had two — leaving two free sections, kitty-corner. Fedor claims one quarter section, his father-in-law, Ivan Svarich, the other: "This forest must be mine" (Svarich 148). The Svarich men are pleased with their choice, with its provision of sixty wooded acres for building materials and fuel. Of his own quarter section Fedor says, "It too has some trees but rather young ones — suitable for corrals and fence posts" (Svarich 149).

The very next day, if Peter is to be believed, they are cutting down dry trees and burning a smudge against the ravenous mosquitoes, while the horses graze. They erect a *buda* — a shelter half-dug into the earth and roofed with clumps of sod — and dig a well. At the same time, for fifty dollars, they rent a quarter section of land, thirty acres already cleared by an earlier homesteader. There is still time even at this latitude (53°) to put in a crop and so "we went to work." Fedor is there, obviously, and within a week they have plowed, harrowed, and seeded. Wheat, oats, barley, and seed potatoes.

That they became familiar with edible wild plants, berries, and mushrooms — that stock Ukrainian Canadian anecdote told

of the "Indian" woman who showed them the bounty of saskatoon bushes — must have meant contact with itinerant Indigenous
families who regularly travelled through the settlement area. "An
Indian once told me that to have healthy teeth you had to chew on
wood from a poplar tree that you saw being hit and split open by
lightning. I am 91 and still have my teeth" (qtd. in Mucz 190).

In his exhaustively researched and illustrated *Zhorna: Material
Culture of the Ukrainian Pioneers,* Roman Fodchuk alerts us to the
dire necessity of homesteaders who, having arrived in the fall,
"didn't have the opportunity to gather and store wild edibles," but
gleaned what they could "from the wilderness." The "wilderness"
offered edibles in season — mushrooms and berries — and eventually homesteaders also gathered rose hips and willow bark as
medicinals and for tea. How did they know where to pick them?
Fodchuk tells us:

> As Helen Solowan Boychuk, an early settler I interviewed
> in 1976, recalled, "The gooseberries were so big and thick
> in those days. We had big lovely strawberries and nice
> raspberries and saskatoon berries along the river. We
> had a patch of blueberries near the house, and we were
> waiting for them to ripen fully. The Indians came, and
> I asked them not to pick. Well, they got there first and
> picked them all, saying, 'God gives to you and God gives
> to me.' So we had no blueberries." (16)

When the lakes to the north of the settlements had frozen
over, the men would fish for whitefish and pickerel and stack them
"like firewood" on the sleigh box (Fodchuk 99). Or had Indigenous
fishers already made the rounds of the homesteads, bartering
frozen fish (for Ukrainian Christmas Eve) for flour or a yard or
two of cloth?

"For our first year we did very well" (Svarich 171).

Peter and Fedor are yoked together in labour. In his *Memoirs,* Peter enumerates their tasks as they build two houses, two granaries, two stables. Fedor cuts trees in the "forest" (parkland bush) and together they cut and hew logs, join logs, lay floor beams, raise walls. Within one week the walls of a two-room house with an entryway have been erected, its roof still open to the sky until bulrushes are laid over the rafters, to be covered in turn in the summer "when the swamp grass reached its full height" (Svarich 152) and bound into small sheaves in imitation of the straw thatch of their house in Tulova.

On the Svarich quarter section they plaster a granary and stable, thatch the granary with sheaves of reeds, and Ivan — powerful on a Canadian harrow — disc-harrows a small, cleared patch, while his wife, Maria, pulls up roots. "They" (a pronoun that includes Fedor) stack hay, fence the house, build corrals, a pigpen, a chicken coop. They've been on the land since the end of April (and they've worn me out just reading about their labours): by Pentecost (June 3) they are ready to pay for their homesteads and make the trek back to Edmonton.

They were expected. Hon. Frank Oliver, Minister of the Interior in Ottawa, welcomes them to the Last Best West, Canada-West, a Land for Millions, who had earlier pressed for, and won, the removal of Indigenous bands right off their reserves to make room for farmers.

They put up hay, and now it's July — their first July — and they drag out the hay mower and rakes: Ivan and Fedor fill sixty wagon loads in one week, their first "harvest" off virgin black earth before they slash it open — ploughing and preparing their own fields for spring sowing — and, no longer peasants who consume all that they produce, become farmers. They buy heifers, a horse, more pigs. They have the cows for milk and cheese, and for meat they take a rifle (they have cash for this too) and go into the bush, shooting rabbits, ducks, and prairie chickens. Peter says nothing about what the women made of this bounty: they know how to pluck and dress fowl, but skinning a rabbit? Apparently, no one seriously considered bagging a deer: back in Tulova, deer belonged to the *Pan*.

From their thirty acres of rented fields, they thresh more than 300 bushels of wheat from ten acres, 600 bushels of oats from fifteen acres, 150 bushels of barley from five acres. They dig up forty bushels of potatoes and cut fifty heads of cabbage. The total yield is more than three times the produce from their fields in Tulova. Peter: "My father now felt like a wealthy man" (Svarich 171).

There is even time to read a German-language newspaper subscribed to in Winnipeg, which draws the Svariches'/Kostashchuks' neighbours to Peter's oil lamp and table: "What is happening out there in the world?" And what he read to them was only a week old: O marvel of postal service from Winnipeg to Beaver Hill!

I am humbled by this prodigy of industry and offer apologies to the ancestors for having dismissed as pioneers' fables these matter-of-fact accounts of dogged, sweated fortitude. I picture a speeded-up film whipping through a projector, almost flying off its sprockets, figures that jerk rapidly to and fro, logs flying up off the woodpile into their hands.

But I wonder how Fedor, who had been counted among Tulova's village intelligentsia, now bent to this labour so doggedly. Back in Tulova, he would have been the husbandman of land cleared generations earlier. Of animal stock of lengthy, painstaking lineage. Of (modest) crops scythed with a blade honed on an ancient whetstone. In Royal Park, Fedor, starting from scratch, was neither very imaginative nor resourceful, and detested the chores that went with pigs. The pens were never well built and were inevitably evil-smelling. The fences never kept the pigs in.

Rounding up the escapees and mending the fences was a chore assigned to the boys. In a poignant memory of his father, Dad sees him "carrying two five-gallon grease or oil pails, slowly and painfully up the path from the well to the pens. The economy of farming in those years demanded such endless and soul-killing drudgery."

And there is the clue to the Kostash economic insufficiency: those families who placed little value in education kept their sons at home, used their help to develop their homesteads. To Fedor, however, the homestead was merely a means to an end: as quickly as possible to send the sons to school, urging them, in his words, "Study, boys, so you won't have to work as I do."

A photo album

"Do you remember the first tractor on the farm?" I asked my father on his 87th birthday.

"Oh yes. Brother Elias was in charge. He fiddled with it all the time. Was always taking the wheels off, greasing it. He built a shed to keep it warm, as though it were a member of the livestock family."

"And why was it so memorable, that first one?"

"It made our family feel that we'd finally entered the twentieth century."

More and more often, as my relatives pass on, I am the recipient of family photo albums. They have become precious as archives, yes, but also in their unchanging materiality, in their indestructabil-ity. I hold the photos, turn them over, put them into plastic envelopes to protect them, and then take them out again, add a sticky note to the back, get some photocopied. They have out-lived their subjects and their photographers, and they will outlive me, never fading beyond retrieval in a digital cloud. "Thingness matters" (Wagner). Dad's older and much-admired brother Elias kept one such album of black-and-white photos meticulously captioned, so that I am able to see how the Kostashes had progressed from the first labour-intensive plowing to the industrial age: Elias, being an engineer, took pictures of the family's machinery. In 1925 the whole family were still breaking sod but now they also worked with a monstrous machine, an assembly of giant steel wheels propelled by what seems to be its very own steam turbine between the front wheels, trophies of labour in the Machine Age. But for fields that were already cropped, a team of four horses still brought in the 1925 harvest. And good-looking fields they seemed to be, tall stands of wheat laid down in thick swaths behind the retreating buttocks of the team that pulled the swather.

With no living informants from my grandparents' immigrant generation, I have come to rely on photographs such as these, loosened from albums and haphazardly handed down, to contextualize or illustrate (holding clues) biographical and autobiographical narratives, largely remote from my time of writing. The celebrated American documentary photographer, Dorothea Lange, said of her own modus operandi that "the best way to go into an unknown territory is to go in ignorant" (qtd. in P. Gross 30). She is speaking of literal territories, but if we think of the "territory" of our own family history in photographs, it is not possible to "go in" ignorant. It is because we already have memories.

Our own memories, or what cultural historian Marianne Hirsch calls the "postmemory" of "postgeneration" (Hirsch 2012). Hirsch wrote particularly of the memory held by the generations that came after the one that experienced collective trauma, the Holocaust (I add: occupations, mass murder, terror in Ukraine and, in Canada, "the clearing of the plains"). But as I make my way through family photographs — Old Country, Alberta, studio, snapshot, black-and-white, coloured, portrait, group — I wonder if this postmemory can also apply to the experience in their new world of the gap in family memory opened up by the passage of time from one generation to another once the initial trauma of migration has been alleviated. For Hirsch, postmemory is not concerned with history's facticity but with its own memory-making: each time I look at an old photo that conveys only limited information as to its facticity — setting, clothing, hairstyles, and so on — and does so rarely with captions, I "remember" a past with which I feel deeply connected but only in my imagination, by means, Hirsch tells us, of the "stories, images and behaviors" with which I grew up (Hirsch 2012).

Fedor becomes Fred

In 1903, Fedor Kostashchuk, having slid from one empire to another, became a British Subject. Identified as "formerly of Galicia, Austria," and still eleven years away from the world war that would rip through the Kostashchuks of Tulova, he was now resident at Vegreville, NES 18, T53, R15, W4 and "entitled to all political and other rights, powers and privileges, and is subject to all obligations to which a natural born British Subject is entitled or subject within Canada," with one qualification, that he cease to be a citizen subject of Austria. Agreed! Signed, "D.L. Scott, Judge of the Supreme Court of the North West Territory, June 13, 1903."

He had arrived in Canada as Kostaszczuk, the passport's spelling (Polish orthography), which became, according to Library of Congress transliteration, Kostashchuk. Shortly after receiving his naturalization papers, Fedor adopted the name Fred Kostash, largely because the name was shorter and easier to spell and to pronounce by his fellow Canadians. The telltale "chuk" had been dropped, to produce the first Kostashes of North America.

One hundred and sixteen years later, as an aging grandchild who never knew him, how do I reconstruct the emotions of that moment? Naturalization was the culmination of his in-laws' plans, a family he had married into with no forethought of his own, I assume, of emigration. He had completed the three years of high school offered in Kolomyia's imposing *gymnasia* (high school) and was a man of some means, living in a land-hungry village, when he married Anna Svarich and began raising two children. I have no other story of his life in Tulova before Peter's and Ivan's clarion call to quit the village and strike out for the "wild lands" of Canada — and to trade his comfortable status for that of an "alien" and the prospect that lay ahead: to homestead, with no real aptitude for the task.

Having been yanked out of Tulova by the enterprise of his brother-in-law, did he feel betrayed when Peter, barely having dusted his shoes in the "free earth" of the Svarich homestead, made straight for Edmonton? Fred stayed behind to become a farmer. What then of the accumulated cultural capital of his education in Sniatyn and Kolomyia enabled by his father's financial capital in land?

In 2013 in Sniatyn, I took a photograph of the building purported to be the elementary school "where your Dido went to school," but it seems too grand for such a middling institution: balustrades, three Ionic columns, engraved lintels. His own children in Canada would go study in a shack.

I cannot shake the melancholy impression I have of a man written between the lines of Peter Svarich's memoir and later in the recall of my father: a man who, through no intention of his own, eluded a destiny he was marked for in Galicia to grub for one in Canada. All my life he had been set squarely within our family's pantheon of homesteading heroes; for the first time, my heart now aches for him as he trades in Fedor for Fred.

A homesteader's progress, gleaned from the Vegreville Observer

1907: Shandro Bros. are successful in selling farm machinery.

1908: The area is more prosperous now as many are exchanging oxen for horses and thatched roofs for shingles. They cultivate a small patch and have a remarkable garden.

1909: Girls are giving up shawls for more modern dress when they go to work in towns. As reported in a *Globe and Mail* editorial: "All political and economic positions [in Western Canada] are being held by Easterners and there is no danger of the west becoming Slav" (*Ukrainian Pioneers* 136).

1915, December: Dm. Nykyforuk, Peter Svarich, Mike Petruk, Was. Stefanyk, Thos. Petruk, Joe Wynnychuk, Steve Rusnak, and Fred Kostash contribute to Vegreville's Patriotic Fund.

1916, March 8: thirty-four more names: Paraftey, Diordi, Onufry, Artemy, Wasyl, by Christian name, and two women, Daria and Weronia. Peter Svarich has donated again in January 1916, and for the year more names trickle in, including Fred Kostash again, and one more time, Peter Svarich, then a surge in June from contributors in Pruth, Chrapko, Tkachuk, Ropchan, Chmilar.

1917, January 3: "Workers for the Patriotic Fund" meet, with a reporter from the *Observer* clearly in attendance. Unattributed "reports" (about local farmers' responses to the Fund appeal) mention indifference and even hostility to the Fund, with dark suggestions of "treason" ("Canada best country"). A veil has been pulled briefly aside: these are settlers "unfriendly" to Canada but friendly to the Austro-Hungarian Empire (whence they had arrived on Canada's shores) and to Emperor Franz Josef or to Ukrainian Catholic bishops in Poland or to revolutionaries in Petersburg (not quite yet the Bolsheviks, but soon). By May 1917, Peter Svarich, an indefatigable correspondent, is protesting vigorously in a Letter to the Editor the proposal endorsed by a Returned Soldiers' Association that British subjects, now naturalized but immigrants nevertheless, from "countries who are now at war with Great Britain," be disenfranchised. The "unscrupulous" socialists have arrived.

June 1917: Joe Knight (anarchist organizer in Ontario and a sympathizer of the underground communist movement in Canada) has been campaigning against conscription. There are "agitators" in Pakan (near present-day Smoky Lake in Alberta). In January 1918, the *Observer* finally airs the scandal of "alien enemies": veterans of the Great War demand all such "be set to work on works of national importance and the rest interned" (qtd. in *Ukrainian Pioneers* 174). Anxiety of Ukrainian Canadian settlers is palpable as the *Observer* reports meeting after meeting: What to do? How to respond? They crank up their patriotism — no case of sedition has ever been proven, settlers' contributions have poured into the Patriotic Fund, the Red Cross, the Victory Bonds. They abhor Bolshevism! The Svarich-Kostash men still on the land keep on farming.

I visit my cousin, Orest Fodchuk, in Vegreville, in 2009.

My notes: *He's 86, going on 87. Dad was 88 when he died, already fading, but Orest is still very much "with it." But he's a terrible rememberer! Just look at the task I've set myself: to recover Canadian memories of 1900–1930 in my family when the oldest (and failing) relative is cousin Jennie, born in 1920. Alice said: "We saw her just before Thanksgiving. If you want to talk with her, don't wait."*

Orest says: "I don't remember Dido very much."

That was my Dido too, Fred Kostash. Orest was 16 when he died in 1939. (What do you mean you don't remember very much? Except, it has to be said, excellent recall of the price and brand of tractors in the 1940s.)

Fred was my grandfather

It seemed that Fred had arrived in Canada with so few stories that it was years before I took note of the fact he had left behind in Tulova six brothers, unnamed among us. Naturally taciturn, he was not a very outgoing man — perhaps he told no stories because no one asked — but, according to my father's memoir, among his neighbours he was honest and hated sham of any kind. He was not dour and on occasion showed "unexpected wit and a sense of humour," a damning by faint praise by my father whose expressed love for his mother was extravagant. (Anna was "the epitome of kindness, patience and understanding.")

Fred's voice was most authoritative in those earnest discussions that were frequently held around the long dining room table after the evening meal. Or, repeatedly, in Dad's memoir, when Fred expounded on the deficits of religious faith and belief, the result, apparently, of his higher education and mingling among young socialists before emigrating to Canada. Fred had a dim view of the "sacred cows of the church" (Galician intelligentsia considered going to church beneath their dignity), and an ordained priest had once confided to him that much of Christian dogma and doctrine was merely "legend, such as the Virgin Birth and Christ's Resurrection." As for kissing a priest's hand, Fred simply would not perform such servile practice in "free" Canada. And thus, my father concludes, he and my uncles grew up without formal religious education and soon forgot even the simple prayers my Baba had taught them at their bedside.

Photo

Besides the oval, oak-framed, and colour-tinted studio portrait of Fred together with those of his wife, Anna, and son Peter (deceased 1921 at seven years old) that now hangs in my Ottawa cousin's home, and the vanished snapshot of Fred in his open coffin, I have now seen another image, a black-and-white photo such as those taken by a box camera circa 1925. Mum, family archivist, about Dad's family has written on the back: "Bill's father standing," meaning Fred standing, behind two companions in a horse buggy, sans horse. He is of medium height, well-built but lean, and of dark complexion.

Dad has written of this photo: "The earliest photo shows him standing on the back of a buggy, the seat being occupied by two neighbours, American bachelor brothers about Father's age. Their influence is obvious in father's appearance — a grey Stetson hat, open-neck shirt and a generous moustache — a veritable Kentucky colonel."

I see: the shadow of the photographer and his own wide-brimmed Stetson cast on the front board of the buggy, my grand-father's hands each resting on a shoulder of the Americans, visibly darker than their pale hands resting on their thighs, his finger-nails whitened by the contrast of the skin (swarthy Slav or just sun-burned?). I don't see his shirt unbuttoned; I see that he is tie-less, unlike his neighbours, who also wear no facial hair. They are all handsomely jacketed, although Fred's jacket seems a size or two too large for his frame. But he stands straight-backed, his head tilted slightly up, the brim of his Stetson pushed back off his high forehead, his moustache framing a long chin. By all appearances he is proud of his station in life in the New Country.

Yet Fred never mastered English; he was married to a woman who was virtually illiterate all her life, as were many of their neighbours in Canada; and his children left the farm for schooling and never came back. It has occurred to me in its full poignancy that Fred must have hated being a farmer. By all accounts he assured his family's survival and well-being, but beyond that? Religion was no consolation — far from it — and he seems never to have engaged in local politics, except in tandem with his brother-in-law, Peter Svarich, making contributions to the Patriotic Fund in Vegreville. Instead, he seems to have foregone intellectual nourishment in Canada in order to ensure that of his sons'. We are always told that this was why families emigrated, why Fred Kostash and the Svariches — from families of means in the village — emigrated. *Anastasia and Hrytsko Kostaszczuk, relatively well-to-do peasant farmers …* They gambled that the initial steep decline in their standard of living would soon be outpaced by Canadian incomes and, more to the point, by their educated children's assimilation into the Canadian lower middle class.

And yet there is this, a story that is a kind of last hurrah from the Old Country as it is folded into the new on Ukrainian Christmas Eve, Holy Eve, on a Ukrainian Canadian homestead, sometime before World War I. A story where the Ukrainian Canadian settler dissolves back into the village patriarch. My father writes — and I quote him in full, not wanting to supplant his voice, his literary persona, observant, lightly ironic, a bit sentimental, and completely immersed in a memory I could not even begin to paraphrase.

Then the last night before Christmas, at dusk, we would troop out to help Father with the final barnyard chores. We went into the barn, spread dry straw for bedding, and stuffed the cribs with fresh hay, in the firm belief that on this Holy Night the animals deserved the best of care. Until we reached the age of sophistication (about 6 or 7) we firmly believed that the animals talked at midnight — we did not wish them to complain that the straw was wet or the hay was stale. Although we often talked of it, not one of us was bold enough to stay up until midnight to listen to what the animals said to one another. Long before midnight we would all be too drowsy and too stuffed with food to stay up that late. Maybe the hired man would venture out to get more cordwood for the box stove; but he never looked in on the animals. We suspected that, being somewhat super-stitious, he was really afraid.

Then one of us would spot the star, rush into the house and loudly announce that the Star of Bethlehem was vis-ible and it was time to sit down to eat. By which time Mother had spread some hay under the tablecloth, strewn some of it under the table, laid out the dishes, set the braided bread (*kalach*) in the middle and lit a candle stuck in it. Then Father and the hired man came in, took off their mackinaws, their lumber socks, washed their hands, smoothed their hair, and sat down at the table. We took our places (all seven of us) around it, and Mother motioned for Father to lead in prayer. He said it rather bashfully; we suspected that he did not really believe in all this ritual. And long before the brood was grown up, prayer was omitted from the Holy Supper.

Settler colonialism

On lined yellow paper inside a file folder labelled "Galicia," I discover that I have already written (undated) what I've had in mind to write now.

> In the recitation of the quintessential story that lies at the heart of every Ukrainian Canadian family in Western Canada — How Baba and Dido Left the Old Country and What They Went Through Over Here — there is a recurring image: viewing its quarter section of parkland bush, the Galician pioneer family rejoices, for here in these poplar groves and tangle of willow and saskatoon bush is an unfathomable bounty of wood. Free. Wood for building, wood for burning. Free, free. This deciduous harvest, even more than the virgin loam (for soil was good and deep and black in Ukraine too) came to represent what the immigrants had come "for."

I pause here to make room for my own discomfort. While I accept the sincerity of the sentiment, the ambition, the yearning to escape the economic and spiritual stifling of the Galician village, from my perspective as their Canadian grandchild the assumption of their own future mastery over the "wilderness" now rings also of assumed mastery over those undefined "others." If they were imagined or conceived of at all, "Indians" loomed in the Galician imagination as the savages of popular lore (though I wonder how such lore penetrated a Galician village circa 1900). Peter Svarich's neighbours mocked his ambition to found a "colony of Ukrainian settlers.... If I survived the ocean voyage and found myself among the Indians, if they would not scalp me, they would certainly paint me from head to foot, give me a crown of feathers and call me their chief" (Svarich 75).

Cue Peter's gaze out the train window as the family made its way across Canada: "In several places, looking out the coach windows, we saw some Indians. Some of our people, scrutinizing them closely, thought they looked rather wild and dangerous, and worried that they might have some of them for neighbours" (Svarich 110). Cue the "faint trails" through the bush down which they would drive to the eastern edge of the incipient colony to select their homesteads. A mere generation later, from a perspective unavailable to settlers staring out windows, seeing only their future farms, a Canadian-born historian would account for the absence of those who had trampled down the trails. "The crushing of the Riel Rebellion had broken the hearts of the Indians and treaties had pried from their grasp these lands of their fathers" (MacGregor 24).

Peter Svarich writes a poem

What kind of hut is this, what are these things,
Where did they all come from?
Especially since but a week ago
There was nothing there?   (SVARICH 155)

Nothing?

We who were now Ukrainian Canadians didn't puzzle over this omission of Indigenous presence in the family history. Our grandparents had come to Canada in a great gamble to secure a future for their children and grandchildren, a gamble that had already required a leap of the imagination away from the foreshortened future in Tulova. At least, that was how the story was told from my earliest recall, the immigrants' foundational story that evolved into the narratives of official multiculturalism.

Its main elements were gratitude for the security of land tenure, secondary public-school education, freedom of religion, universal suffrage eventually, and the right to form ethnic associations (labour and socialist not so much). It was narrated in tones of ingratiating thankfulness to Sir Clifford Sifton, Wilfred Laurier's Minister of the Interior and the man Ukrainian Canadians most revere for his vigorous immigration policy that opened up the Canadian west to their huddled masses. Sifton: "These men are workers. They have been bred for generations to work from daylight to dark. They have never done anything else and they never expect to do anything else" (37), which, come to think of it, is rather like the view the Ukrainian Canadians themselves held of their blighted brethren who never emigrated.

At the same time, the presence offstage of Indigenous peoples so recently subdued in the resistance movements of 1885 is never acknowledged in Ukrainian Canadiana, and yet —

Lost on the prairie

On a rainy day under a darkened sky, Peter Svarich set out to round up cows for the milking. (No date provided.) He walked in large loops until he realized he was lost: no cows and no direction home. It grew darker. He took shelter in a small thicket, lying sleepless to the accompaniment of coyotes, then arose at dawn and walked steadily west, he hoped. In that direction, more or less, lay the homestead.

"At last I heard the barking of a dog and felt thrilled.... I came upon an Indian teepee, in front of which was an open fire. Seeing me, the Indians, who were squatting in front of the teepee, stood up, said something to one another, and out of the teepee appeared a number of children. I approached and said 'Good day!' in English. They replied in like manner."

What follows in Peter's recitation is, in some ways, the familiar trope of Indigenous-Ukrainian relations: the "Indians" rescue the hapless immigrant from his ignorance of the environment. Peter is lost, weary, and hungry, his accidental neighbours feed him and point the way west. But what they have fed him is roasted musk-rat, which he does not recognize but gestures for more; the woman skins some fresh ones for the fire. At this, our settler goes behind a bush and vomits.

At least he had the good manners to apologize — "I was very embarrassed in front of my host" — and then accepted dry bread crusts for his journey, and went his way.

Peter is the resident alien in this story. He is disoriented in a landscape without the markers of rural life (a homestead, a fence, smoke rising out of chimney, cows lowing in tall grass), but with markers legible to the Indigenous resident — the course of a stream, a copse here, a marsh there, an animal track. He does not have even a few words of the local Indigenous language but offers words from an assimilated *lingua franca*, English: "Good day!" The cultural and physiological shock of consuming flesh of local wildlife over-comes him. And, for all their help, it is not the "Indians" who finally show him the way back to his people but a "cowboy" — "luckily a man on horseback approached me" — who speaks of Ranges and Townships and directions. Peter walks southwest until he hears the "welcoming, angelic sound" of the bells clanging on home-steader Cherniawsky's horses. Saved! And the "Indians" of this story? Spoken of without a trace of curiosity and never to reappear (Svarich 174–175).

Until I read this anecdote in Peter's *Memoirs*, I had no know-ledge of it. It had not been passed along, as though there is in fact no need of such stories once the settlers are no longer depend-ent on Indigenous knowledge for survival. So we had no idea that the "Indians" — those dubious characters as viewed from a railway carriage, and here probably an itinerant Métis family — had been such gracious and helpful hosts to our great-uncle, who without their hospitality may never have found his way "home."

In short order, the Svariches and Kostashes will have become proficient, and bilingual, in the vocabulary of possession in which land becomes property: title, boundaries, road allowance, ours, mine, homestead, home/place, not to mention "here." Later generations, conscience-stricken, would come to view Canadian settler-forebears rather like squatters on public land, given the vast disproportion between public (Crown) land and the land assigned by Treaty Six to the Plains and Wood Cree signatories. Thus "reserves" enters the lexicon of settlement: "Her Majesty's Government of the Dominion of Canada, provided all such reserves shall not exceed in all one square mile for each family of five, or in that proportion for larger or smaller families" (Copy of Treaty No. 6).

"We [Peter and Fedor] felt in our hearts the eagerness of suitors, about to meet their brides for the first time, and somewhat nervous, hoped to make the right choices," Peter wrote in elaborate metaphor for imminent possession (147). "Every section [of homestead land]," he goes on to say, "there is good and free for the taking; there were almost no signs of human footprints, only deeply trodden trails, which had been buffalo trails in former times, but were now overgrown with grass" (148).

No wonder our families never gave a moment's thought to the question: had someone once lived here? So they named their new possession as though the land lay as blank as a slate before them: Look, there was nothing here and then we arrived and named it piece by piece. Appropriately, I suppose, they even named the place for one of their churches north of the North Saskatchewan River, Dickie Bush. "Dickie" for "dykyi" in Ukrainian, meaning wild, savage, ferocious; odd, absurd; unsociable.

They named better than they knew — because the "clearing of the plains," to make way for the railways and land surveyors in anticipation of the immigration in their many thousands of all our Babas and Didos, had been "wild, savage, ferocious" to the point of physical and biological violence upon the very bodies of Indigenous women, men, and children. Once the buffalo were gone in the 1870s, starvation stalked the Peoples who had now utterly lost what James Daschuk calls the "nutritional advantage" that the bison provided. Calamity upon calamity: malnutrition, famine, tainted government rations, TB and smallpox, deliberate refusal of food despite Treaty obligations, "until the Indians are on the verge of starvation, to reduce the expense" to the Dominion's purse, in the words of the prime minister, John A. Macdonald (Daschuk 123). Not to mention the agricultural ravaging of an entire ecology that was the literal clearing of the land.

Once corralled onto reserve lands that HM the Queen had agreed and undertaken "to lay aside ... for farming lands," the prospective Cree farmers were promptly prohibited from "selling, bartering, exchanging or giving any person grain or root crops" grown on any reserve on Treaty Six territory (Daschuk 122). While the policy was intended to ensure that food produced on the reserve would feed its population, it had the happy side effect of keeping this production out of competition with that of the incoming hordes of homesteaders, the future agrarian mini-capitalists of the parkland. Recall Peter's boast of 600 bushels of oats from fifteen acres, 150 bushels of barley from five acres, and 40 bushels of potatoes from the garden plot after a single season on the land.

From another context altogether, I paraphrase: "the ability of the settler to go unexamined is one of the characteristics of power and privilege" (Enright). There it is: all that has gone "unexamined" in the self-regarding Ukrainian Canadian narrative, from the Treaties to the reserves to the TB sanitaria to the residential schools. Here was a yawning vacated space opened up for our enrichment and advantage that we have boasted as entirely of our own making.

This overlap and continuity of Indigenous and settler circumstance and outcome since the signing of Treaty Six means that we are in a relationship, however contested by either party, Indigenous and settler. Chelsea Vowel (Métis) describes treaties as "living documents.... Treaties provide a framework for Indigenous folks and settlers to live in a good way as community partners and neighbours. They were supposed to be lasting documents ... not agreements to surrender land titles" (qtd. in Laboucan).

I may chafe at the identity of settler assigned generations beyond the initial and literal act of settlement on Indigenous traditional territory. But it is inarguable that, if the trauma of colonization experienced by Indigenous Peoples is continuous and ongoing, so then is the identity and activity of settlerhood. This, for me, is an implication for settlers, that of being "in relationship with" Indigenous communities: the fruits of our colonization — property, urbanization, education and the self-serving narratives that obscure their origin at least partly in the initial appropriation of Indigenous territory — are likewise of ongoing and continuous benefit to us.

But I also owe a debt of thankfulness to my forebears who by turning sod and planting seed (metaphorical and actual) generated wealth I would go on to inherit.

I think of the on-again off-again dialogue between Saskatchewan Métis writer and community activist, Maria Campbell, and the Toronto actor, Linda Griffiths, published in 1989 as *The Book of Jessica: A Theatrical Transformation*. Working together over a series of improvisations and script revisions, they confronted each other's demons. I read it in 1989 and I reread it now, and the provocation is as I remember it.

Griffiths is burdened by her feelings of "whiteness" and "guilt" as a White person, overwhelmed by the history she is just learning of the oppression of Indigenous Peoples such as Campbell's own forebears. Campbell pushes back, challenging Griffiths to "go find your own spirits, your own power" (17) in the history of her own people, the Highland Scots. This bewilders Linda, the notion that there was something there, in a *European* history of violent displacement and cultural shaming during the period of the Highland Clearances 1750 to 1860 that brought her into affinity with that of the violence perpetrated on the Canadian plains. There is a story they could tell *each other*:

Campbell: "You could say, 'This is what happened to my grandfathers,' and I could say, 'This is what happened to my grandfathers.' The same conqueror who had taken my [Scottish Campbell] grandfather's land away, outlawed his culture, did the same to my grandmother here on this land" (35).

This is not a perfect fit in my case, with the wholly-European history of feudal and authoritarian power unleashed on ancestral bodies in Galicia, but in taking up Campbell's invitation to say what I "could say," here is a story:

A Roman Catholic priest tells of conducting a Galician and his wife to a quarter section he had helped them secure for homesteading. The man could hardly believe that the land on which he stood was, on certain conditions, to be actually his own. When he was assured that such it might be, he knelt down and kissed the sod (Woodsworth 1972, 112).

Who am I, a lucky one, to revile his gesture? It is an ancient one, an honouring of the power of the gods of the black earth in "Old" and "New" Worlds and a gesture of gratitude for its fecundity. So I am torn between the obligation to acknowledge that my forebears' legacy is far from concluded and the ancestral duty I have to honour their lives. Both impulses are at play in revisiting the

Canadian stories from the long intellectual and moral perspective of my own life and age, and in playing sleuth among the artefacts of the ancestors in Galicia.

The dedication, "For Fedor Kostashchuk," is handwritten in ink in elegant Cyrillic script on the back of a studio portrait, framed in decorative cardboard, of a family group.

No names nor place nor year. My Kostash cousin in Ottawa had found it among her parents' memorabilia. We have no idea who these people are. Fedor Kostashchuk was our grandfather. He emigrated from Galicia to western Canada in 1900, and dropped the "chuk." The photo could be a hundred years old. We are barely into the era when, "for the first time in history," John Szarkowski tells us, "even the poor man knew what his ancestors had looked like" (98). Had there been even earlier images that frugal Kostashchuks could afford? There is now no way to reconstruct the connection between "Fedor Kostashchuk" and the story that the image wanted to tell about itself before it was mailed off to Canada.

Off-frame there is a photographer for whom they are posed. They are not so much under his scrutiny (that will be the role of Fedor Kostashchuk) as under his control. They have been instructed to keep still ("frozen"), unspeaking, unsmiling, with all the inexpressive "power and dignity of icons" (Wright Morris 69). All seven adults and five children sit motionless as statuary in startling clarity (only the baby is a little fuzzy for having fidgeted) in their village finery, elaborately embroidered sheepskin vests, strands of coral beads, hair neatly tucked within kerchiefs, clearly all decked-out and on display for the relatives in Canada. They are seated in front of a studio curtain painted with trees in a woodland. I try to match faces as those of siblings or mother and daughters and discern a relationship from a hand resting on a shoulder, a baby on a lap.

None of this group resembles the Canadian relatives whose family portraits I know by heart (many reunions on the homestead farm). Our family photographs go as far back as my maternal Baba's wedding in Edmonton in 1911, to early threshing scenes on the Kostash homestead in the 1920s, then move on through funerals — Fred in his open coffin — and Mum and Dad's courtship and wedding, other weddings, reunions, then my baby pictures, and so it goes, the "inexorable extinction of the generations" (Barthes 84). If indeed they occupy the "postmodern space" of which Marianne Hirsch writes, in which "leftovers, debris, single items" compose memory (1997, 13), then I as their inheritor and collector may reassemble them any which way and even in the end refuse to disperse them.

Two Writers Named Kostashchuk: Part One

A cemetery

In 1988 I was travelling in Ukraine as the guest of the Union of Ukrainian Writers, no longer an invitation to be regarded with misgiving. In 1984, as a tourist, my program in Kyiv had been carefully managed by the Ukraine-Canada Friendship Society, but now this was the era of perestroika in the Soviet Union. Even members of such a historically compromised institution as the Writers' Union, which had once exposed, denounced, and then expelled those members accused as dissidents, was now participating in *Rukh* (movement) that blew fresh air through its ranks. Reputations were being rehabilitated, drawers opened to yellowed manuscripts, and this Canadian writer, at her request and without objection, was supplied with a car and driver who drove her to Tulova.

I was the first Canadian Kostash(chuk) to see the place since 1922. I retain now a memory of a thriving village dappled by June's lovely sunlight filtered through the lush linden trees along the dirt streets. I remember being driven along a country lane — cows on the verges, gooseherds crossing our path, a horse and battered wagon, as though brought to life from the nostalgic scenes on stage flats in Ukrainian Canadian auditoriums — and into the village proper. I remember the green sward of the commons, and the stroll around the village with Hryhoryi Kostashchuk, tractor machinist, who, I was surprised to learn, was a first cousin of my father.

———————

Beyond the common lay the extensive and productive fields of the collective farms and the sowers, reapers, ploughmen, and machinists who worked them, including steel-toothed Hryhoryi, who next took me, wondering, to the cemetery, furiously overgrown with grasses and weeds. Among the headstones I deciphered the family names of those whose forebears had made the same trek out of Tulova as my grandparents, leaving these unbroken lines behind, including a whole row of boys from Tulova buried in 1942, 1943, 1944. We stopped, Hryhoryi gestured, and I looked on a gravestone with my familial name on it.

An upright slab of stone bore the likeness of "Vasyl Kostash-chuk, author, 1896–1973," his sculpted head with furrowed brow bent over to consider the open pages of a book in his hands. I stood dumbfounded.

This was 1988. My grandfather had left eighty-eight years earlier. As far as my Canadian generation imagined it, if he had time travelled to Tulova in the twentieth century he would have found it pretty much as he had left it — oppressed peasants toiling under the lash not of the *Pan* but of the Party. But, look, here was a writer and scholar who seems never to have left Tulova. Nobody had ever told me. No one in Canada seemed ever to have uttered his name. The great memoirist of the Canadian family, Great-Uncle Peter Svarich, so proud (justifiably) of his own gift of words in several languages, wrote not a single one about Vasyl in his *Memoirs*. Writers in the family? *I* was the writer. In my travel notes I wrote that "I sat down on the grass in the cemetery to take the measure of this information: I had not come, miraculously, from illiterates." And then forgot that I had written it. It is a measure of the fog that obscured so much of our family's collective memory that I had taken it as a given that I was descended from village semi-literates.

In my mind — and I had no reason to disbelieve it — my immigrant grandparents came from the same stock as those folk, barefoot and unschooled, who lined up in groups on the train station platform in Strathcona to be photographed, stunned by their drastic transfer from the village. They had so recently — in my mind — been bowing and scraping, cap in hand, in front of the *Pan*'s manor house, before setting out for his fields. Now they were about to lay claim to land of their own in Canada's western "wilderness." In the photos they may still be in a state of shock but they are no longer abject. Within two generations they will have produced the likes of me, university educated and in the precarious self-employment of *writer*. What a marvel.

It was a cliché of our Ukrainian Canadian pioneer narratives that the original settler, i.e., immigrant generation, had been virtually driven out of Galician darkness by despair: land poor, cycled through generations of poverty, illiterate in their own language, brutalized by landlords, and fleeced by tavern keepers, and offered only the thin gruel of salvation at the Communion cup, emigrants hastened to Canadian shores for the promise of productive labour on their own "free" land. Back-breaking it would be — and there would be crushing setbacks — but, hey, these were the dogged homesteaders welcomed as immigrants for their sturdy backs bent to the plow. It was their children or grandchildren who would go to school. Because the point of the whole adventure was finally *to leave the farm*. It was a given that the Kostashchuks who had not got away from Tulova, who were now bound and bonded to state-owned enterprise in Soviet Ukraine, never did leave the farm that, in any case, they no longer owned. In Canada, owning land was only a temporary investment in the future, which lay in the education of sons.

I was complicit in reproducing this narrative.

Here is how I open the first chapter of *All of Baba's Children* (1992): "Squeezed between the Polish landlords and the Austrian army, reduced to a strip of land that could support fewer and fewer people, *denied literacy and cultural self-expression* ... the Ukrainian peasant was at his wit's end precisely when the Canadian government opened the North-West Territories for settlement" (3–4; italics added).

This, in spite of the evidence of my own relatives in Canada, two of whom had arrived as high-school graduates of the Austrian school system and neither of whom would farm. The evidence was all around me that the immigrant generation in Canada had published and written for newspapers; run bookstores; organized drama groups; composed manifestoes, petitions, constitutions, and bylaws; learned English; addressed labour demonstrations and legislatures; and eventually wrote the first pioneer histories. But such was the power among us Ukrainian Canadians, and later reinforced by our folksy image in multiculturalism, of the foundational mythology of the barefoot Galician in a sheepskin coat that I stood stupefied in Tulova, before the resting place of a relative in benighted Soviet Ukraine who had been a writer.

Who was Vasyl Andriovych Kostashchuk and what had he written? Whoever he was and whatever he had written, he was grafted onto a Canadian family tree that had taken no notice of him. But I would track him down and, by doing so, marvellously construct a literary lineage for myself forged in darkest Galicia.

A bookshelf

On my return to Kyiv from Tulova, I was the lunch guest of the Pavlychko family (Dmytro Pavlychko, noted editor and poet, was secretary of the Writers' Union and active in *Rukh*), in their vast apartment with its voluminous furniture and heavy drapes that framed the windows overlooking Kyiv's main and grandest street.

After pleasantries and the soup course, Pavlychko inquired after my name, Kostash. "Where are your people from?" Among Ukrainian Canadians this is a familiar question, a way of calculating in distances of one ancestral village from another, our degree of likely kinship. "Tulova," I said. Pavlychko was delighted by this information. Tulova wasn't so far from Stopchativ, his birthplace, therefore we were almost kin. He embraced me warmly. "My relatives there have kept the name Kostashchuk," I added. He brightened some more. "Would you then be related to Vasyl Kostashchuk, the writer, also of Tulova?" Would I? I described my visit to the village cemetery and my astonishment at the site of the grave of a Kostashchuk writer, and that I had had no idea.

My host rose from the table and walked over to one of the ceiling-high bookcases that lined a long wall, pulled off a book and handed it to me without comment but with that bright expression still on his face.

The book Dmytro Pavlychko handed over to me — I have it still — bore the title, *Volodar dum selians'kykh* (plausibly, *Ruler of*

Peasant Dreams), a 1968 edition published in Uzhhorod (originally published in 1959 in Lviv, western Ukraine). Visibly moved, Pavlychko told me of how he, a humble Ukrainian born into a lumber worker family in western Ukraine near the Carpathian Mountains, was a poet-in-the-making during a bit of a thaw in state control of Ukrainian publishing, when he seized upon this treasure. It is Vasyl Andriovych Kostashchuk's memoir of his friendship with Vasyl Stefanyk, the celebrated modernist writer of short stories. I was impressed. Even I had heard of Stefanyk, in fact I'd read him in the sole Ukrainian literature class of my academic career. The very fact of the publication of a work by a contemporary writer who lived right there in Tulova (and whose one book would be translated into Polish and Czech) signalled to Pavlychko that "*our own* Ukrainian literary figures were worthy of biography" and indeed worthy of being included eventually into the canon of Soviet Ukrainian literature. I have not forgotten that moment of Pavlychko's delight. I shared it vicariously, as a Canadian writer of a generation that had seized on its own literary antecedents in memoirists and modernists of the Canadian West.

I turned the book over in my hands. It had a decidedly Soviet look to it, in its grey cover that was pasted onto layers of pressed cardboard, layers of which were already poking out of the corners. It was not hefty, only 190 pages, and its cost sixty kopecks, which was pretty cheap considering the kopeck was a denomination of the ruble. On the final page, Vasyl Andriovych tells us he wrote his modest reminiscence in Kolomyia between 1937 and 1958. On the equivalent of a copyright page, the printer tells us, in Russian, that this is a work in the Ukrainian language.

I held the book as though I was the custodian of a family secret entrusted to me by sheer happenstance. I didn't know what to do with it. Over the years I would remember I had the book and would open it up, flip through it to see just how complicated

it would be for me to read it, take note that it seemed quite readable, then, wondering what would finally goad me to the task and
whether I should do so sooner than later given the state of the
yellowing pages and uncertain binding, I would shelve it again.

A booklet

And there the book rested, for twenty years, until in 2008, fellow
parishioners from my church in Edmonton, having returned from
a trip to see their own family in Tulova, presented me a booklet.
Of some sixty pages, rather cheaply produced in 2002, its authors,
Vasyl Kharyton and Mykola Biiovskyi, village teachers and community activists, had borne the costs of publication "with financial
support of a local dairy." Titled *Tam, De Dobri Lovy: Narysy Istorii
Tulovy* (*There Where the Hunting is Good: Sketches of the History of
Tulova*), they said it might be an "interesting" read for me.

"Interesting"? As I made my way through it, fragments of
worlds of an array of Kostashchuks opened up before me, leaving me dazed. The only Kostashchuk that had ever been named
in Canada was my paternal grandfather, Fedor Kostashchuk, who,
anyway, had become Kostash at naturalization, and that was it for
the "Chuks." But here in these pages were Kostashchuks galore,
Mykola and Dmytro and Ilia and several Vasyls — a son of Ilia, a
son of Hrytsko. In their variety, they were members, and head,
of Tulova's Enlightenment Society, vice-chair of the reading club,
a librarian of the club, an archivist. And then on page 31, Vasyl
Andriovych's biography (hereafter Vasyl A.).

His education is duly noted, then the interrupted enrollment
in a teachers' college (he never returned) when he was called to
the Austrian army in 1915. In peacetime he did become a teacher
in Tulova itself and wrote, throughout the later German and Soviet
occupations, short pieces on literary themes for newspapers

(hiding in plain sight in Tulova from German then Soviet surveillance). These contributions included the reminiscences that would bring him into the view of admirers of the renowned Ukrainian writer, Vasyl Stefanyk, who was his neighbour. On the basis of recollected conversations with Vasyl Stefanyk and family in their home in Rusiv, some ten kilometres distant, he wrote *Ruler of Peasant Dreams*.

He was already sixty-three years old when *Ruler* was published. Three years before his death in 1973, his literary importance was duly appreciated in a scholarly tome published in 2010 and dedicated to critical and memoiristic comment on Stefanyk's work. I sense the true dimension of Vasyl A.'s literary reputation: he's a footnote to Stefanyk. Fittingly, and proportionately, a street in Kolomyia has been named after him, not, however, on either of the two streets where he actually lived. "It would be appropriate," suggests the tome's editor, Vasyl Kharyton, "to place a memorial plaque dedicated to the biographer of Vasyl Stefanyk on one of the schools where he taught, in Kolomyia or in his native village" (126).

In a photo from 1935, Vasyl A. is thirty-nine years old and is living and working as either a teacher or an inspector in Galicia, then part of Poland. He is lucky to have this job: in a semi-dictatorial Poland, the number of Ukrainian schools in Galicia declined from 2,420 in 1921–1922 to 352 in 1937–1939. Surrounded by ranks of boys and girls in traditional embroidered blouses and shirts, he stands, a slope-shouldered sad sack.

The stone cross

Vasyl Semenovych Stefanyk (1871–1936) wrote stories and novellas whose protagonists were the peasants among whom he lived in his native Rusiv. Literary scholar Marko Pavlyshyn wrote me that Stefanyk showed "ordinary people from the Ukrainian village struggling with the injustices of peasant life.... Poverty, land-hunger, and emigration are among the themes of his prose." As a political radical he represented them in parliament in Vienna (1908–1918). As a political radical on the left, he made it into the Soviet Ukrainian literary canon but died before Eastern Galicia was incorporated into the Ukrainian Soviet Socialist Republic in 1945. So you could not claim him for Soviet literature but, plausibly, for "world progressive literature."

In 1988, I visited the museum dedicated to his life and work in Rusiv. I've kept the pamphlet I picked up in which I wrote in the margins, in Ukrainian, the words inscribed on his memorial stone: "I still have not written all my words nor wept all my tears." They move me still. They had touched the heart of the pamphleteer as well: "The love of his wretched people ignited Stefanyk's words. And this love inspired faith and hope in the hearts of simple people for better times.... but his thought and vision are here, with us. Feel them, and with trembling in your heart step across the threshold of his *khata* [cottage]."

The Soviets were very good at assembling atmospheric literary museums from the everyday artefacts of a writer's life — the hand-loomed table runner, the Kazakh carpet, the pen-and-ink sketch, the manuscript pages, and, under glass, examples of multiple international editions published in translation in the brotherly socialist republics. When I stepped out onto the porch, I saw, a distance away, on the crest of a sloping field, the "stone cross" of his classic novella published in 1900, *Kamennyi Khrest* (*Stone Cross*), the piece I had once studied in Ukrainian literature class and then forgotten.

In 1899, while studying at the medical faculty of Cracow University and a year before the novella was published, Stefanyk had written in a letter his emotional reaction to watching the Galician emigrants move through the Cracow train station to

Canada: "I see them as oaks ... driven away like logs for firewood. I feel their pain — all those threads that are broken between their hearts and their native village — are broken in me. I feel their sorrow and torment" (88).

I look out to the cross planted in the field as though itself an oak and feel the tug from its roots.

"Cracow station," a painting by V.I. Kassian in Kosiv museum, shows a bedlam of peasants, whole families of the old and the young, women in headscarves and shawls, men carrying boxes tied with rope, bodies jostling and shoving and reeling, as though an undertow may suck them under the train itself. In Canada, we only told the story of their arrival, safe and sound. But in Tulova, in 1885, Ivan Svarich, my paternal great-grandfather, had placed his own stone cross near a well and had inscribed on it, in Old Slavonic, "This cross was erected by God's Servant Ivan Svarich with his wife, Maria, to the glory of our Lord God." But it is in Canadian earth that they will lie, buried under a cross that is inscribed in English, *John and Mary, asleep in the Lord*, long past glory in the mother tongue.

A letter

As the sole family member who would or could or cared to make sense of it, I inherited at my mother's death in 2010 everything among her belongings that was plausibly related to "Ukrainian." This included a packet of airmail letters from Ukraine, all addressed to my father in a good hand, which must have been kept stashed away in his file cabinet and of no apparent interest to the rest of the family until, now intensely interested, I had them on my desk.

They were written in the 1970s and 1980s and mailed from Tulova. Dad's correspondent was his cousin, Dmytro Kostashchuk — another cousin! — and I made a mental note to start building a family tree. Perhaps these letters themselves would contain some clues of genealogical relationships. I did not have Dad's side of the correspondence, so I relied on Dmytro's answers to any queries he may have posed. Most of what Dmytro had to say was banal, the sort of letter we were used to reading from Ukraine, of news fit to pass the postal censorship. He thanks Dad for the *banderoli* (boxes of used clothing and items suitable for trade on the local black market) and for not forgetting the family. It was a lean year (no details). Then Dmytro advises Dad, on his and Mum's plan to travel to Ukraine, to include Chernivtsi, and how from there, it was an hour's drive to Tulova. (My parents never went.) "Please overlook my ungrammatical writing." (In fact, it's grammatical.)

I was starting to lose interest when on March 1, 1973, Dmytro answers a question. "You ask, cousin, who is this Vasyl Kostashchuk, is he a distant or a close relative?" Well, I'll be damned: my own father knew of the existence (if not much else) of Vasyl Andriovych Kostashchuk, enough to wonder whether they were related. If so, how? What he learned was never incorporated into the Triumphant Saga of the (Canadian) Kostashes and I will never know why he kept it to himself, even when he knew I was planning a trip to Tulova.

Related in my father's memoir: *Once upon a time there lived in old Tulova a certain peasant, Yuri, of the tribe Kostashchuk, who begat two sons, Ivan and Mykola. Ivan begat all the Kostash(chuks) on our line, Mykola begat the other line including, ultimately, Andryi, Vasyl A.'s father. They all lived, begat, and died in Tulova.*

I had seen for myself Vasyl Andriovych's own grave in the cemetery.

Were we close relatives? Not really. But not so separated as to be genealogically vague. I am Yuri's great-great-great-granddaughter, Vasyl A. is Mykola's great-grandson. And we share a name of some literary repute.

The book

I think of Vasyl A.'s literary reputation as a footnote to the life of Vasyl Stefanyk, but I do not mean to trivialize it. When he died in 1973 at age seventy-six, a "group of friends" wrote a eulogy in a regional Party newspaper, "In Memory of a Comrade": "Implacable death has taken from us a human being who had given many years of labour to community education and who, it must be said, left to our literature a remarkable and interesting book of memoirs of V. Stefanyk, *The Ruler of Peasant Dreams*" (Kharyton 130).

Vasyl Kostashchuk and his wife Hanusia had been "intimate" friends of the Stefanyk family and it was their meetings and conversations that provided their visitor the rich material that became the much-reprinted 1937 reminiscence, "Christmas at Vasyl Stefanyk's" and, twenty years later, the memoir, *Ruler*, "a gift to upcoming generations" (Kharyton 114).

It was time that I read Vasyl A. for myself, for his writing style and a hint of what he had to say about Stefanyk, that "ruler of peasant dreams." I opened and began to read, from the beginning.

Seven kilometres from the northern exit of the town of Sniatyn in Ivano-Frankivsk district lies the village of Rusiv. It lies hidden in low-lying land surrounded by hillocks. Knolls similarly run across [maybe "through"?] *the village.* (I'm the translator and I can't make up my mind.) *On one such knoll, the school, on another, the church, on others, the cemeteries. There are five of them, by which one understands that Rusiv hearkens back to primeval settlers. In 1622, when Tatars burned the neighbouring village, Stetseva, only five farms were saved. Frightened, people abandoned their village and hid in the forests of Rusiv.*

(So far, a whole long paragraph translated, the dictionary consulted only eight times: I should have started reading this long ago.)

Vasyl A. continues: *On the highest hill, according to local lore, there once stood the castle of Boyar* [nobleman] *Rus, from whom the village took its name. The southern edge of the lowland is forested. This is the "Rusiv thicket* [or copse or grove]*." The forest and the rolling landscape lend the village its particular loveliness and attraction. In summer or winter, Rusiv charms with its scenery. Neat white houses spill out from the greenery; and in the winter, from across the sea of snow, against a background of the dark copse, one would say the village is enchanted.*

We are moving in on Stefanyk.

Two main roads run across the village — one from east to west, the other from south to north. The roads are narrow and the houses of the collective farmers of Rusiv are scattered on both sides.... In 1939, the fields of the landlord, Josif Teodorovych, unfolded all around the village. After the unification of Western Ukraine with Soviet Ukraine, this fertile land became the property of the Stefanyk Collective Farm.

Suddenly, I am ejected with a thump from the enchanted village to land on a Soviet collective farm, a *kolhosp*.

The code

In 1952 Vasyl Andriovych wrote a single-page formulaic account of himself for the Union of Ukrainian Writers titled "Autobiography." Stalin died in 1953 and in 1952 we are still two years away from the publication of *The Thaw* by the Russian writer Ilya Ehrenburg, the novel that stunned everyone who, East or West, followed such literary upheavals in the Soviet sphere. "It broke open the frozen crust of Soviet literature," to quote from conversations with my Australian friend, Marko Pavlyshyn, professor of Ukrainian literature in all its eras. Eventually I would read that novel as a student of Russian literature, in the era of the Soviet literary dissidents who came after Ehrenburg. But in 1952 Vasyl A. writes his "Autobiography" in an atmosphere when the Central Committee of the Communist Party of the Soviet Union in 1946, pronouncing on issues of literature, had decreed that writers must be guided by "Party and Social realism." So Vasyl A. writes in a kind of code.

He is a teacher in High School No. 1 in Kolomyia, not so far from Tulova. He has not yet published *Ruler of Peasant Dreams* (but I imagine him composing notes, journal entries, drafts, for his desk drawer), though by 1937 he has published at least two locally celebrated literary sketches that he mentions not at all. For all the world he is simply a teacher of Ukrainian language and literature in a provincial town in western Ukraine. Not just modest, he may also be prudent.

The fact is, Vasyl A. has lived through a period of tumultuous events that represent, for an intellectual, an artist, a series of unexploded bombs. He treads very carefully as he discloses the salient facts of his life (he is fifty-six years old). He was born in a village during the time of the Austro-Hungarian Empire but he is writing this "Autobiography" as a resident in the Ukrainian Soviet Socialist Republic. This is my first glimpse of him not as a cemetery monument but as citizen of an imposed literary culture of Socialist Realism, and of fear and self-censorship.

Olya Pavlyshyn, herself a product of Soviet Ukrainian education, perused Vasyl A.'s text (included in a published collection of literary documents in 2010) and explained to me that it was written "within the rules of official legitimacy."

Who was Vasyl Andriovych as he accounted for himself to the Soviet censors according to the current Party ideology? Although he was born in Eastern Galicia well before its incorporation into the UKRSSR, by the time he is composing this for Soviet scrutiny, he is at pains to be reassuringly of the peasant class. He was born into a family of "middling peasants," so not *kulaks,* the savagely

persecuted class of "rich" peasants during the period of the collectivization of agricultural land (1928–1933). He was only nineteen
when he was mobilized to fight in the Austrian army in the "first
Imperialist war" of 1914–1918. Curiously, he writes that he was
"resettled" away from the front to lower Austria, perhaps under
suspicion of potential disloyalty, as an ethnic Ukrainian, to the
Austrian Emperor, Franz Josef. Vasyl A. thus signals to the censors
that he was anti-imperialist from youth.

We move on. Forced to withdraw from Lviv University in
1923 due to "lack of resources," he signals that he may have been
an aspiring intellectual but he was too poor to fulfil such aspirations. Suitably, he became a village teacher in Tulova, living quietly
under the radar of both Soviet and German occupations (1939–1941,
1941–1944), away from the hotspots in the cities that harboured
Ukrainian nationalist conspirators. Vasyl A. was then forty-five
years old and had already lived under three repressive regimes; he
was about to live the rest of his life as a citizen-subject of the USSR.

Ukraine was liberated from the "fascist invaders" in 1944 and
from then to 1952 Vasyl A. continued as a teacher. Could any biographical sketch be more innocuous? But he has family members
to account for. "My father died in 1938, my mother in 1950. I have a
brother and two sisters. They work on the '1917 September' collective farm in Tulova, my brother as a brigade leader, one sister as a
foreman." Decode: he has no worryingly bourgeois family connections. There is no mention of a wife, although, as I have learned,
she was Anna Fodchuk, called Hanusia (1901–1956), a teacher much
loved for her singing voice.

"I have never belonged to a political party and none of my
relatives lives abroad."

none of my relatives lives abroad...?

With this he closes his account. And with this I have finally
closed in on him. He has kept his head down and saved himself,

even as a footnote, for the future of Ukrainian literature. In Canada, we Kostashes have never heard of him because he denies we, I, exist.

But here's the thing. He died in October 1973, the same year that my father read his cousin Dmytro's letter mailed from Tulova in March. Dad had already heard or read something, somehow, about Vasyl Andriovych, enough to make an enquiry about his degree of relationship to us. But he never said a word of this to me, even while I was setting out on my own writing life. I confess to a bewilderment as much emotional as intellectual that my father, with whom I shared so very many lively and mutually respectful conversations about my various literary projects up to and including my research trips to Ukraine — to Tulova! — had failed to engage me with what he already seemed to know. It's in hindsight that I feel bereft, for I no longer recall whether I confronted him in 1988, back home in Edmonton from the visit to the cemetery in Tulova. It's now that I feel the pain of his withholding that conversation with me.

From the last pages of Vasyl Andriovych Kostashchuk's *Volodar Dum Selians'kykh* (*Ruler of Peasant Dreams*):

On Sunday, December 6 [1936], I arrived in Rusiv. I entered the house. Utter fright on everyone's face. They walked on tiptoe, spoke in hushed voices. A minute later the doctor arrived. Stefanyk had had another attack overnight, his temperature had risen. This the doctor ascertained from his inflamed lungs, and said his condition was hopeless. The sick man's favourite niece, Paraska, emerged from his room, her face streaked with tears. She told us that her uncle's condition was even worse after the cupping therapy — heated cups applied by two village women, their neighbours.

"I know," the sick man had said to them, "that you are kind-hearted women, Good Samaritans, but leave me in peace, stop torturing me!"

A moment later I went into the sickroom with Kyryl [Stefanyk's son]. *Before our eyes, Stefanyk was waging his final battle for life. The death mask shadowed his face, his eyes blazed. He recognized me. 'Vasyl!' and looked over at the chair where I should sit. He said nothing more.*

The disease was winning. The sick man was delirious, threshing about, then, a moment later, regaining consciousness only once again to sink into bottomless delirium.... At half-past three in the morning, his great heart stopped.

Now, as I read this poignant conclusion of Vasyl A.'s deeply-felt and solemn witness at the deathbed of his friend, I wish my father was still alive so we could read the book together. He could help me when I stumbled on a word or phrase — "from the horse's mouth," so to speak — and belie Vasyl A.'s contention that he had no relations abroad. We would not just be his relations; we would be his readers.

3

Anna Svarich
1879 – 1964

A patience that would have made the angels weep

In 1986, all the descendants of a certain Ivan and Maria Svarich —
my Baba Anna was their daughter — had gathered for a reunion
in Edmonton. For the occasion a cousin had helpfully drawn up a
family tree and reproduced a vintage photograph — Ivan and Maria
were long departed, but there they were, my forebears in Canada,
in an oval frame, photographed in their Canadian finery: Ivan in
suit, tie, waistcoat, and watch-chain, Maria in a ruffled white blouse
and black skirt. The photographer, likely in Vegreville, had seated
them in front of a studio backdrop depicting, sketchily, a flowering

arbour. I had seen this portrait hung in the farmhouse's living room when we would visit the Kostash relatives there, but I had never been curious enough to ask more about an Ivan and a Maria Svarich I never knew. In any event, they had arrived in Canada ages earlier from a village we had no connection with. Relatives, such as those gathered at the reunion, were all Canadians.

By the time I was born in what was still the Cold War era between the West and the Soviet Union, the silences between families across a continent and an ocean were vast. Unlike descendants of immigrants from England and Scotland, or Calabria and Iceland, we Ukrainian Canadians could not keep the channels open by visits and reunions — except on carefully chaperoned group tours after the 1960s — and even with difficulty by correspondence. The only story that interested my generation was the one that opened up all the others: Baba Anna and Dido Fred Kostash bought a homestead in Alberta in 1900 and genealogical time flowed only forward from there.

But now that I am thinking about Anna Kostash née Svarich, time begins to flow backwards. She had a life *before:* before emigration, before the homestead, before birthing Canadians.

At age sixteen in 1895, she marries. I try to imagine the intense negotiations between two families who know everything about each other — Tulova is a village of fewer than a thousand souls — while Anna anxiously awaits her fate. When she is affianced to Fedor Kostashchuk, eldest of six sons, she cannot believe her good luck. Fedor is tall and handsome, and a teetotaller. The whole village knew that the entire Kostashchuk family had taken a vow of sobriety (the church had roused an enthusiastic campaign) into which I insinuate a subtext: Anna would not be beaten up by a drunken husband, reeling in from the alehouse.

Anna was still five years away from a Canadian homestead, but even there, years later, she was still so in love with Fedor (now

Fred) that, when he came in from the fields, like a young bride she would run out of the house to greet him and help him unharness the horses.

Who were these lovers? Dido Fred was already a gaunt and grey-haired old man laid out in his open coffin before my parents had married. But my father described him as kind by nature but uncommunicative, in his own way an Old Country patriarch, the unchallenged head of the household with rights over his wife and children and hired hands. This much Anna, remembered by my father as "meek and uncomplaining," knew to expect of married life. But I want to ask her if she had also freely given her consent (was it even solicited?) to move lock, stock, and barrel halfway around the world to 160 acres of unbroken parkland, with the nearest womenfolk, also bush-bound, a mile away?

From my book, *Bloodlines:* "Anna Kostashchuk walks backwards out of her house, stopping at its stoop, and genuflects deeply, three times, in propitiation to the gods of the hearth. Then, on hands and knees, she kisses the stoop and rises, brushing the dust off her apron. Fedor is already on his way to the church with his neighbours; there will be one last Mass and the funeral hymn, *Vichnaia Pamiat*. Eternal memory. It is a kind of death. Anna and Fedor are leaving forever" (237–8).

Dido Fred was a quiet man. Did he and Anna ever have conversations? Speak to each other of their feelings? Or am I projecting my sensibilities back into a patriarchal household where the point was not what each member of the family felt or emoted but what they *did*? Fred, *pater familias*, fulfilled his paternal responsibilities to break his back, if need be, to feed his family. But once he stepped over the stoop and into the house, he relinquished all responsibility to Anna and, to a certain extent, to his sons (my father was in charge of the butter churn), to maintain and reproduce the household.

Of Baba I have a single but persistent memory. Our family has come out to "the farm" for a visit — cousins are in the picture as well — and Baba, widowed since 1938 is, to me, very old, although she was still in her fifties. But she is this crone, in a crocheted black cap, with rheumy eyes, who ladles out her famous chicken noodle soup to a small tribe of her grandchildren, who accept it wordlessly as if it came from someone who had been waiting for us, who had nothing else to do, no other role to play in our lives, than to shuffle to and from the wood-burning stove, carrying the flat soup plates: globules of chicken fat left floating on the aromatic broth.

I don't suppose I ever spoke more than a few words to her.

I had heard it all my life: "Your Baba and Dido came to Canada to give their children and grandchildren a better life." Not just better, spectacularly better, as it turned out, for the grand- and great-grandchildren.

Much else was understood in this formula: my Kostash grand-parents' emigration from Tulova was a sacrifice; they were willing to leave behind material and spiritual goods for the sake of children still to be born. They had the foresight their more timorous neighbours lacked to see that the link to the ancestral soil had to be broken if ever the story of future Kostashes and Svariches were to be written in another script. And lo! it all happened as they had hoped.

I absorbed all this and accepted the virtue of it. When we Canadians compared our circumstances with those of the relatives still in Ukraine (what we knew of them), we breathed a sigh of profound relief that Baba and Dido had "got away" and spared us lives as dairymaids on a collective farm, putting up with short-ages of soap, winter boots, and greasy sausage. The transplanting had been worth it, as seen from the perspective of my generation. It never occurred to me that Baba Anna may have had a perspective all her own. After all, she was never heard to complain. Complain?

Why would she complain? Everything had turned out as she, Fred and Peter, Ivan and Maria had wagered. As for the perspective of the relatives whose descendants would become loyal Soviet Ukrainians, their forebears' emigration from Tulova was a tragedy of compulsion, entire villages "forced" by the knout of landlordism to take their chances inside the machinery of capitalism in North America. Good luck with that!

She hadn't always been a crone. I work backwards from the studio portrait, undated, of the face I knew, grooved and surmounted by large, round spectacles, from behind which her bleary eyes seem to strain for focus, a little upturned smile, ears tucked into the black crocheted cap. On July 1, 1951 — so I have captioned it when I pasted it into my childhood album — perhaps exactly on the Dominion Day holiday weekend, she is surrounded by the generation who have redeemed her sacrifices, her surviving children. They all smile, as well they might; she sits hands folded, clothed in black, and with the crocheted cap, head slightly tilted, not so much unsmiling as pensive. She is seventy-two years old, younger than I am now, but ageless in the sense that I never knew her to look any other way. When I was still a toddler, perched on her lap with her scrawny, sun-darkened arm gripping me while I suck my thumb, she already looked exactly as I would remember her until her death. Backwards to her middle-aged widowhood — about 1940 — unsmiling, with a little frown between her eyebrows, looking out at the photographer from behind those round glasses, her hair in a no-nonsense bob, probably cut in her kitchen. In a small photo saved by my mother, she stands stolidly (same haircut and glasses) in the yard outside the farmhouse. Three daughters-in-law, though not my mother, stand grouped around her, each in a rather fashionable outfit, their long shadows thrown across the grass. Joey is in black velvet, Mae in a floral, open-necked frock, and Elsie has a corsage and crimped hairdo. Baba is draped neck to shoe in a dark, long-sleeved sack.

Back further to circa 1925 when Fred is still alive and Baba still pleasingly fills out her small frame. It is a family reunion on the farm — my father, in a city slicker suit and tie, is about twenty years old — and Baba, knees apart under a long skirt, sits next to Fred who, already greying, holds a toddler grandchild on his lap. Further back still she is a matron in a fur coat, her features slightly discomposed but with no hint yet of their collapse into the creases and folds of her old age, until, finally, I see her at age thirty, young and handsome, her parents still alive, Fred still dark of hair and moustache. They are perched outside the house on straight-backed wooden chairs that have been brought out from the kitchen and Anna holds her own toddler — her five other children arranged around her and Fred — for all the world the proud and satisfied matriarch of a lineage whose Ground Zero was here, Royal Park, near Vegreville, epicentre of Ukrainian settlement in Alberta. It has been ten years since the dashing emigrant hauled her out of Tulova.

My father's memoir: *The Zwaryche/Svariches of Tulova — numerous Zwarychyes have populated Ukraine — boasted of a lineage, probably apocryphal, from an authentic Kniaz [Prince] Zwarych in Ukrainian history. They were disinclined to reject him as a progenitor.*

————

When I visited Tulova in 1988, I made note of the dirt road that led off the highway to the settlement and then of the green sweep of the common, the tethered cow, the church, and the splotches of colour of the small houses sheltered in the village greenery.

My host and guide, Hryhoryi Kostashchuk, proposed a short walking tour of Tulova. A real *muzhyk* (peasant), he was a tractor operator on the "1917 September" *kolhosp*, with a grizzled, knobby, close-shaven skull and steel teeth.

I had brought with me a photocopy of the layout of Tulova in the 1890s, a map Great-Uncle Peter Svarich, Baba's elder brother, drew from memory in Canada. In a precise hand, with ruled lines and angles, he shows how the village was arranged around the common: he locates the properties of Hryts Onyschuk, Vasyl Poraiko, and the blacksmith Budakovsky; the schoolyard with its two swings; the orchard, the woven willow fences, the conical haystacks, the reading room, and the three-domed church.

We started at the church.

The sexton threw on the switch and Hryhoryi and I stepped in. Versions of the icons, banners, and embroideries must have hung here in this very space when Anna and Fedor married, standing side by side, their hands tied together with a *rushnyk* (embroidered towel), kneeling together on a *rushnyk* before the altar, from which she rose and put on the white kerchief that would be her brand ever after as a married woman. She expected then that she would spend her life as her female forebears had done, in the village of fewer than a thousand souls, moving from a father's regime to a husband's down the road, no longer a daughter but a daughter-in-law. But patriarchal strictures were softened by the rounds of village life, religious and pagan rituals re-enacted communally generation after generation, and her own sisters and mother and aunts were only a garden or two away.

The orchard: This would be Baba's first nostalgia in the New Country; dumbfounded by the relentless prairie winter, she longed for Tulova's early spring and the blossoming of the pear and plum and cherry trees. She would learn to make do with sour little crab-apples and the bounty of the parkland bush.

Smack in the middle of the common, enclosed in a small plot and shaded by two cypresses, Peter sketched two crosses, monuments "to the abolition of corvée 1848" and "to the institution of [illegible] 1856." There are no generations alive who would remember the pomp and circumstance of the annual celebration that took place on May 3 commemorating their emancipation, when the villages would drape the cross with garlands and ribbons and crowd together for a prayer service to remember — *Eternal be their memory* — those who had died unfree. Now it is a desecrated plaster monument effaced of its cross, knocked down by "them, from Moscow in the 1950s," Hryhoryi said with a nudge and a wink.

I looked up from the map. Tulova in 1988 seemed shrunken as though half its inhabitants had moved on, taking with them the disassembled corn cribs, beehives, pigsty, well, and gates. The ancient tilled fields, furrows, groves, and ravines had been flattened, rolled out as horizon-sweeping acres of the *kolhosp* from which the villagers now drew their sustenance. They fed themselves as well from the legendary household gardens of prodigious fertility and (when they dared) nourished themselves spiritually at the same three-domed church that Peter had drawn.

There is nothing left of the Svarich home on the property — from here Baba had been courted by Fedor — two lots down from a newish home plastered a brilliant blue with chickens pecking in the gravel of the yard.

In the corner of the Svarich property in 1890, Peter has drawn the house and sketched in a tile stove, a cupboard for bed linens, and that's it, presumably the limit of Peter's interest in domesticity. The hearth, the home: he takes no closer look.

But page upon page of farm tools (scale 1:35): whetstones, scythe, rakes, flail, shovel, seed drill, mallet, oven rake. Outbuildings: well and trough, winch and bucket, the funnel and ladder of the corn crib, the opening in the fence. He has drawn all this from memory in Canada in 1920, an exercise in obsessive recall, but only to a point. He's drawn a house, a *khata,* the thatched roof with smoke vents, shuttered windows, a plank door, doorpost, bench, but no hint of the life within. Peter is not interested in the lives of his mother and sisters in a kitchen, at a stove, at the icons, in the marriage bed, in the childbed. But I am.

I have depended on his *Memoirs*, his village map, his meticulous sketches, for a glimpse at least into the materials of Anna's domestic life before she left for Canada. Peter's right there, laying it all out. I suppose I have naively hoped that a man (especially a brother) admittedly of consummate patriarchal values would take a little longer look at those parts of the village that would illuminate the lives of women (he had six sisters).

Anna would not know the place now, but in 1900 it had everything she needed and could want; she left it all behind and all of it would have to be put together again.

Peter has sketched the bird's eye view of the country crisscrossed by roadways, a tangle of lines connecting villages every which way, and all of it bisected by the Royal Highway. Tulova is no farther than a kilometre by footpath to the nearest village. According to Peter's scale, I count fifty villages and towns in an area roughly fifteen-by-twelve kilometres, a human geography there for all to see, laid down by the ancestors, all the way back to Kniaz (Prince) Zwarych himself. Tulova is *ancient.*

Alberta: Northeast quarter, Section 18, Township 53, Range 20, West of the 4th Meridian

Anna and Fred almost had a village — the contiguous quarter sections claimed by her brother and parents. Granted, it lacked amenities of a long-standing settlement — a (rutted) road, a freshly-thatched roof, a cow and her calf, the dome of a church poking up from the poplars — but from the menfolks' point of view there was much of value: a spring to water the livestock that they were in their minds already herding, nature's own windbreaks to break the force of the prevailing northwest winds, dry wood litter for fuel, land for the house rising away from a flooding creek in spring. Did they choose well? Even when laid out according to these principles,

Anna would later find herself walking several hundred metres back and forth between well and house and would discover that the bluff of trees that had promised her wood for her stove funnelled all the west winds straight at the house. The men had put up a chicken coop in the willow bushes from which the hens routinely escaped, to make nests and lay eggs in patches of weeds.

But this is to get ahead of her story. First there must be a shelter before the winter closed in on them.

It was called a *burdei* or *burda* and it could be constructed in an afternoon. Dig a pit three-metres wide, four-metres long, and a metre deep, and erect above it a roof of smooth saplings with one end thrust into the ground. The stove they had bought and hauled from Edmonton was placed at the centre of the earthen floor. They made their beds of poplar branches covered with meadow grasses. Fragrant, for a while.

The *burdei* was cramped, dark, and smoky. And there Anna gave birth to Elias in 1901, her first Canadian-born child, who would later recall woodsmoke and the damp rising out of wet laundry strung along a rope between saplings.

Was the Canadian homestead the great leveller of Old Country fortune? In his memoir, Peter will remember how, in the rooming house in Sniatyn, his Polish landlady served coffee with sweet cream for breakfast and spoke to him in Polish, "the language of the aristocrats" (Svarich 23). I can almost hear him calculating: "One day I will sit in a café in Cracow and order *kawa ze słodką śmietaną* and then another one ..." but he wagered on Canada instead. Despite the money the family had brought with them and exchanged for agricultural goods, their first home was a hole in the ground.

I stand by Baba as she watches the men at their shovels, now chest-deep in a pit, dirt flying overhead. She will, eventually, live in a real farmhouse, but at the moment she is offered dirt, sod, and slender green tree trunks still oozing their sap. In Tulova she lived in rooms with shelving, a wardrobe, lamps, icons, shuttered windows. She owned cookware and tableware, woven and embroidered linens, and pillows. Not for the first time I have the thought: maybe she never wanted to come to Canada. Her father, husband, and brother chose for her, and so here she is, at the edge of a pit in the ground and told to make herself at home.

The men cut down trees, dug wells, laid floor beams, plastered granaries, and so on, but I struggle to see Anna at work. Her brother has not once mentioned her in his Memoir — I am beginning to get the measure of his self-centredness — but I want to know what she has been up to, a five-year-old and a toddler underfoot in a sod cellar, a babe at her breast as she hacks a garden out of the matted roots of native grasses to get at the loam beneath. Six years into homesteading, she is still arduously hauling dry poplar branches and logs from the thick bush they had coveted as their fuel supply.

Retrospectively, this cataloguing of the remarkable labour of homesteaders in setting up a homeplace feeds the nostalgia of their descendants, rendering lyrical that which had been necessary for survival. Settler lore of the Indigenous neighbours who showed them where to find berries and mushrooms, how to make medicines from native plants, and how to follow deer trails, were told for one generation and then forgotten.

And they break sod. All of them: at this task Baba is just another (ungendered) hand. Brute labour may have been men's work — Fred at the reins of three plow horses harnessed to a breaking-plow tough enough to cut through the roots of tree stumps — but Anna followed behind, walking and stumbling over the stumps, flattening the overturned sod by stomping on it before it flipped back grass-side up. Even in the 1920s, when my father was a teenager, he and Fred were still breaking sod, fifty-three acres in one summer alone.

Is haystack-building men's or women's labour? Anna prided herself on her architect's skill as a haystack-builder, the only one in her extended family to build the stack as a perfect beehive. Sloping neither left nor right, her work was the boast of any farmer.

By 1910, the Kostash family — Anna had now borne seven of her eight children — lived in a two-roomed thatched-roof house, its walls of logs plastered with clay. When this house burned down in 1913, the Kostashes built the wood-framed farmhouse that I remember from family reunions on "the farm," a house indistinguishable from those of the "Canadian" neighbours.

Its southern wall features two four-paned windows on either side of a "front door" that was never used, for we all entered through the door in the kitchen extension, only one-storey high under a sloping roof. But the roof over the house proper is a conspicuous affair with its gabled dormer window. It is a feature I am noticing for the first time, looking at the photograph captioned, "Our House" — I think of it now as "Anna's House" — that I have torn out of Uncle Elias's album, along with all the pictures he lovingly took of the farm's machines.

From age five, my father was turning the crank on the large wheel of the washing machine seventy-five times each operation, agitating fresh cream in a tumbling barrel until it became butter, washing dishes and floors, peeling potatoes, shelling peas, plucking chickens. On the way home from school, he "went for the cows" that had roamed freely over a still-unfenced countryside. He fetched water from the well thirty metres from the house, chopped and split wood, helped weed the garden half an acre in size — a chore he loathed — and milked the gentler cows.

The list of Baba's responsibilities is overly familiar, almost a refrain from any family's recollections of how things were — from the family photo album to the community's local history compendium to feminist scholarship on the economics of domestic labour — but still I feel winded by the recitation, from my father's memory, of Anna Kostash's domestic routines.

"As a matter of course" she milked the cows, fed the chickens, set and monitored the brooding hens, attended the farrowing sows, pounded laundry with a paddle on a smooth rock by the well — it was cold water, and hard. Her enormous garden — there would always be something to eat even in the leanest days before spring planting — with all its provisions for borshch, sauerkraut, pickles, and, for protein, broad beans. Indoors, she was supervisor of the kitchen, feeding hired men as well as her own large family. A feast for the threshers, for instance, would have Baba serving borshch, roast chicken, corn, new potatoes in cream, beets, preserved saskatoons, and dried apples. Late into the night when her menfolk were already asleep, she baked the next day's bread, washed the pots and pans, and, tired and sleepy, wearily sewed patches on a pair of overalls, before herself going to bed.

My father even includes "raising the family" as domestic labour, but there were some occasions when even Fred realized that the mother of his numerous children was overburdened with tasks and that she needed help with a squalling infant or two while she tried desperately to get the evening meal to the table. It was then, my father remembers, that Fred would pick up an infant and croon a simple lullaby, *hai tsiu loo loo loo*, as it giggled and gurgled and waved its little limbs at him, finally lulled to sleep in his arms. There is something reassuring in seeing this man, of so few images, in a moment of gentlest paternity.

Meanwhile, Baba's younger sisters, still unmarried, were transforming into Canadian women on their way to urbanization. They wore navy blue sailor middies trimmed with lace, their hair upswept Queen Alexandra style. No farmhouse drudgery for them. Two of them would leave the farm for housemaid employment in town, extend their education there, learn English "and the ways of the 'upper classes,'" which is to say of the Anglo elite of Vegreville. Consequently, they "married well," into enterprising Ukrainian Canadian farm families. Eventually all lived in Edmonton and wore hats when they left the house.

I grew up in the city, and by the time our family made its visits to "the farm," it had long since been a more-or-less successful Canadian farm. Of course, I had only the sketchiest notion of the work that had been invested in it as a homestead, let alone of the kind of farm they had abandoned or sold on in Tulova. What I could see of the Kostash operation was the usual complement of heavy steel plows, the seed drills and binders here and there on the fields, the granaries stuffed with Marquis wheat, the cows at the milking machines, the tractors that had long replaced the draft horses whose stalls stood empty in the cavernous barn that smelled so pleasingly of meadow grasses.

From her point of view, Baba counted as progress the cream separator (a contraption of bowl, crank and tentacular spouts which I viewed warily in the milk house), an incubator for keeping eggs warm, the brooder, heated to keep chicks warm, and a flock of egg-laying Leghorns whose glossy white plumage and flaming red comb I greatly admired. Three purebred sows grunted contentedly in the mud. A soft-eyed purebred Guernsey or two grazed quietly while being in the business of producing 6,000 litres of buttery milk per cow per year. Splendid progress, which entrenched Baba's labour at the butter churn, the separator, the incubator, in the family's expectations of *more*: more butter, more eggs, more milk, more piglets.

Meanwhile, the progress made out on the fields was reinvested in bigger, newer, more efficient machines: profit from the larger crop yields would eventually be diverted to pay for the Kostash boys' higher education. Even improvements to the farm's outbuildings and fences or the purchase of a gasoline engine to pump up the well water were foregone.

As for that other site of productivity, the 1913 house remained essentially unchanged for forty years. For decades, then, when Baba was hardest at work, it had no indoor plumbing or central heating or running water, and electricity didn't come down the municipal wire until the 1930s. (Even I can remember the large box telephone with the wind-up crank and mouthpiece into which the caller bellowed, all up and down the party line, in its day a miracle of telecommunication.)

Anna supervised the kitchen with a large frying pan, cheap pots and saucepans made serviceable in spite of the holes plugged with a small bit of rag. She baked bread in the traditional clay oven in the milk house. If she yearned for "the finer things in life," such as comfortable furniture and a better class of tableware, these would have to wait until the farm produced a surplus — good crops, good prices — and even then, the cash went to purchase goods necessary for the farming operations, not creature comforts.

That would be the Kroehler davenport, a folding sofa that took up most of the living/dining room and required two beefy men to open and unfold, and fold it up again. Fred was not an unreasonable man (my father gives him his due) but this hundred dollar "luxury" had tested his good will past the breaking point, and he made it plain that "no more cash would be thrown away on silly things."

To be fair, in Fred Kostash's accounts book for 1928, I read that several items of clothing had been purchased from Eaton's Catalogue, although it is not clear whether the "sveder"/sweater or the "spidne shmate"/underwear or the "robory"/rubber boots are men's or women's nor for which child the 10¢ scribbler has been purchased, but I am willing to bet that, as the only woman in the household, Anna was the beneficiary of the "blouse" ($1.00).

Here and there in my father's narrative I get a glimpse of the household's poverty, a deprivation shared equally among its members: the treasures they could not afford on display in the pages of Eaton's Catalogue, from "fancy" pig fencing to cast-iron frying pans to toy soldiers. Baba may have been too preoccupied with her work to watch with a wince her boys at make-believe play with a buffalo skull (a threshing machine); a dry, twisted willow root (a binder); a broomstick or stout poplar pole for a horse in games of Indians and "bandits."

The Kostash farmstead itself was a woeful sight where proper landscaping or fencing of the yard seemed to be out of the question. There were no walks, and muddy boots tramped right into the kitchen porch or into the kitchen itself. The boys slept in the unheated second-floor attic, its walls sweating so profusely in cold weather that the interior mud plastering fell off the sloping walls in loud clumps. It seems no male in the household knew how properly to attach the flashing around the kitchen chimney; inevitably, rainwater leaked through the roof's cedar shingles, seeped down the sides of the chimney, and stained Baba's cupboards and the shelving itself that held up the chimney. Dad writes in his memoir: "And in this far from convenient set-up Mother performed her housewifely duties with a patience that would have made the angels weep."

On the occasion of the Svarich family reunion in Edmonton in 1986, we women of the third generation compiled *The Svarich Clan Cookbook*, coil-bound with a plasticized cover that displays three Cossacks leaping. All the recipes were submitted by female descendants — by birth or through marriage — of Ivan and Maria Svarich, and they are much as you'd expect: family favourites you'd bring to a potluck, crab mousse, Ambrosia salad, salmon loaf, layered *pyrohy* (dumplings) casserole, rhubarb dessert squares.

I have not made use of any of these recipes except for that of my sister's "maple mousse," a cousin's "malt vinaigrette," and for a while my own submissions, "winter sauerkraut salad" and "cherry tomatoes French-style." But over the years there is one page of the cookbook that has proved over and again a Godsend for us forgetful third-generation descendants: the Family Tree of the first and second generations.

I look at it now for a new reason: Anna Svarich's progression through motherhood. The sequence of children is neatly laid out, one pregnancy after another — the first child, born in Tulova in 1896, when Baba was seventeen years old, the last, born on the Kostash farm near Royal Park, Alberta, in 1914 when she was thirty-five. Eight babies over an eighteen-year span. These were farm families, the wisdom goes, who needed lots of farmhands. (Her sister-in-law, Parania, bore ten.) And in Canada, all of Baba's children survived to adulthood save one. The irony — it would turn out — is that they all left the farm for a university degree. And then, still of child-bearing age, Anna stops bearing them. I consult the Tree again: her last child, Peter, born in 1914, was dead seven years later, and perhaps she swore that she would not bury another.

Or perhaps Baba's mother, Maria, the redoubtable Boss Lady and midwife to the entire clan, read Fred Kostash the riot act, in the one serious quarrel they had. Having just delivered Anna's sixth child, she turned dramatically on her son-in-law and warned him that his wife's health was at stake should she be made to endure one more pregnancy. It is a scene of unnerving intimacy — someone must have overheard it or perhaps Maria herself told and retold it with satisfaction within my father's hearing — but in the end it had no enduring effect: Anna bore two more sons. It is the only allusion my father made to his parents' sexual relations. He was a man of circumspection, and it would not have been easy for him to decide to preserve the incident. But I think he may have done so from the fierce solidarity with his mother he felt even as a little boy but which, only now, as a grown man with a typewriter, could he transcribe.

Menopause had not yet intervened to disable routine pregnancies when, somehow, it seems that Anna and Fred no longer
shared their marriage bed. Or, sharing it, lay together companionably and celibate or, more likely, exhausted. I've heard of forms of
birth control practised with knowledge of certain abortifacient
herbs and infusions, both Old Country remedies and those passed
on by Indigenous neighbours. As midwife to them all, Maria would
have knowledge of how to induce miscarriage. I've heard that
women who feared they were carrying an unwanted pregnancy
would jump off tables or sit in mustard baths. I've ruled out, perhaps too hastily, the "rhythm method" of natural birth control or
coitus interruptus because they were not foolproof — yet as far
as I can tell by the dates, there were no "accidents" among the
fifty-two recorded births on the Family Tree, except perhaps that
eight-year gap between Parania's last and second-to-last babies.
Did Fred wear a condom? Did he even have access to condoms,
imported from Germany, in a homesteading economy, or would
he dare ask for them — euphemistically "rubbers" — in a whisper
in the pharmacy when it was still illegal to sell or advertise birth
control in Canada, and the more comfortable latex had yet to be
invented?

There was another way to escape the long sequence of bi- and
tri-annual pregnancies: elude the farm by marriage to a man in
town. There you could see for yourself that even a Ukrainian housewife could acquire real luxuries such as a sofa and an armchair.
And space out her children rationally. Baba's younger sister by sixteen years, Parania "Pearl" Salamandick, who lived in Vegreville,
spaced her five babies between 1915 and 1933. It was in her home in
town that my father paid visits as a boy, enamoured of this "angel
Mother" who was his aunt, so much younger than his mother, a
soft, gentle, gracious creature who sat beside him on the plush
sofa next to an armchair in a roomy living room and served tea for

two. On china plates she laid out slabs of "Canadian" orange chiffon cake turned out of its tube pan and slathered with frosting, sugary enough (white sugar!) to make a boy's teeth ache.

Meanwhile, back at the Kostash farmhouse, with its wood- or coal-burning stove, oil lamps, and an unheated parlour kept shut and gathering dust, Baba raised her boys, dreaming, hoping, praying that the next child would be a girl to replace Helen, her only daughter, who had married at fifteen and moved with her husband to Athabasca country. It was a loss, a subtraction that Baba mourned all her days until her son Elias brought his bride, Anne, to live with them on the farm. The two women grew to care deeply for each other: the daughter-in-law who had grown up motherless in Saskatchewan's Dust Bowl now had a mother and Anna, a daughter she took into her heart.

A photo

The photograph has been reproduced in multiple copies on the walls of Kostash homes, in newspapers, in Ukrainian Canadian pioneer histories, chronicles, and memoirs. I have one in my own study. It is a group photograph, in the sense of separate portraits of six sons in graduation garb who surround, like a garland, portraits of Fred and Anna Kostash, now in their encroaching old age. Has Anna been included as a courtesy or even as an afterthought — a lifelong illiterate, she is surrounded by men who are all educated — and is her sons' rich education understood to be the outcome solely of one parent?

"By 1948 the Kostash family had earned nine more degrees," J.G. MacGregor wrote with breathless admiration in *Vilni Zemli*, having remarked on Harry, the Kostashes' eldest son, as an early Ukrainian graduate from the University of Alberta in 1921. "All six of Frederick Kostash's sons graduated" (258) — and here I break off, stung on Baba's behalf that Fred should be named as the single pro-genitor of all those clever boys.

Anna Svarich grew up in Tulova where the village school provided basic instruction — three grades of two years each to complete — for all children. Even if they never left the village, over six years they would have learned the basics — reading, writing, arithmetic, religion as taught by priests, and Polish language lessons. On offer for girls from grade three: domestic science. Short-sighted anyway, Baba was kept back from school to look after younger siblings, Maria and Ivan producing them every two or three years. Recalling in his memoir, Peter had shrewdly cal-culated that, because "there were already enough children in the family to take care of the cows, the sheep, and the pigs," his parents could be persuaded to let their eldest son leave the village (Svarich 21). That would be him.

From a typed and photocopied text of Peter Svarich's self-authored "Biography of Peter Svarich": "At the age of fifteen went to the *gimnaziia* (*high school*) in Kolomea and had the highest stand-ing in all subjects in High School. He studied five languages and three other subjects in High School and took painting privately. He was instructor to his schoolmates in various difficult subjects, for the remuneration of $5.00 per month from each pupil."

So Baba had remained unschooled while her elder brother Peter made it all the way to university entrance in Austrian Galicia; Fedor graduates from *gimnaziia;* Helen, the only daughter, is vir-tually unschooled as well except for the occasional lesson from immigrant schoolteachers who boarded a few weeks at a time on the Kostash farm and brought her up to the reading level of grade three while she baby-sat her younger brothers.

A family's resources, the surplus, invested in the sons.

You can see the Svarich parents' reasoning in keeping Anna home at that point: she would learn all she needed to know of "domestic science" in Tulova, right there in their own house, at the stove, at the butter churn, the cradle.

Tulova boasted a reading club, a *chytalnia*. Here even the most irredeemably illiterate could listen to newspapers, pamphlets, and entire books read aloud by the literate. In the summer, students from the capital of the region, Lviv, toured the countryside giving lectures. Some village clubs had their own choirs and theatrical troupes — their skills transferred intact to their settlements in western Canada — and organized commemorative evenings in honour of the "people's poet," Taras Shevchenko, to declaim his poetry, this also a tradition that emigrated to Canada.

I don't suppose that Anna ever went to the *chytalnia* to listen to the learned visitors who read aloud about agricultural innovations and political developments in Vienna or even to listen to her brother Peter who read aloud from the Ukrainian American press about the "free land" opening up for settlement across the sea. If not, then she was at home milking the cow and rolling dough for the *pyrohy*. And the announcement from Peter, that she and her husband and two children would be joining the rest of the family on the journey to the free lands, would have struck her dumb. "The leadership of the national movement" among the local intelligentsia "was quite indifferent to [women's] presence in the clubs" (Himka 1988, 134).

Neither brother nor husband nor her sons ever broke through Anna's intellectual solitude. (Did they even try?) She grew up totally illiterate. In Canada the most she could do in the English language was to sign her name.

On Sundays and holidays in the Canadian household on the farm, the family is gathered around the supper table, father and sons in round-table discussions led by Fred. Baba would pause her labours at the stove — and here I want to stand beside her — and try to catch what they were talking about as Fred read from the newspapers. This then was her "further education," her hand above the pot of boiling potatoes stilled, so she could hear something, some thing, of a report about a local election, about the progress of armies in Belgium, about the price of binder twine. My father wrote: "She had a keen mind."

Then, to his "astonishment and pleasure" (he was still a small boy), Baba, at rest, would recite, like fragments of old nursery rhymes or nonsense syllables, Latin conjugations.

amo, amas, amat, amamus, amatis, amant

Of course she did: all those evenings at her girlhood chores she had listened to Peter at his homework, hours of his monotonous oral repetition, in preparation for exams, of Latin declensions and conjugations. She had memorized the sounds.

"If you *must* go to town," Peter told his sisters, "you will dress like ladies." Or words to that effect. He had fretted while still in Tulova: "I insisted that all those who travelled with us should not be clad in peasant style, lest they become laughingstocks among strangers" (Svarich 75). Dressed in long black skirts that reached the tops of buttoned black boots, and white blouses with puffy sleeves, perhaps a straw boater on one of the younger heads, they piled into the wagon and cantered off to Vegreville. Not a sheepskin jacket in sight.

Each clutched a penny in a handkerchief to weigh herself, giggling, on the pharmacy scale: what else would bring an unmarried girl to town? The menfolk always had a reason, and here's Peter with Baba's shopping list as well as his own, cantankerously settling a bill at the haberdashery. *Somebody* had to pay for that straw boater. And darning yarn. And a replacement chimney for the kerosene lamp.

And Peter went to the post office to pick up newspapers, initially ones from New Jersey and Hamburg, later the Canadian paper from Winnipeg, *Ukrains'kyi Holos*, the press organ of the enlightened, proudly hyphenated-Canadian spokesmen of an assimilating generation. *Holos* was established in 1910. Baba couldn't read, period. Her sons, Elias and Bill, read it. Her granddaughters, my cousin Liz, my sister and I, never did.

By the 1930s, the immigrant-settlers and their children had recreated much of what they had left behind in their villages — but upgraded to Canadian standards — usually in this order: the general store, the post office in the store, a church, a community hall, and within each township a school (Fodchuk 14). Forty years later when I was doing interviews in Two Hills, another Ukrainian Canadian town in the bloc settlement east of Edmonton, I made the rounds of two churches, a high school, auto repair shop, jeweller's, hardware store, the Co-op, the hardware for bulk kerosene, hotel and coffee shop, government liquor store, seniors citizens' club, and so on, in other words the full complement of amenities and necessities of life for townspeople and farmers alike. By this time, in the 1970s, as a third-generation Ukrainian Canadian, I had no interest in the pioneering generation who, in any case, were in the cemeteries.

Vegreville had built its hall by 1914, active up to the Second World War, with a reading club, political meetings, lectures on farming practices, dances, church suppers, and a drama club, whose production of a play called *The Old and the New Country* everyone was urged to see by the editor of the *Vegreville Observer* himself, A.L. Horton.

There is no suggestion in any source that Baba ever went to the Hall.

But Vegreville was my father's and his brothers' funnel onto the highway to Edmonton and beyond. Within a year or two of schooling in town, the process of assimilation by anglicization had begun, the "veneer of WASP culture." Some veneer! It began with speaking English almost exclusively. Classmates were English-speaking. The Kostash boys joined them reluctantly, if sporadically,

at the Presbyterian Sunday school. All the town's notable citizens —
lawyers, the mayor, the druggist, postmaster, station agent, grain
elevator operators, and "all" the teachers — were anglophone, while
the town's *untermenschen* (janitors, store clerks, shoemakers,
tailors, and carpenters) included Ukrainians, Poles, Jews, and
Germans. As young scholars, the Kostash boys were effectively
unaffected by Ukrainian influences; in fact, they were being effectively assimilated into WASP culture, "and we never have felt since,"
he wrote, "that we were in any way crippled by it."

Dad and his brothers may not have been "crippled" by anglicization, but Baba? Her boys have disappeared down a rabbit hole only
to pop up again in Edmonton, Copper Cliff, Ottawa, Minneapolis.

Anna and Fred had first sent their sons to school in the one-
room structure named for Kolomyia, the Galician town of Fred's
and Peter's *gimnaziia.* They trudged the miles of winding trail
around swamps and through heavy willow bush, and there, in
that schoolroom — tall windows on two sides, a raised platform for
the teacher's desk — they memorized "great gobs" of *Macbeth* and
the poems of Walter Scott, and broke the rote learning with songs.
"Keep the Home Fires Burning" (a patriotic song from Britain in 1914)
and, of all things, "Sur le Pont d'Avignon" (from 15th century France).
A rickety set of stairs led up to the attic where, my dad writes, the
teacher "cooked, wept and slept."

The younger Kostash boys began their departure from the
farm in 1914. Having outgrown the one-room schoolhouse in the
back of beyond, they would continue their schooling in town.

And so Fred built a two-room shack on a patch of wasteland
in Vegreville. He furnished it with a tin wood-burning stove, two
beds, a table and four chairs, and for the next fourteen years all the
Kostash sons lived and studied there in succession.

Dad took up residence in 1915 at the age of nine. In his narrative, Baba disappears from view, but her presence — "dear soul" — is

palpable when the boys eagerly open up the "grub" that Fred brings the boys from the farm — bread in a cloth sack and a gallon of milk in jars, potatoes from the root cellar, sometimes a roast chicken — for the treats she has tucked, somewhere among the jars of sauerkraut, jugs, and boxes, something very special, deep-fried doughnuts or half a plain cake marbled with the red cake dye that was a popular item bought from Watkin's itinerant peddler. These sumptuously broke the monotony of pork and fried pota-toes — fried potatoes every day of the week for the six years Dad lived in the shack.

Baba still had three young boys at home, too young to be of much help with their chores, let alone hers. And there I leave her: she is thirty-six years old in 1915 and will not come into view again until 1938 when Dad brings his fiancée home to meet her.

And in all this I mark the place where Dad began to slip away into the new world where Baba would not follow, along the weedy trail that led ultimately to *A Connecticut Yankee in King Arthur's Court* and *Treasure Island.* Many times as I was growing up, he would recollect how exciting it was to read books that took him miles and eras away from the farm: how else to loosen its grip?

Years ago I read a slim paperback, *The Injuries of Class,* which made an impression that has never left me. It was the revelation about the psychological and emotional lives of people like my grandparents, my father, my uncles, how, in securing a modest place for their children in the middle class entirely by seeing to their education, Fred and Anna Kostash forfeited the millennial continuity between generations that has sustained forebears on the land of Galicia. Of course, what other sense could there be to having abandoned those graves?

Anna's boys left home for further schooling when they were still in short pants, and she would see them again only in summer when they worked in the fields alongside Fred. It was Fred who made the trip to town and the Kostash shack to deliver food supplies, and it was he who witnessed how they were growing up, mastering their school subjects, making "Anglo" acquaintances. If he related any of this to Anna, she would have been proud, not without some misgiving, of their cleverness, but she would have fretted about their health, the condition of their clothing, attendance at church, their remembering to say their prayers. Did they send her any messages to reassure her?

In town, Peter and Fred had become adept at dealing with merchants, grain buyers, weed inspectors. But the boys were way in front of Fred: they all spoke fluent, unaccented English, which would increase their social confidence as they moved on to Edmonton and university classes. For Baba, the distance from her kitchen stoop to the neo-Classical portals of the Arts Building at the University of Alberta was immeasurable, and when she saw her boys again they were all suited up in three-piece suits and had taken English middle names because that's what Anglos had (Dad chose Ellsworth, unfathomably), earned enough money from their employment (teaching or engineering, we wouldn't have lawyers for another generation) to send some of it home, married women from families with whom Baba was unacquainted (how then do you judge the match? Two daughters-in-law weren't even Ukrainian), and may or may not have their children, *her* grandchildren, baptized, preferably in the Eastern Rite.

By the time her sons had reached "the age of intellectual snobbery" in their freshman year at university, my father wrote, they had became iconoclasts, a memory that he recalls with shame, how they challenged Baba "to prove the existence of God," to "explain the Holy Trinity," challenges they never would have set themselves. As each of her sons entered freshman year, she went through this six times, sacrificed to the university motto, *Quaecumque Vera. Whatsoever Things Are True.*

Baba never went back to Tulova even to visit, and she left the farm, with Elias and his family, only to move down the highway to a bungalow in Vegreville. She found a place for herself, a wooden chair that fit in the space between the kitchen stove and the chimney wall, and she took her comfort there, her hands stroking the cat in her lap, at rest.

To me, it seemed she had no past, only the much-endowed future she was handing on to me, with even more education than my parents had. I would learn to speak French, I would travel hither and yon, I would be at home in cities even bigger than Edmonton, I would spurn the church and take up women's liberation. I would write books, and when I did see her, little old wrinkled lady in a black shawl, I wouldn't be able to say more than a few words to her about any of it. I had always believed she must have nevertheless been gratified — and by all those other grandchildren who were a federal civil servant or social worker or high-school teachers abroad or an interior designer — but now I feel her overwhelming loneliness in the midst of us all.

In Tulova, had Fedor and Anna moved into a new *khata* (cottage) of their own, a vested priest would have blessed it, sprinkling it with holy water, and then, into a space in each cornerstone, have inserted a small paper icon and sealed it in. These holy duties were joyously followed by a dinner at which offerings of *kalachi* (small, round buns) were handed out as gifts to the neighbours (Fodchuk 62).

But on the Alberta homestead, a modern, disenchanted world had long superseded Baba's world of reverence that saw meaning in the simplest incarnated objects and gestures. But Baba hung on — if not always at church, then at least observing the major Fast periods marked on the Julian calendar. The forty days of Great Lent (not counting weekends) was the most important and she was particularly strict in following the rules for herself. No meat, of course, and no milk or dairy products during the last week before Easter Sunday. On Good Friday she would not take even water, infuriating her son, Elias, who shouted at his wife and daughter to "make her stop." She was already so tiny, so old. But who could stop her?

Is this discipline of starvation all that was left of her piety after a lifetime of marriage to an educated "freethinker" and mothering a brood of future freethinkers? Fred argued loudly that all the rites and rituals of the church in the Old Country were mere inventions of the priests who took selfish advantage of the ignorance and superstition of their peasant flock. What could Baba have said in her own defense — perhaps that a priest here and there had been kind to her, that she felt the exquisite relief of his blessing when she had confessed her sins, and the satisfaction of filling his travelling bag with *kalachi,* a boiled egg, spring onions? So what if, in his own home, he ate it all with relish while, back on the farms, Lent was an occasion for semi-starvation.

"Give us this day our daily bread." Baba served it up in an invariable routine of perpetual labour. Ordinary Saturday evenings, perhaps mindful that the next day was nominally a day of rest, she scrubbed the floors and ironed clothes, and before heading out to church, she plucked a rooster, boiled cabbage and rice, washed the milk separator, sorted out socks and stockings, and polished shoes with carbon black scraped off the bottom of a stove plate. By the time Fred had ridden up to the house with horse and buggy, Baba, as usual, was the last to get aboard, carrying her shoes and stockings in her hand and pulling them on, lurching, as the buggy drove off.

There, at church, Baba stood with her children at prayer before the icons. This may have been just another one of the expectations of "women's work," actually to enter the church with the children and stay there, while the men loitered outside, having tethered the horses, dropped some oats on the ground, and looked around to see who else had arrived. But for the next couple of hours, a devout if unlettered Christian, Baba would be in God's House; she had no other obligation. She took her rest. She believed life's tribulations were fleeting, my father intimates, but that eternal bliss, "of which she had so little on earth," awaited her after death.

But rest on earth?

For Christmas Eve, she cleaned wheat for *kutia*, boiled fish, and removed the bones, rolled out dough, mashed the potatoes, cooked sauerkraut and prunes, and made the *pyrohy*. She sautéed onions "until you could smell them in your woolen socks," my father wrote. But in her heart, I believe she was preparing the Holy Supper, whose twelve dishes were a reminder of the Twelve Apostles; the fine hay scattered under the table, of the manger of the Christ Child; the three rounded and braided loaves of *kalachi* on the table pierced with a candle, as the symbolic centrepiece of the prayers for the family's prosperity. Surely, at the most important Feasts, Nativity and Easter, her mundane routines of feeding the family had taken on a kind of sacralizing, and she consecrated them to God.

4

Two Writers Called Kostashchuk: Part Two

When Mum moved out of her house into assisted living at age ninety-three, my sister was tasked with the responsibility to set aside, for my consideration, all materials that had accumulated in the basement rooms loosely categorized as "Ukrainian stuff." As well as the letters from "cousin Dmytro," this included an impressive number of files and books in my father's study that had sat undisturbed since his death thirteen years earlier.

Dad belonged to an inordinate number of organizations, and the group photos in plain black frames of their executives, councils, and boards decorated his study walls. They meant little to us.

Uniquely, however, hung the tinted portrait of a young man dressed in (I'm guessing) a high-school uniform very much Old Country, with thick waves of hair atop a high forehead. Looking out into the middle distance, he bore an expression of remarkable serenity. He had hung there for decades without my once having asked my father, "Who is that?" "Where did the picture come from?" "Why do you keep it?" The frame alone, of polished oak, was eye-catching: *someone* had gone to some trouble to conserve the photograph. (My Kostash cousin in Ottawa wrote me: "The portrait probably belonged to our grandparents. It hung behind a door in my parents' bedroom on the farm and later in a spare room in the basement in the house in Vegreville. I always found the frame most odd. I thought Mom gave it to you but she may well have given it to your father.")

In the event, my sister sold the portrait to an "antiques and collectibles" merchant for the value of the frame: forty dollars.

Some weeks later, in the same booklet of uncommon interest, *There Where the Hunting is Good: Sketches of the History of Tulova*, loaded with genealogies of families from Tulova, I flipped through it again and was stopped dead on page 33: there inside an oval was the exact same portrait of that young man, a little cloudy in black-and-white reproduction, minus the frame. Without reading further, I rushed over to the antiques shop where, to my relief, the portrait remained unsold. I bought it back from the dealer and hung it prominently in my study, very pleased with myself. I especially admired his expression of untroubled youthfulness, a schoolboy after all, retrieved from certain oblivion by my quick-wittedness.

I returned to the booklet and to page 33. There is a caption under the photo: "literary scholar Vasyl Mykolaiovych Kostashchuk." A relative! This is exciting, another literary antecedent from the Galician homeland. But so young! What had happened to Vasyl Mykolaiovych after he left that studio for his graduating picture?

Vasyl Mykolaiovych (hereafter Vasyl M.) shows up in a number of places in the narrative of the village's intellectual and social history. But before I begin to translate these, I notice discrepancies in information. On page 46 he is simply Vasyl Kostashchuk, born in Tulova in 1884, who died in 1931 in Kyiv. On page 58, he is Vasyl Mykhailovych Kostashchuk, born in Tulova in 1926, died in 1947.

These could not possibly be the same V.M. Kostashchuk. In my excitement and reading the Cyrillic, I had failed to notice a salient difference between the two names. Among Ukrainians and Russians, one's middle name, the patronymic, is derived from one's father's first name. Reading more carefully I see that the two Vasyl M.'s have two different patronymics, therefore two different fathers: Mykolaiovych, whose father was Mykola, and Mykhailovych, whose father was Mykhailo. In my haste to learn anything at all about Kostashchuks of ancestral Tulova, I had made these two Vasyls interchangeable. (And muttered in some irritation that Tulovians might have bothered to come up with a few more names for their children instead of endlessly recycling Mykola, son of, Mykhailo, father of, Mykola, father of, Mykhailo, son of.)

But my confusion persisted. On rereading my father's memoir, *A Gift to Last*, I was startled to learn that he had in fact accounted for this very portrait that was now hanging on my wall. His parents had been beguiled by the smooth-talking travelling salesman, "working both sides of the range line," who counted on at least some of the settlers having brought precious family photographs with them in their steamer trunk, along with the family Bible and flour mill. So it was with Fred and Anna Kostash, who paid for an "entire gallery" of oak and gilt frames so that the touched-up photographs of the relatives in Tulova could be hung in pride of place in the parlour.

Among them, my father continues, was a "cousin," dressed in the uniform of a graduate of the *gimnaziia*. So far Dad and I are on the same page. He adds that the frame bore the made-in-Canada inscription, in bold and gilded relief, "For King and Country." The gold paint has worn off, but a festoon of maple leaves encircles the letters. And Dad, commenting, has caught the irony: here was a cousin, son of a Mykola Kostashchuk of Tulova, respected by the homesteaders in Alberta as a member of the "intelligentsia," who would fall as a soldier not in defence of his King, Franz Josef of Austria — nor any British king here, Dad pounced — but in mortal combat "against the Reds in the Russian Revolution."

Well, well, portrait of the young man as an anti-Bolshevik. How on earth had this snippet of tragic family lore made its way to the Kostash homestead? But wait: according to the caption on page 33 of *Where the Hunting is Good*, Vasyl M. died in 1931, long after the Bolsheviks and their Red Army had overwhelmed Ukraine.

No wonder, then, that I was growing increasingly befuddled by two different histories that I was trying to conflate into a single biography. Vasyl son of Mykola was still the literary scholar who had died in 1930s Kyiv. But Vasyl the son of Mykhail (no identifying photo) is mentioned as a sharpshooter in the post-Second-World-War underground army known as the Ukrainian Insurgent Army and had been killed in a battle with the Soviets in 1947. Now that's a Kostashchuk who had given his life in a battle with the Reds; *my* Vasyl M. probably died peacefully in bed.

I put aside the sharpshooter in order to return to the literary scholar, about whom the booklet has quite a bit to say. He completed *gymnaziia* in Zalishchyky in Galicia, and university in Chernivtsi. Apparently, this much the doting relatives in Canada knew. From 1912–1914 he was a teacher in a private *gymnaziia* in Horodenka, not far from Tulova. At the beginning of the First World War, he was mobilized (one of some 300,000 Ukrainians) in the Austrian army. Was wounded in battles with Russian forces in the Halych-Rohatyn region in Galicia and taken a prisoner of war of the Russians. He lived some time in Kursk and Penza (provinces in western Russia). In 1917–1923 he was a teacher and director of a school in Boryspil south of Kyiv. This is all rather tantalizing: a village scholar in Galicia, a prisoner of war in Imperial Russia, a schoolteacher in Soviet Ukraine, all by the time he was twenty-eight.

I look again at the caption on the picture on page 33 of *There Where the Hunting is Good*, which adds another snippet of information that yet another Kostashchuk of Tulova, Ivan, has the photo in his archive. Perhaps this is the source of the large-tinted version hanging on my wall as well as of the sepia-toned postcard-sized version that spills out of one of my father's manila folders. Someone from the Old Country — Ivan the Archivist, perhaps — has written on it, in English, "Cosin Bill Kostash." According to the booklet, Ivan Kostashchuk was a man of few words who kept his own counsel at meetings until all others had exhausted themselves, all the while quietly assembling a village archive.

It was time to get out of these loops and coils of memorabilia and consult Ukrainian Wikipedia, a stub last edited in October 2014. I didn't know there was such a site until my hosts in Melbourne, Marko and Olya Pavlyshyn, directed me to it: "There's a lot more information in Ukrainian about all things Ukrainian" than on English-language Wikipedia, they explained. And so there was.

Vasyl M. takes on new proportions, bulking up as a historian and bibliographer as well as a literary scholar. (There are no details about his areas of expertise but perhaps I missed the hyperlink.) He had a political life in Galicia, as a member of the Ukrainian Radical Party, the Party that defended the social interests of the Galician peasantry and articulated their still inchoate yearnings for an independent Ukraine as well as the more sophisticated yearnings of a young intellectual such as Vasyl M. How did he "spend" those years in the Russian provinces of Kursk and Penza? "Not exactly interned," Marko conjectured, "but perhaps as a prisoner of war compelled to work on a farm or in a mine, and living outside the camp." In any event, he was able to escape during the turbulent events of the collapse of the Russian Empire in 1917 and returned to Ukrainian territory — to Kyiv, not to the "motherland" in Galicia that had passed into Polish control, not to Tulova, which he seems never to have seen again.

Why would a Galician *independentiste* choose to live and work in Kyiv in the midst of nerve-wracking political turmoil, not to mention violence, battered by multiple deployments of hostile and invading troops, ultimately to be overcome by Bolshevik forces in 1921?

"Given his political affiliations," Marko continued, "he had a socialist vision for Ukraine." Ah, a vision, a "yearning" ignited first in Tulova. In 1917, before Ukraine's fate was sealed within the USSR, Vasyl M. would have rejoiced in the short-lived Central *Rada* (Council) in Kyiv whose delegates represented mainly parties of socialist orientation, "clearly a place where a left-leaning patriotic Ukrainian intellectual would want to be." Perhaps, desperately, he even took heart in the proclamation of a Provisional Workers' and Peasants' Government of Ukraine in 1918 that vowed "All power to Soviets," and with that to complete the Socialist Revolution.

In 1922, after Ukraine's long agony, when its territory had been the arena of war among Bolshevik, White, and Polish armies, what had been Tsarist Ukraine finally became one of the original constituent republics of the Union of Soviet Socialist Republics (USSR). Eastern Galicia, however, had been annexed into the newly reconstituted Polish Republic. Ukraine was "socialist." Vasyl M. would stay.

Weeks later at home, I strolled over to the floor-to-ceiling set of bookshelves that held my collection of books loosely labelled "Eastern Europe" and carefully read the spines of all the books in the Ukraine section. Ah ha! *Literary Politics in the Soviet Ukraine 1917–1934* by George S.N. Luckyj.

Professor Luckyj had been my professor of Ukrainian literature at the University of Toronto in 1968 where I was a graduate student in Slavic Studies. He led a semester in the work of Nikolai Gogol/Mykola Hohol whom he reclaimed for Ukrainian literature. After graduation, I pursued my own curriculum of Slavic studies as a writer and itinerant traveller in Soviet space in the 1980s. Now I fell upon Luckyj's book as a portal to Vasyl M.'s time in Soviet Kyiv, and was rewarded on page 74.

It was January 25–28, 1928, and a new literary organization, the All-Ukrainian Union of Proletarian Writers (VUSPP) sponsored by the Communist Party, had its first Congress. Its timing was no coincidence: the First Five Year (Economic) Plan for the mass industrialization of the Soviet Union had been announced only a month earlier. And now the writers and publishers in Ukraine were called on to do their part. Literature was now subsumed within the "book industry" and assigned a single task, to serve the needs of the socialist construction of the USSR. This entailed the fight for the success of the Plan and to meet the demands of the workers and peasants, above all to "inspire" them.

Even as a student of Russian and Soviet literature in the late 1960s, during the interminable Cold War, I experienced this rhetoric as hackneyed, stale, manipulative, and worthy of my derision. Slogans thundered their ecstatic exhortation: "With shock labour we will ensure prompt delivery of the giants of the Five Year Plan." "All power to the Soviets! Peace to the peoples! Land to the peasants! Factories and plants to the workers!" I hung up Soviet-era posters alongside great black-and-white news photos of Angela Davis and "Hanoi" Jane Fonda: Old Left meet New Left. I was not being ironic.

And there was nothing ironic about the VUSPP. I knew that Vasyl M. was back in Kyiv, was published in the literary quarterly *Ukraine* in 1927 and 1928, and worked on a dissertation, "Issues of Folk Daily Life."

So he was in the thick of things — albeit in one marginal sector — and unlikely to be left alone by the VUSPP, who required his "industrialization." I imagine him trying to hide in their plain sight, camouflaged as a reliable labourer in the collective of SovLit's minor leagues, while the Congress went hammer and sickle after juicier quarry. Intellectuals, that is Ukrainian nationalists, they charged, only pretended to be sympathizers of the internationalist Bolshevik order when actually they "worked for the separation of the Ukraine from the Soviet Union, for the imperialist enslavement of Ukrainian workers and peasants" (Luckyj 197). This was an ideological assault full of menace. The pressure intensified: even the most inoffensive apparatchik of the intelligentsia working in the bowels of the All-Ukrainian Academy of Science lined up behind the VUSPP's cringe-worthy declarations of loyalty. By 1929, intellectuals were offering their services as "active builders" of socialism, "disciplined fighters" in the class struggle, "commanders" of an army of "Ukrainian revolutionary Soviet literature." Vasyl M. was a radical/Radical, but had he signed up for this?

For Vasyl M. there was still a safety valve of sorts. For writers just like him — Galicians who had migrated to the Ukrainian SSR to work for the success of the revolution in Ukraine — the Party encouraged the formation of an aspirational organization, Western Ukraine. No need to pine away for the Galician homeland he had abandoned, lost anyway to Polish fascism, when there was a place for him to belong in the Soviet system.

From 1927, Vasyl M. worked as an associate of the Commission of the History of Western Ukraine within the All-Ukrainian Academy of Science, presumably his comfort zone, all things considered. In 1929–1930 he worked in its Bibliographical Commission, "cataloguing the full scope of publications in a particular field," Marko explained. Four years after Vasyl M.'s death in 1931, counterrevolutionaries having been found plotting against the Party, whole sections of the Academy were "liquidated."

And that was as much as I could flesh out of the life of Vasyl M. who was hanging so uncommunicatively on my wall. Behind the bare biographical details of the life of a minor man of letters in Soviet Ukraine, what was his story?

Among Ukrainian Wikipedia's sources is *Kyiv Historical School: Fate of Its Scholars* (no date). Fate. *Dolia.* Lot, fortune, luck, destiny. What had been the luck of Vasyl M.?

I have read nothing in his own words.

He hangs on my wall in sweetest youth, broad full-lipped mouth under a respectable moustache, a rather long but narrow nose and full eyebrows arched symmetrically above that unerringly serene expression. Nothing has happened to him yet. Not the war, nor the labour camp, nor the collapsed hope of an independent Ukraine, nor the declaration of the First Five Year Plan, nor the serious intellectual pursuits in Bolshevik Kyiv. And nor the ominous Communist Party attacks on "deviation towards local nationalism" that would eventually swell, after Vasyl M.'s rather timely death, into full-scale denunciations and purges, arrests, imprisonment and executions of literary figures throughout the 1930s. In the period 1930–1938 long lists of Ukrainian writers, condemned as "traitors" and "enemies of the people," were silenced, imprisoned, tried and often executed. "Thus the purging of nationalist deviations went on claiming ever more victims. It never ceased" (Luckyj 237).

I have one more source in my files, *Pokutiany* (*People of Pokutia*), a compendium of literary documents, given to me during my second visit to Tulova in 2013. I had already rummaged through it for details about that other Kostashchuk writer, Vasyl Andriovych (b. 1896), the biographical sketches and his correspondence with the celebrated Galician writer, Vasyl Stefanyk. Now I open the book again, looking for Vasyl M. (b. 1884). The book's editor, Vasyl

Kharyton, has done a good job of scraping together the materials he could find, mainly letters and parts of letters to Stefanyk. Of course, Stefanyk is the reason why Kharyton has retrieved Vasyl M. from the archive in the first place — as evidence of a valuable conduit of correspondence for Stefanyk with writers in Soviet Ukraine — but for me almost a century later I am grateful for his effort. Vasyl M. has a voice.

Until 2010, only one of Vasyl M.'s letters to Stefanyk had been published (in 1970) and was on display in the Stefanyk Museum in Rusiv. Perhaps I had even glanced at it though a glass pane. It was written in 1927. Recently, writes Kharyton, six other letters of Vasyl M. to Stefanyk have been found: "Read them, and you will understand why they could never have been published in Soviet times" (19). In 1918, for example, as a briefly independent Ukraine struggled for political sovereignty while menaced by Bolshevik forces, Vasyl M. was writing from Kyiv that "life was going well for me, Ukraine was independent" — and the democratic and parliamentary Central Rada had been passing a series of reformist laws and a constitution — "but then the Bolshevik campaign overturned our Central Rada and was sowing anarchy. In short order, they grabbed power but anarchy will sink them. And so Ukraine will return to its independent existence" (Kharyton 19).

Not so. In January 1923, Vasyl M. confesses to Stefanyk that "my life is completely broken, broken are all our hopes and aspirations in these fractured times that we have come to endure — unless, after us, things will get better" (Kharyton 22). He writes often of his longing to return to Tulova, but it will not happen. Instead, from 1917 to 1923, he is part of a teaching collective in Boryspil high school. In a photograph from the collection of the indefatigable Ivan Kostashchuk, he stands first on the left in the second row, in suit and tie and moustache. He is expressionless, but as Kharyton observes, his miserly teacher's wages meant that life was lived very frugally; worse, in this "insignificant town," Vasyl M.'s circle of friends was very constricted (23). Visitors travelling from Galicia (by then incorporated into Poland) were infrequent and "nothing changed in principle." His isolation would have been total had it not been for the solace he found in his scholarly work — perhaps collecting ethnographic materials for when he would return to his dissertation — and in domestic life with his wife, Lydia, with whom marriage was the "logical, natural step," and the source of a "quiet happiness for an aching heart" (Kharyton 18).

On page 10, I look at an undated studio portrait of Vasyl M. and Lydia Kocherzhynska. He is no longer the dewy school graduate, but now, with a fully grown moustache, white shirt with collar pin and dark tie, dark suit, he's a husband and scholar, his right eyelid noticeably drooping as though he has spent years reading under a poor lamp. Lydia is turned slightly toward him; they are not looking at each other, but she shares his expression of serenity, utterly unsmiling, as though they have settled into the solidarity of connubial affection in a time of social misery.

By January 1924 he is back in Kyiv. The Ukrainian Soviet Socialist Republic had been formed in 1922, and it was perhaps with some residual optimism about the prospects for social and economic justice for the Ukrainian people and most particularly for an efflorescence of Ukrainian arts and letters in this new socialist motherland that Vasyl M. settled down in its heartland. But a letter to Stefanyk at the beginning of the year expresses rather the sorrow of his perpetual estrangement from his first homeland, Galicia, and from its literary life. "Very scanty news has reached us here that you are once again writing, that new work has been published in the literary papers. But we are unable to get hold of them here [in Soviet Ukraine] and we are waiting for those waves that will topple all barriers, when we will be able to enrich our own experiences with your new works" (Kharyton 22).

Vasyl M.'s letters are suffused with nostalgia for his youth in Galicia, or, as Kharyton puts it, with an "autumnal melancholy for his nearest and dearest, his family and friends," whom he had not seen in ages. "Every word, every bit of news, every little detail is such consolation for me ... that I have longed immediately to go back to my native land" (22). And yet he never does.

In the only letter Vasyl M. had written to Stefanyk that was published in the Soviet era (in 1970), he writes in a "voice" that comes from a very different place. It is now 1927. He and his wife Lydia are living in an apartment on Lenin Street in Kyiv. He informs Stefanyk that an all-Ukrainian convention of proletarian writers has taken place, one that (to his evident satisfaction) is "ideologically consistent" and able to "carry on the struggle with every national and petit bourgeois deviation." Does he choke on this formulaic language, he the literary scholar who yearned for a free literature? Significantly, he mentions that, thanks to the Union of Revolutionary Writers of "Western Ukraine," an evening celebrating the twenty-fifth anniversary of Stefanyk's literary debut had been held January 28, 1927 in Kyiv (Kharyton 7). This was the group, Western Ukraine, formed to give sanctuary to writers, like Vasyl M., bound in solidarity with Stefanyk's and their own hope for the eventual reunification of all Ukrainian lands within the socialist project of a liberated people's literature and art. The evening concluded with the audience in unanimous agreement to send a telegram of "warm greetings from Soviet Ukraine" to the honoree, Vasyl Stefanyk, "who was living in the difficult circumstances of Polish oppression" (Kharyton 18).

It is November 6–16, 1930. *Kharkiv hosts the second International Conference of Proletarian Literature in Ukrainian SSR. Western European leftist writers have gathered here — along with their Soviet hosts — among whom "great prominence" is given to the members of the literary group, Western Ukraine. Myroslav Irchan speaks for its members as their delegate. He has recently returned to UKRSSR after several years as a cultural activist among "progressive" Ukrainian Canadians and their organizations, especially in Winnipeg, where he was much feted. At this conference he is still exhilarated by the vision, the dream, of a unified Ukrainian people and a unified Ukrainian culture, gathered together from among the "temporarily" dispersed Ukrainian workers and peasants "under the heel" of Polish, Romanian and Czechoslovakian fascism — he doesn't include the "dispersed" Galicians of western Canada — "separated from their mother country, the Soviet Ukraine" (Luckyj 162).*

The luck of Vasyl Mykolaiovych Kostashchuk

Was he ever a happy man? He had deep but unsatisfied yearnings for a literature of his Galician homeplace, for that homeplace itself, and for an independent Ukraine that would uplift peasant and poet alike. But his nostalgia for Tulova was never quenched, he lived an exile of perpetual spiritual loneliness in Soviet Ukraine, and his political dreams were broken when he was still a young man.

On a gloomy November 10, 1931, in Kyiv, Vasyl Mykolaiovych Kostashchuk peacefully fell asleep in the Lord. (Kharyton 26). Two years later, Western Ukraine was disbanded. Irchan, among many others, was arrested in 1934, accused of acting as an agent of "national fascism" and working to violently overthrow Soviet rule in Ukraine, and shot in 1937. Vasyl M. had already been dead six years. It was a well-timed death, perhaps his only real luck. On page 59 in *Where the Hunting is Good* I find his brother, Dmytro Mykolaiovych, born in 1898 in Tulova. He outlived Vasyl by seventeen years, perishing in Karaganda, Kazakhstan, of hunger in the Gulag archipelago.

5

Nikolai Maksymiuk
1886 – 1918

12518 – 83rd Street, Edmonton, Alberta

I know five things about Nikolai Maksymiuk.

He died in 1918 when his daughter, my mother, was four years old. That's one. After labouring in coal mines somewhere in Poland or Germany, he emigrated to Canada in 1911. That's two. He settled in Edmonton and sent for his betrothed, my grandmother Palahna Kosovan, from the village of Dzhuriv in Galicia. That's three. He worked at a packing plant. That's four. By age thirty-three, he was dead. That's five.

I ask my second cousin, Petro Kosovan, in Zabolotiv, Ukraine, what he remembers of family lore about Nikolai. "Nikolai went to Germany, earned extra money to go to Canada, went there, built a house and then brought your grandmother over in 1912 or 1913. At first, they were poor. They worked very hard." End of story.

I had hoped for more from Ukraine, some thread of the story of Nikolai that they had passed on about the (fantastical?) journey away from the village that had also taken their kinswoman, Palahna Kosovan, with him. The point of view of those who stayed behind. Something to add to his life story as we told it in Canada. But it turns out that from our very different vantage points, a century after the main events and on different continents, Petro and I "remember" exactly the same things.

But there are places, nooks and crannies, where I go looking for my grandfather, or someone like him. He does leave a trace of his brief life in a couple of civic and church documents, a school report, and three photographs; in the transcript of an interview by a researcher with my mother and in my father's unpublished memoir; in a video ballad, on websites, in a Soviet Ukrainian Gazetteer; and, finally, in one of Edmonton's cemeteries.

Nikolai Maksymiuk was born in the Galician village of Dzhuriv, at the time inside Austria-Hungary. No documentation was produced, I just always knew it. Baba always spoke of Dzhuriv as her and Nikolai's birthplace, as did my parents, teaching me how to spell it in Cyrillic and to pronounce it. Джурів. *Djoo-riw*. That's how I could identify the otherwise mysterious airmail letters that came from Soviet Ukraine: I could read the return address. Often they included family photos that I would briefly look at and make no further enquiries about.

Tucked into a hanging file folder that had missed my scrutiny in a file cabinet, I find Nikolai's Baptismal Certificate. As it's in Latin as well as in an unfamiliar, to me, form of Ukrainian, I can't make head or tail of it. I invite a friend to dinner, a historian whose roots also lie in Galicia, and ask him what it reveals. As he strains to read the faded ink in the dim light of the restaurant and I butter bread for both of us, out tumble the names. Nikolai was born in Dzhuriv on June 18, 1886, and his parents, Ivan and Maria, are named, and the Maksymiuk forebears and Maria's, the Lukeniuks, not to forget the godparents: Andryi and Anna Nikiforuk. "All farmers," my friend says, reading from the column *Parentes et conditio*. The midwife is named: Anna Nykoliuk. As is the priest: Fr. Philemon Ponovski. Suddenly, out of the void I had assumed was my grandfather's genealogy, I have great-grandparents and great-great-grandparents. Ivan, Hryhori, Mykhailo, Anastasia, Anna, and two Marias.

In a folder of archival odds and ends assembled by my father ages ago, I find Nikolai's sixth-grade school report, glued on a large sheet of heavy brown paper and drawn up entirely in Polish. I take this over to a Polish neighbour who rattles off the school subjects — arithmetic, geometry, natural history, religion, reading, drawing — all of them *dobrze* (good), as well as *bardzo dobrze* (very good) in the study of the Polish language and in singing, as recorded by the teacher with a flourish of his pen. What to make of this document? That probably there were no more reports, the village school having no more to offer; that, for all Nikolai's scholarly successes, he would go no further, no adventure down the King's Highway and the *gimnaziia* in Kolomyia. He would go down the mines.

On (Ukrainian Canadian artist William) Kurelek's last visit to Borivtsi (his paternal village) he went to the fields to paint and a child found him with his face in the dirt. "I'm alright," Kurelek assured him. "I'm only searching for my roots" (qtd. in Kishkan).

Notes: 1984, visit to Dzhuriv

Sunday. As my relatives drive me through the countryside, I am impressed by how lush it looks, with stands of big, soft trees and rolling, swollen contours of farmland, the fields laid out in large splotches and not on the grid of the Canadian prairie. Ukrainian Canadians like to believe that the vast spaciousness of the prairie and parkland felt like home to the Galician pioneers, but I am thinking how dismal Alberta must have looked — bush and slough and stands of scrawny aspen — compared to this effulgent vista.

Dzhuriv is tidy and colourful. I walk around it and take pictures. An abandoned blue cottage, overwhelmed by its ancient, thatched roof sinking somnolently into a yard gone wild with grasses and yellow daisies. Click. The field behind the Kosovans' house, Baba's people — the celebrated fecund private plot of Soviet agriculture — scrupulously clean of weeds and bordered by fruit trees. Click. A neighbour, stout, baggy-bosomed, and kerchiefed, knee-deep in red and yellow tulips. Click. The church where Baba used to go, still in good shape, white-walled and tin-roofed with a single, squat, hexagonal dome. Click. The very pathway along which the village girls drove the sheep out of the village and into the upland meadow. Click. The family and neighbours in front of the Kosovan house, the little girls with those oddly affecting, enormous white bows on top their heads; at the edge of the group, an aged, stooped crone who seems to have wandered into the picture on her way to the bus stop. Click.

The land is rich and broad and generous. Why have so many people starved here so often? Why do people in the north never taste the fruit of the south? Why do people still shuffle around the cities with their plastic shopping bags looking for a bin, a stall, somewhere that is selling something to eat? Something that is not last winter's soft and shrivelled carrots and beets? Why do they have to buy Canadian wheat to make their bread? Would Baba still have to emigrate?

Years later, when I visit his home office in Hamilton, retired professor of political science Peter Potichnyj sweeps his hand along the
spines of a row of large books bound in blue cloth that are shelved
under a windowsill that supports pots of ferns and geraniums, a
nice touch of homeliness I am thinking, as the professor gestures
again toward the books.

"Where were your grandparents born?"

"Dzhuriv, in Halychyna [Galicia]."

He extracts a volume, explaining that it is part of a Soviet
Ukrainian gazetteer published in the 1970s, and flips its pages until
page 564, where I can read for myself the half-column of potted history of the village of Dzhuriv, population 1,989 souls. It entered the
historical record in 1394, after which nothing seems to have happened there to interest Soviet scholars until the 1860s when a coal
mine was opened. I wondered why Nikolai had left home for the
mines of Silesia when he could have stayed in Dzhuriv and eked
out the bride price for Palahna at the coal seam in his backyard.

The making of a proletarian in Edmonton

At Christmas 1979, my father had distributed his photocopied
memoir, *A Gift to Last*, among Kostash relations in Canada. This too
had been one of his labours at the Remington about which I made
no enquiry, absorbed as I was at the time by research and travels
across Canada for my own book (*Long Way from Home: The Story of
the Sixties Generation in Canada*). Although mine would be a kind of
generational memoir, of our two books it was my father's book that
most affectingly deployed the first-person singular in the act of re-
constructing memory: did I think or say so at the time? Did I even
open the book in Dad's presence and begin the conversation, writer
to writer, that he so obviously invited in dedicating the copy he gave
me: "because you have a genuine interest in your roots"? May it be so.

I did read it at some point because I now remember that Dad had included some little account of the life of Mum's father, Nikolai, and that of his younger brother, Andrew, and so I open *A Gift to Last* again. Dad begins when Nikolai was seventeen and Andrew fifteen, and there was nothing to hold them in the village, neither their father's "pitifully small farm," subdivided each generation, nor the grave of their mother. Ivan Maksymiuk had married three wives and buried two of them when the boys, old enough to shift for themselves, shook the mud off their boots and tramped out of Dzhuriv for the Silesian mines.

My father had obviously done some research, for he claims that the coal mines of Silesia were expanding production and required all sorts of brute labour — the cheaper the better — just when young men like the Maksymiuk brothers were seeking it: "Poor and untutored young Ukrainians were leaving their homes to seek fortunes elsewhere." Because Nikolai was, by my father's account, ambitious, energetic, and intelligent, he was soon selected by bosses "for easier and more responsible work." I do some research of my own and come upon the website of the Caledonian Maritime Research Trust:

A nineteenth-century colliery in Britain, "hot, dusty and wet." The mine could be 500 to 1,200 metres deep, and into this sooty and pitch-black crater the workers were dropped, in a cage, to then walk miles to the coal face (on their own time) and work doubled-over at the coal seams, swinging pick and shovel while women and children loaded the loosened coal onto trucks that were hauled by "miserable" pit ponies to the shaft. At the pithead, women and older or injured miners cleaned the coal, a job they were fit for.

Nikolai may well have been "ambitious, energetic and intelligent," but how, in this scenario, are you compensated what you are worth? Nikolai gave four years to the mines until "he got the itch to go to Canada." But he wasn't after the land, the "free" quarter section. Land — earth, soil — the true measure of a peasant's wealth. But if there wasn't enough of it, it was just muck. He never home-steaded, sinking his luck into a small city lot and the modest house he built on it in Edmonton, then struck out for the packing plant. He would not live to reap the privilege of this landless settlement, his daughter's and granddaughters' public-school education, free and without title.

> My field, O my field!
> By my grandfather won,
> Why dost thou not give
> Me the means of life?
> Bitter toil! With my own blood stained,
> My heart's blood is there.
> How bitter for me, my field,
> To look on thee!   (LIVESAY 76)

From one of my mother's cupboard drawers I retrieve a plastic bag that holds Nikolai's Immigration Inspection Card registering his arrival in Canada (Steerage) from the port of Rotterdam on May 8, 1911, on the ship *Gothland*. Stamped: Passed Medical Examination. Initialled by the Ship Surgeon.

The card, a little yellowed but still impressively stiff, is not large — I line up my metric ruler — 13 cm by 11 cm. I turn it over. "This card should be kept carefully for three years. It should be shown to government officials whenever required." This is repeated in German, French, Dutch, Hungarian, Swedish, Polish, Italian, Bohemian (Czech), Russian, Ruthenian (Ukrainian), and Hebrew (Yiddish in Hebrew script). The document is a curiosity, tangible evidence over three years of Nikolai's evolving Canadian status. But now I wonder whether it sounds rather menacing in those languages, such as Russian and Ruthenian, spoken in unluckier countries of origin than, say, Italy or Sweden? A language spoken by a semi-literate villager from the far side of Europe constantly menaced by officials who represent some unaccountable authority such as the monarchy or the army or the constabulary or, even, the church? So in Canada such cardholders could be similarly stopped arbitrarily and confronted in a language imperfectly understood under suspicion of what, exactly?

It seems the typesetter of this document had no access to a Cyrillic keyboard for he has made a valiant, if nonsensical, effort to represent Slavic sounds with Latin letters. What on earth did Nikolai make of this: *Cro kapmky mpeda mpu poku sobamu?* (My best guess: The bearer must have this card on his person for three years.) His vulnerability to "carding" was acute.

> The Gothland lies sleek and low, almost feline, in the water — in the photo, steaming in a bay alongside a picturesque village of stone houses on a rising hill — her masts furled but her stack belching out a flue of steam. She lies so low in the water that all classes of passenger, not just steerage, are accommodated below the water line. Built at Cessnock Bank Yard, Scotland, in 1871, she moved immigrants and cargo around ports in South Africa, Liverpool, Hamburg as well as Quebec City before passing into the ownership of the British Admiralty as HMS Gothland in 1915 (war booty from the Huns?) and sold on three more times until "laid up" on February 2, 1920. Broken up November 23, 1924, and scrapped by Hendrik-Ido-Ambacht, Germany, she outlived my grandfather by five years. ("Gothland")

On a visit to Halifax shortly after my mother's death in 2010, I wandered into the Canadian Museum of Immigration at Pier 21, vaguely curious about the waves of Galicians who disembarked here in the mass migration of 1900. Not at this pier, apparently, and so I was invited instead to visit the Genealogy Centre for information about specific immigrants. The youthful researcher had more enthusiasm for the search than I did: I had never been persuaded that genealogical databases would yield much of anything about the so-called ancestry of Galician peasants.

But there Nikolai was, on the purser's page of the *Gothland*'s manifest: age twenty-five, born in Austria, of the Ruthenian "race of people," destined for Winnipeg (?), by previous occupation a "farmhand," and for his intended occupation in Canada, "farmhand" (really, Dido?), a "Catholic," travelling inland by CPR, with forty dollars burning in his pocket. No one else on that purser's page had half as much, perhaps not having gone first to the mines.

Wait! I want to ask him: why didn't you say you were a coal miner by "previous occupation"? How were you destined for Winnipeg when in fact you were making a beeline for Edmonton? As for your "intended occupation" in Canada as a farmhand, it was no such thing. You would get off the train in Edmonton and never leave its boundaries. Those hallowed 160 acres of "free land," towards which the hordes streamed from the Strathcona train station via Edmonton's Land Titles Office? You never made the claim. You would try your luck and fortune at the Swift Canadian Company Plant, on the killing floor.

Nikolai settles in the city

In 1911, 692 Edmontonians, or 2.8% of the population, were of Ukrainian origin (Swyripa 431) and worked mainly as unskilled labourers and domestic servants but also as aspiring merchants and teachers. According to *Henderson's* Winnipeg and Edmonton City Directories for 1911, the largest unskilled category of male

Ukrainians in Edmonton was one hundred "labourers." Also in that category are fifteen miners and three farmers. Among the skilled, one clergyman, three students, seven carpenters, and six blacksmiths (qtd. in Martynowych 132). Out on the homesteads? *Thousands* of Ukrainians, and more on their way.

But Nikolai was on his way to becoming an Edmontonian, and I look for him and try to picture him in the urban institutions of "Anglo" Edmonton that had the resources to give a semi-skilled, semi-literate immigrant a hand up. Methodist clergy, for example, Ukrainian converts among them, founded missions and perhaps Nikolai wandered into one of their Ukrainian-language services — Palahna Kosovan had not yet arrived — grateful too for their storefront operation on Kinistino Avenue, not far from the farmers' market, where the Methodists helped publish a Ukrainian-language newspaper. They competed for Galician souls with the Presbyterians, who opened a mission on the same avenue, in a converted smithy.

What was in it for Nikolai? Assimilation of a sort, into the city, its civic institutions (schools, hospitals, tax offices), an economy (that farmers' market, a lumberyard, coal mines in the river bank, a stockyard), roads that intersected as streets north-south with avenues east-west, and houses erected on narrow lots that formed Edmonton's rudimentary neighbourhoods. And jobs: ditchdiggers, draymen, housepainters, blacksmiths, slaughterhouse workers.

Not everyone would be lucky on the land, and, perhaps, on those trips to downtown (for that newspaper, that Lord's Prayer in Ukrainian, a sack of potatoes), Nikolai saw the luckless ones, down-at-the-heels, the lousy and unshaven, succoured by the Protestant Mission workers. In his memoir of touring the North-West Territory (today's Alberta and Saskatchewan) in 1897, Rev. Nestor Dmytriw, missionary priest from Pennsylvania, surveyed the representatives of "his" people from villages near Borshchiw in

Galicia and found them destitute: penniless, cheated by CPR agents, now "ill-clad, half-naked, barefoot, dirty." He declared that they brought "only disgrace upon our nation" (Hoerder 164).

Nikolai spent his small hoard of dollars on the purchase of a city lot in the northeast end of town, built a house on it and got a job in a packing plant even further east in Edmonton's Packingtown. He may have been processed by the Immigration officer in Quebec City as an intended farmhand, but once through and out the sheds on the pier, he had no more intention of wheedling sustenance out of dirt, thick and black and loamy as it was, than of sailing the sands of Araby.

"Along These Railroad Tracks"

> There's new folks rolling in like waves of grain / Nothing to
>   lose and everything to gain
>
> For an honest job, with honest pay / We'll put up with the
>   squeals, the squeamish they won't stay
>
> Who doesn't need a place to break her bread? / Who doesn't
>   need a place to lay his head?
>
> (Here's) a chance to leave old poverty behind / With a willing
>   hand for any work you find.
>
> (DUNN ET AL.)

The Swift Canadian Company had opened operations in North Edmonton in 1908. By 1913, the plant employed 400 people slaughtering cattle, hogs, sheep, and poultry.

How my mother remembers Nikolai, the Dad she never knew

My mother was eighty-nine years old in 2004, ten years widowed, of sound mind and still living in her own home, when she was inter- viewed for several hours by a researcher for the "Local Culture and Diversity on the Prairies Project" at the University of Alberta's Ukrain- ian Folklore Centre. He was Andryi Chernevych, from Ukraine, at her kitchen table to get the stories of her generation of Ukrainian Canadian teachers. Mum's stories of her girlhood growing up at the near edge of Edmonton I knew almost by heart, so often did she repeat them as she grew older. But I transcribed the hours of this interview nevertheless because now I was looking for Baba Palahna.

There are three extant photographs of Nikolai Maksymiuk, and my mother held up one of them, taken on his wedding day, to show the university student-interviewer. "Look," she says, over the tape recorder on her kitchen table, "Wasn't my father a hand- some man?" The small photograph, still in excellent condition in its wooden frame — the expressions, on the faces of the bridal couple, are of startling clarity — now hangs on my bedroom wall. (What does the university student see?)

I see a short, stocky, and swarthy man with a moustache that frames his upper lip and ends in a little twist. His dark brows are drawn together above a fixed, almost glinty, gaze, his nose and ears are finely shaped, and he is as unsmiling as his bride. He's short but with a manly set to his shoulders. He had, after all, built the house on the stoop of which the couple stands before he sent for her.

There is a second photo of Nikolai and Palahna's wedding day. It was quite a party. In the three years that Nikolai had been in Edmonton, he had acquired a sizeable community of friends and compatriots to judge from the crowd of men, women, and chil- dren, either sprawled on the grass or squished together in front of the house, 12518–83rd Street. My grandfather is distinguishable in his suit, white shirt, and tie, from the unjacketed men, while my grandmother is a standout in a long white dress with its veil falling back from a floral crown. There is not a single embroidered shirt or sheepskin vest or headscarf to be seen.

To my eyes the only visual clue to this being a Ukrainian wedding party is the dulcimer player seated in the front row, his traditional *tsymbaly* secured on his lap by a thick strap around his neck, his hands lightly holding the two wooden hammers as though poised any second to hit the strings, just as the fiddler next to him, knees crossed, rests his bow lightly in position on the fingerboard. If they were invited, I assume this means there was singing and dancing soon after the photo was taken.

There is no priest.

But their marriage certificate — in a language neither groom nor bride could read — certifies that "Nykolai" and "Polame" (*sic*) were indeed duly "united in the bonds of matrimony" on May 2, 1914, as witnessed by Fedor Nykoluk and D. Semeniuk. Witnesses but no clergyman's signature. I begin to suspect a wedding party of a bunch of socialists but, no, for my father in his memoir records that a "genuine minister," a Rev. Wilchinski, had officiated. He's not in the photo; he couldn't even stay for lunch.

Nikolai Maksymiuk is now twenty-eight years old. He has a wife, a house, neighbours, and a job for seventeen cents an hour as a labourer at the Swift Canadian packing plant. And he has an Anglo name, Nick.

Postcard circa 1920s

You could buy this image of the Swift Canadian Company Plant as it stood in 1914 and mail it to someone to impress, that Edmonton had its own "industrial centre." And over it loomed the great stacks of the packing plants, as slender and upright as the abattoir and packing operations were squat, crouched under the weight of a million bricks. In the 1920s, the Swift Canadian plant was merely functional — swathes of featureless cubes of brick, walls punched with rectangular windows no better than squint. But the smoke-stack soars right out the top of the frame. The first time that I contemplate this image, I think: "If my grandfather has a grave, it may as well be here."

In his memoir, *A Gift to Last*, my father included some brief notices about my mother's origins, that she was born March 27, 1915, in Edmonton to Nick and Palahna Maksymiuk, but was "orphaned" at the age of four when Nikolai died, most likely of pneumonia. "No one at the time seemed to know what ailed him."

My mother to interviewer: "My father died of pneumonia, walking to and from the meat-packing plant."

The Maksymiuks did not live in Packingtown (the community established in the early 1900s near packing plants) but a kilo-metre west of it in a working-class neighbourhood with "English" neighbours — that is, anyone for whom English was their mother tongue — among the Ukrainians. They were families who raised chickens and even, as in Baba's case, grazed a cow along the rail-way tracks across the street. The question arises: if they had lived in Packingtown, sparing Nick the long slog to and from Swift's in all weathers, might he have been spared the pneumonia?

Or was it the work itself that weakened him, a working day in which 350 cattle, 1,200 hogs, 500 sheep and lambs and 500 calves were slaughtered, their carcasses hauled around by men and not by machines? Workers on the killing floor lost fingers, hands, whole limbs to their own butcher knives while in the tankhouse, where all the inedible parts of an animal, its bone, guts, horns and hooves were rendered into oils and fertilizer. Alex Goruk worked at Canada Packers in the 1940s: it was a "dirty place to begin with, you know, all the guts and the blood and the hair" (qtd. in Chambers 5).

If Nick worked in the room where blood was dried to a powder for use in animal feed, this job alone, month after month, may have killed him. When the blood was dry, workers scooped it into gunny sacks, and after about ten minutes of this operation, "you couldn't see the fellow holding the bag and he's standing only two feet away." The tankhouse air was thick with fine dust, blood dust, and for the next two days, you spat and choked, coughing up blood (qtd. in Chambers 5). Is this what happened to Nick? Yet my father wrote that no one seemed to know what "ailed" him, and my mother, grieving and mourning a father she never knew, could narrate no details of his dying that would pinpoint a cause.

Pneumonia was to take my paternal grandfather too, in 1936, but he had lived his whole life on a farm, so you can't say that there is a special fate meted out to slaughterhouse workers when the lung's sacs, inflamed by bacteria, fill with pus and you drown in the fluid of your own lungs. There is no penicillin for anyone. "And no one knew what ailed him."

Meanwhile, at 12518–83rd Street, up in the attic: Andrew, who had worked at Silesian coal faces alongside Nick, his older brother by two years, then waited to be sent the steerage ticket to Canada, arrived in 1912, and was settled into the attic room.

There is another photograph of Nick together with Andrew, with no caption, cropped top and bottom and lifted untidily from the black paper of a photo album. This must have been taken in Canada, to judge from the Canadian style of shirts, jackets, and ties the men wear. They stand side by side against a backdrop of a tall hedge (looks like caragana with mature pods). They don't look much like siblings, Nick having a darker complexion and thick, dark brows and moustache that give him a martial air compared to Andrew's youthful hairless face and woebegone expression. What might have been the occasion for such a formal pose? Perhaps they wanted a picture taken to be sent back to Dzhuriv, to confirm that Andrew was indeed in the care of his older brother, that they were prospering, that they could afford the making and posting of a photograph, but I have no recollection of any correspondence mentioned, discussed, or reread between the Maksymiuk brothers and their relatives in Galicia. In any event, the photo seems never to have been sent off and became, I imagine, a kind of keepsake for my mother — among whose papers I found it — of her handsome father who loved her very much.

I don't suppose Nick died in a hospital. Who would have had the money for that? Was a doctor even summoned? Perhaps neighbours were summoned or were aroused by the sounds of my grandmother's unintelligible panic, my mother's wails, Andrew's helpless groans as he realized he was about to be set adrift in this grieving household. When it came time to bury Nick, I hope it is true that, according to a history of Ukrainian labour in Canada, funeral costs were paid from the wages he had earned but never collected (Petryshyn 118–9). Not a pauper's grave, then. There were gravediggers. It was winter. Did they lay him deep?

What if?

Of Nick's enduring memory in the family, I heard my mother's recitations so many times that it became impossible to discern where my mother's "real" memory blurred into a received one before becoming a newly constructed memory that was her own. Nick never shouted at her or Baba. He was kind. He "doted" on her. Mum had grown up knowing, from his widow's repeated recitations, that he had loved his little Maria with all his heart. When he came through the back door still stinking of the slaughterhouse (I'm adding this detail), still in his coveralls, he would scoop her up and whirl her around the tiny kitchen, her still-pudgy arms locked around his neck. She giggled with delight as he brushed his moustache back and forth across her chubby cheeks and only then turned to embrace his wife. He "spoiled" her as the only child. That's it. And now this is how I too "recall" Nick Maksymiuk.

For the next ninety-one years my mother suffered the inconsolable melancholy of the plaintive question: "What if?" What if Nick had lived out his allotted years as a loving husband and father, what then would have been the lives of his wife and his daughter, my Baba, my mother? Would they have been sweetened by his kindness, his steadfastness, his solicitude? I feel a small shudder of the melancholy myself: what if Nick, my biological grandfather, had survived to be the Dido of my childhood and not the man I called Dido all my life, Nick's brother, Andrew?

Mother tells the interviewer what happened next: "And when a bachelor would come courting her — her, a good-looking widow, a good cook and housekeeper, with a cow (who was tested every year for TB), chickens, a garden — I would scream my head off. So hard that mother was afraid I'd faint. Mother didn't know what to do. She needed a man to help her make money."

The solution lay in her own home: Andrew up in the attic bedroom, quiet, sober, familiar to the child. They married in February, 1919, barely two months after burying Nick. The family carried on — a daughter, Anne, was born to Palahna and Andrew — but Andrew was only my mother's stepfather, to whom she owed and showed respect but never filial love.

In 1918, just as he had depended on Nikolai for the job in the coal pit, just as he had waited for his brother to pay for his steamer ticket and set him up in the house in Edmonton, so now he could not even court and wed a woman of his own nor raise a family of his own: instead, he inherited this hand-me-down widow and a child screaming her head off.

Afterlife

> Chautauqua is the name given to travelling tent shows which originated in the USA and flourished in Canada 1917–35. Of Seneca origin, the word 'chautauqua' has been translated variously as "place of mists," "place of easy death," and "where the fish was taken out." ...
>
> In 1918 chautauquas took place in 294 Canadian towns,... all in the West. A chautauqua offered different programs for each day of its five or six day stay at a given location. Music might be supplied by any combination of soloists, small vocal groups ... choirs, instrumental ensembles, or orchestras. Song and dance acts were popular, as were ethnic music groups.... Novelty acts were booked regularly for tours.... Soloists included the Toronto baritone Ruthven H. McDonald, the Edmonton soprano Edna Reed, and the Metropolitan Opera baritone J. Horace Smithey. ("Chautauqua")

Mum is about fifteen years old. She has girlfriends from the family of daughters two doors down on 83rd Street. A chautauqua is in town.

They all decide to go to a séance conducted by a travelling medium in a tent rigged up in Borden Park. To inspire confidence in the audience, I imagine the medium is dressed in a fringed shawl, jingles a number of bangles, and holds a cloudy globe between her hands, although this is superfluous to her technique. She tells her audience: "If there is someone here who wants to receive a message from the Other World, give me something with which I can make contact," or words to that effect. What does my mother offer? She won't have a watch until she goes teaching, nor does she wear jewellery, so perhaps she hands over a hairpin or a glove.

Stiffening in a trance, rubbing mother's hairpin (or glove), the medium calls out: "There is a message coming in ... from a man, young, dressed well … in a suit and tie … he wants you to know that you are under his protection, he is guarding you, everything will be all right." Back home, bewildered, a bit shaken, Mum tells Baba what has happened. Baba screams. The medium has described Nick's suit, the tie, the shirt and shoes as he was dressed for burial.

My mother told this story many times. And then, as she became more forgetful perhaps even of this story, she stopped.

Baba Palahna did not long outlive Dido Andrew and they are buried together under a flat granite plaque emblazoned MAKYS-MIUK. It was my mother's custom and then mine with her — and is now mine — to visit the family graves and, if it were high summer, to lay flowers from her garden. This was done also for my benefit, so that when the time came for me to make this remembrance on my own, I would know where the ancestral bones lay.

On one such visitation to the cemetery, my mother announced — for the first time ever in my recollection — that she wanted to find her father's grave. We presented ourselves to the genial staff person at the office of the Edmonton Cemetery, the city's oldest, and so the fruitless search through the databases began. Were there alternative spellings for his name? Are you sure it was 1918? Do you have any documentation, an obituary notice? As far as the databases were concerned, Nikolai or Nick Maksymiuk had not been buried in Edmonton in 1918, nor in 1919 or 1920….

Seventy-five years after Nick's death, my mother cannot find his grave. On reflection, I found it extraordinary that Mum did not know the place. Had Baba made solitary visits to the grave, sparing her daughter the pity and the mourning? But my mother did mourn, and as she rose, with a resigned slump of her shoulders, and thanked the staffer for her trouble, I could feel the exhaustion of her mourning, a depletion and beyond repair. Five years after my mother's death in 2010, I would set out in her place to find my grandfather's grave.

6

Palahna Kosovan
1892 – 1979

Baba

There are ways in which my grandmother and I are
more like each other than either of us is like the generation between us — my parents, her children. Baba is
uncontestably Ukrainian or "Galician" as she called herself when she came to Canada.... And I am a Canadian.
Unhyphenated. She has acquired enough English to
make her way with shopkeepers, bus drivers, and me.
I have sponged up enough Ukrainian to be courteous
with priests, great-aunts, and her. We share a mutual but

mystified curiosity about the conditions in which the other was bred and a respectful astonishment that the hardship and bedevilment of the one life underlie the jubilation and ease of the other, mine. We are tourists in each other's history, and conduct ourselves accordingly. In each other's country, we do not try to pass as natives.

FROM MY "BABA WAS A BOHUNK,"
SATURDAY NIGHT, OCTOBER 1976

I wrote the above while working on my first book, *All of Baba's Children*, rehearsing some of its main arguments. "Baba Was a Bohunk" was published under the editorship of Robert Fulford (he had bought my first-ever published piece in 1972), who, despite his ten-year seniority on my generation of fledgling magazine writers, was encouraging of our New Journalism breaches of journalistic conventions. At least, that's how I read my own supremely confident voice, encouraged by his editorial leniency, opining, without presenting much evidence, on the identity and presumed history of my maternal Baba. I had been away from western Canada for a decade, during which I had rarely spoken with her but depended on my mother's news to stay in touch.

The piece's title was formulated by the editors and didn't bother me in the least, because it was true: athough the *Canadian Oxford Dictionary* defines "bohunk" as "derogatory," literally, it means "an immigrant from central or SE Europe" (154). But now, retrospectively, I am truly nonplussed by the subtitle, "And so am I — a stranger, despite three generations in Canada," given that I was making precisely the contrary point. I do not recall noticing this flagrant discrepancy at the time. The titular "bohunk" was doing its job, earning me a notoriety and a prospective readership for the book I was still writing, *All of Baba's Children*.

The piece is illustrated by a handsome black-and-white photograph of the two of us seated shoulder-to-shoulder — I, a head taller — on Baba's sofa. I have no recollection of the event, but there must have been considerable disordering of her modest living room to find a place for camera, cables, and lights, and there must have been instructions to tilt a chin, shift a shoulder. Someone artfully arranged the embroidered cushions that are perched behind our heads while the celebrated portrait photographer Arnaud Maggs, all the way from Toronto, took his best shots. (From the editorial perches in Toronto, there were no professional photographers in Edmonton in sight.) My expression is one of serenest imperturbability, but Baba, who has donned her two-stranded pearl necklace for the occasion, at least has the presence of mind to look bemused.

One photograph after another

August 2004, Edmonton: Mum has brought out photographs to show the interviewer.

> I just want to show you this wedding picture. Wasn't my father a handsome man? And I never knew him. He died when I was four [voice quivering]. That's the house: 12518–83rd Street. It's gone now.... Look at the size of this house. See the haystack by the house? The cow was in the barn, there. That's the shed where we kept the coal, next to the well where my mother kept the milk bottles. See the fence? My stepfather didn't fix it, so Baba tried to. That's my sister and a friend.... And here's my mother on one of her birthdays. She was such a sweetheart, a lovely, lovely lady.

There is a cool formality in that reference to her "stepfather" — not inappropriate in an interview with a stranger to the family — but I catch the implied indictment of a man who was not the handsome father who had, after all, built the house.

My mother's stories were my first lessons in how love works — how a teenaged girl, my mother in the 1930s, could so love her mother (called "Baba" by us all), so empathize with her circumstances and feel the pangs of daughterly duty, that every Saturday she would be down on her hands and knees, with pail and rags, to wash the meagre flooring of the house to spare Baba that chore at least. She would get to her homework later. (My sister and I, teenagers of another, selfish, generation, were meant to "listen up" during the recitation of this oft-told reminiscence.) The washing of floors, pasturing the cow on the lush grass beside the CPR tracks, and hauling pails of drinking water were all outward expressions of deepest filial love.

I am looking at some of Mum's square, black-and-white photographs from her albums. In one of them, the house is not in sight, but I see in the yard a crude pole fence, a shed, and a junk pile on the other side of the fence. Despite Baba's interventions, the fence is decrepit. Unplaned poles are held together by wire, slung lengthwise with wide enough gaps between them to let a cow through. A later photograph, captioned "1920," includes Palahna and Andrew's daughter as a toddler and five-year-old Mum standing in what seems to be an overgrown field bordered with unkempt willow bushes. Perhaps this was the very edge of urbanization, the house just out of frame.

I never knew that house. It was the one attached to all my mother's girlhood stories and the one she meant when she pleaded with me in her last couple of years for a drive "home." I explained that it no longer stood. But, I would add, the one she lived in from 1963 to 2007 was very much standing — "Look, Mum, there's a photo of it on your bookshelf!" — but that wasn't what she meant any longer by "home."

I had forgotten that I have among my own photos one of the 83rd Street house when it still stood. It's a coloured photo cropped square and probably taken on one of my visits to Edmonton when I lived in Toronto. I may even have taken it when on a nostalgic Sunday drive with my parents. I look at it now and can barely see any resemblance to the house in Mum's photographs. It's tucked inside a white picket fence and seems to have been raised in order to build a proper basement. A new blue asphalt-shingled roof and a modest bed of flowers beside the front steps indicate that its current owners are taking care of it. The trees are mature, a cement sidewalk has been laid; there's a garage in the next-door neighbour's yard. It is impossible to imagine the haystack and cow barn of my mother's recollection. I drove down the street just the other day and there is no longer such an address.

The house had two storeys. One main room, a bedroom, and the kitchen on the main floor. Upstairs, one big attic room. Baba kept her milk pails and bottles on a side porch. No running water, no electricity. Mum had to walk three blocks over to the municipal standpipe for drinking water — her job, except in winter.

Is this poverty that the interviewer and I are witnessing? Baba was poor most of her life, or at least frugal; although, as a child, I didn't realize that this was what I was seeing — her stooped body lumped inside the homemade dresses she sewed on her pedal Singer (she never wore trousers), patched dishtowels fashioned from sugar sacks, and chipped enamel ware in which she baked the *holubtsi* (stuffed cabbage rolls).

I listen to the tapes, stopping to type, pressing play for another couple of minutes, hour after hour. My mother is clearly enjoying having this captive audience from the university. They speak mostly in English, and they go back to the beginning. How, for all their frugality, the Maksymiuks — Baba and Dido, Mum and her sister Annie — were never hungry. They harvested a prodigious number of vegetables from the garden, made cheese and butter from the cow's milk, gathered eggs, and occasionally butchered a chicken for meat and soup. Baba baked large loaves of white bread and was an excellent cook with what she had. An apple for dessert.

When Baba had some extra "pin money" from the sale of eggs and cream to neighbours or from taking in the laundry of women whose homes she cleaned or from hoeing for ten cents an hour in the acre of carrots of the "Chinese garden," she might arrive home with candy for her girls, once she had paid for cooking oil and flour.

When Mum regaled my sister and me with the rich details of her recollection, we heard them equally with a sense of wonderment at such a charming, quaint world and as the life lesson we were meant to absorb: "If you don't have it, you don't miss it."

Of course, there was never money for toys, none at all, not even an orange in the Christmas stocking. But "we made our own fun." That old barn in the yard? You threw a ball back and forth over its roof. On the stoop of the house, a game of jacks. Hide and seek in the hedges. In the fall, at the raking up of leaves and ground litter, you built a small bonfire and in the ashes roasted potatoes that you had grubbed for like leftover treasure in the upturned trenches of the potato patch while Annie played cowboy songs on her harmonica, and the next-door neighbour sent over marshmallows.

There was a cow and a barn and a haystack, but this was still a city lot — a "kind of" road ran in front of the houses and the municipal water pipe stood in a community yard — and there was a neighbourhood and neighbours. And it is in the midst of these neighbours that another love is nurtured, one that opens up from the triad of Baba and her daughters to embrace Baba's women friends around the block.

The girl from Dzhuriv settles in

It began on Baba's wedding day.

If the photograph is to be believed, the photographer is standing far enough back from the front yard of 12518–83rd Street to include the entire party in the frame. I count seventy-four people, including the wedding couple; the groom's brother; one baby; a handful of children; and in the front row, the *tsymbaly* (zither) player and a fiddler. The crowd is overwhelmingly young men, presumably still unmarried, all in white shirts and ties, some with moustaches but no beards, bearing fine heads of well-groomed hair. The young women wear long white dresses — this is 1914, none is a "flapper" yet — some belted or pinned with rosettes and some with bits of frippery on their coiffures. An older woman stands in no-nonsense white shirt and tie — could she be a teacher? — but otherwise the female guests look like handmaidens attending the Queen of May. As in the Old Country, this will be a wedding that lasts two days.

The photo, 105 years old, is in its original cardboard frame. I turn it over and read, still legible in a hurried Cyrillic script: "Ukrainian wedding! In Canada, in the city of Edmonton, a wedding took place in the year 1914, the month of May." Another hand in green ink has added: "Comrade Nikolai Maksymiuk." Each face in the crowd is as clear as though illuminated, waiting for the photographer's lamp to flash so the merriment can begin. I am looking, from face to face, and there, at the very edge of the group as though he had just inserted himself, uninvited, is a short man wearing suspenders but no tie or belt. The suspenders are holding up his baggy trousers that are too short in the leg and balloon around his hips. He must be a "comrade," but he is visibly poor and, perhaps like Palahna, feeling a stranger amongst smart immigrants who had already formed a compact community, into which she will eventually be assimilated in the hall of the Ukrainian Labour-Farmer Temple Association (ULFTA). But she doesn't know that yet.

Baba is framed by the doorposts of the house, in front of which the crowd has assembled, and we see the stamp of proprietorship, the numbers 12518, on the same plain, shingled, and wood-framed structure that will be in the background of so many of my mother's photos. But on this wedding day nothing yet has happened: my grandparents stand at the literal threshold of their (foreshortened) future. In five years, the groom will be dead; the clean-shaven youth standing behind Baba's right shoulder in the crowd, a rosette pinned to his shirt, the groom's brother and groomsman, Andrew, will be the new proprietor; and my mother will know him as "father," or formally as stepfather, the man who will raise her and her half-sister, Annie, and I will know him as Dido. It is as though Nikolai's role in the scheme of things was to bring his brother and then his bride to Canada, and then to withdraw from the scene so the rest of the story could unfold through two more generations.

The courtship of Nikolai and Palahna began in the Galician village of Dzhuriv where they had both grown up. The tale circulated among family members as far back as I remember acquired embellishments in the way of storytelling and suffered deletions in each new recital. My father committed it to publication when he repeated it yet again in his memoir, so this is the version I subscribe to, without knowing, however (because I never asked) what was his source or whether he too had created yet another version. And here, in my recounting, is one more. I have no reason to believe there will be another.

Nikolai first noticed Palahna at a church feast when she was still a shy and giggly maiden at the more-than-marriageable age of nineteen. His mind made up, he approached old man Kosovan to let him know that, although he would like to court Palahna, he was on his way to Canada. Once settled there, with work and a house, he would send for her. In due course, the money was sent from Canada to pay for the journey.

Baba had her misgivings. Of course she did, for she hardly knew this Nikolai, except that he seemed to be a nice man, and she knew even less about Canada. But her father, who had three other daughters to marry off and was struggling to sustain the household as a carter — hauling casks of beer to the local taverns and then drinking up most of the profits — gave his blessing to the union, and off Baba went, on her own, leaving behind an entire world of family and neighbours, not to say a motherland she would never see again.

> Marusya, Marusya, dost thou not lonesome feel?
> And tears from thy blue eyes must surely unbidden steal.
> In a strange new country thy wedding-day sun must rise;
> And none of thy kin will be near thee to love, praise or advise.
> This is sung [Livesay notes] by a maiden about to be married
> in a land far from her parents and native land.
>
> (LIVESAY 39)

Someone in the family has kept her passport. It's a pocket-sized document, its pages threaded together by a thin twist of orange and black string, still intact, and bearing the stamp of Vienna's Westbanhof in 1914. Inside, the pages bear German and Polish text with handwritten details in ink, a flourish of German I can't read until I resort to Google Translate.

Build: Medium. Face: Oval. Hair: (I can't make this out). *Ears:* (ditto). *Nose:* (ditto). *This passport is valid until March 11, 1915. Issued at Sniatyn March 11, 1914.*

In the name of His Majesty Francis Joseph I, Emperor of Austria, King of Bohemia, etc., and Apostolic King of Hungary.

Then, shuffled inside other papers I find a vellum page inscribed in English, in a sure-handed cursive, a text that overlaps with that of the passport (it even says so: "Passport for Palahna Kosowan, travelling from Dzurov to America-Canada") and supplies missing details. *Hair: Black. Eyes: Grey. Mouth: Moderate. Character and occupation: Charwoman.*

Perhaps Palahna Kosovan has the moderate mouth of a charwoman, a "woman hired by the day or hour for housework" ("Charwoman"). It is a curious "occupation" for a village girl who had only ever worked for her family, beating their soiled linen down by the creek with paddles on a rock or milking the cow, and so on, for her keep until marriage. But now she would be living in a city, and for all she knew work as a charwoman is what she could expect.

All remaining eleven pages of her passport are blank. She got as far as she was going on a one-way ticket. A woman not yet even legally a person in the Dominion of Canada, she stepped off the train and planted herself in Edmonton, in a wood-frame house built for her and their future children by the man who had left her father the money to send her on, and that was that. Baba was home.

Nikolai Maksymiuk met her at the station platform with a horse and wagon and conveyed her home. Nikolai had been in Canada for three years and so he must have been wearing a shirt and trousers with suspenders, his wedding suit hanging in the closet.

There are no photos of her before her wedding picture in 1914, but having come direct from Dzhuriv, I expect she was dressed in some version of village-style dress, the iconic stranger in the sheepskin coat at a railway station. Immigration minister Clifford Sifton's policy was to bring in "stalwart peasant[s] in sheepskin coats" ("Ukrainian Canadians") to farm the Canadian west; and there they stand, newly-landed, some barefoot, in a famly line-up at the railway tracks. Several layers of handwoven skirts and aprons, an embroidered blouse, a sheepskin vest, a kerchief wrapped around the entirety of her hair. Good boots, I think. Perhaps her dead mother's wealth in coral beads. She was naïve and unsophisticated and would not have known yet to feel humiliated by that wardrobe.

They were married within a week.

Before their wedding day, Palahna had been taken in hand by a businesslike but good-hearted neighbour, Mrs. Hafia Janishewsky, who had been in Canada already fourteen years and knew where to shop.

In her wedding photo, Palahna is dressed in a long white dress, tightly fitted around her waist, collared up to her chin, her hair swept up under a splendid wreath of ornamental pearls and flower blossoms, and from it a gauzy veil flows down her back. Her groom has pinned her arm against him; it hangs listlessly, but there's no missing the white handkerchief she has balled up in her hand. Nikolai, short, mustachioed, suited, stands shoulders pulled back, chin slightly tilted up, and wears on his face an expression of serene gratification. On hers an unsmiling apprehensiveness — "Who *is* this man?"

It was a "traditional" wedding, according to my father, with a Reverend Wilchinski, a church cantor from Bukovyna with a fair education, presiding. Someone had prepared plenty of food for the horde of guests, for by this time Nikolai had embedded himself as a member of the working class at the packing plant and had many comrades.

I look at Baba's face again and I can believe that a few minutes earlier, hanky clenched in her tightened fist, she had been weeping behind the door.

She brought no photographs with her from the village and never owned a camera. But she went to the photography studio in

Edmonton at least once when she was a young mother. The image is printed as a postcard. Mum is about nine or ten years old (although with her long legs and slender arms she could be older). She is wearing a white frock with eyelet trim at the sleeves and hem, and a bow somehow fixed to her straight, flat hair: is this a dress handed down from a woman whose delicate laundry Baba took into her own wash basin? Her chubby younger half-sister, Annie, looks to be about five years old and stands on a stool, slightly knock-kneed in her laced-up ankle boots. Except for little Annie who has kept her head tilted slightly, eyes downcast and half-lidded, with an expression of forbearing melancholy, Baba and Mum stand transfixed, arms at their sides, eyes wide open staring into the lens as though down the barrel of a gun.

Great grandmother

In 1975, directors Anne Wheeler and Lorna Rasmussen made a film for the National Film Board, *Great Grand Mother*, an "ode" to the women who had "settled the prairies" from earliest immigration through suffrage campaigns, world wars, "and beyond." They interviewed my Baba, who they introduce as Pauline Maksymuk. She's in colour, a green sweater over her shoulders, her two strings of pearls around her neck, with an exuberance of cross-stitched pillows behind her head, one of which is now in my home — *and she's speaking English.* (I am gobsmacked by the possibility that she and I did converse throughout my childhood but that I remember none of it.) Her wedding picture, bride and groom on the stoop of their Edmonton house, is on the screen.

I surmise that the interviewer's question is about her emigration to Edmonton from Dzhuriv, for Baba is saying, "No, I don't want to go," and shaking her head. "Why?" asks the off-screen interviewer. "Because I don't know Canada, because I'm scared.

I know it's twenty-three years I live over there [in Dzhuriv], maybe it's danger for me, it's one boy, only one time I see him. It's not handy for me to go but I have to go. Wait one week, wait two weeks, wait three weeks, and my daddy says, 'When you go? When you go?' And I say, 'Later, later.' 'No,' daddy says, 'you go right now.'"

She responds to another, inaudible, question from the off-screen interviewer: "Oh, wedding big. I have some picture from my wedding. It sure is big. All week, cook and eat and drink, cook and eat and drink. But I go upstairs and cry. Because nobody … because all *chuzhi* [strangers]" — on the screen we see the wedding picture — "I don't know the people, they Ukrainian people but no family, so I went inside and cry. For my brother, my sister, I cry" (Wheeler and Rasmussen).

I hadn't recalled the tale in a couple of decades but now, viewing the film on my laptop, I did in its completeness. The jist of it always was Baba's profound reluctance to leave the village and join a man to whom she had been betrothed without her consent, to begin a shockingly new life for which she was utterly unprepared. And yet look at her now! Matriarch of a couple of generations of Canadian women. Loved and honoured by neighbours.

———

Baba stands companionably with Mrs. Barton in a photo saved in my mother's photo album. With snow still underfoot, in their sensible shoes they stand outside, wearing cotton dresses (I surmise the flashbulb for Brownie cameras had not yet been invented, for all of mum's photos are taken outdoors), bright grins on their faces. Baba has the same blunt haircut as her daughters; Mrs. Barton's style has a wave across her forehead. Mrs. Barton's "English" dress, perhaps purchased in a shop, is somewhat fitted to her form, with a pleated flare in the skirt, but Baba's is homemade, basically a long gaily patterned pillowcase with sleeves. But she's looped a bit of ribbon and fastened it to the collar at her throat. Her face and neck have become fleshy, her legs thickened around the calves. Mrs. Barton, leaning into Baba, has extended her left leg forward a bit, almost flirtatiously, toward the photographer.

Who took the picture? In his compact *Photography: A Very Short Introduction*, Steve Edwards makes the observation that, "while it is usually men who take family pictures … [m]others and grandmothers take charge of the album" (122). It is certainly in my mother's and aunt's albums where I have found, scrutinizing the family photos that make up her narrative, so, following Edwards, I assume Andrew wielded the camera. (In others, a man's shadow can be clearly made out — trousers, fedora — his arms bent at the elbows to steady the box while the ladies for their part hold their toothy smiles.) The family snapshots — once my mother and aunt start taking them — show Baba in the kitchen, surprised by the flash while lifting the lid off a large pan; seated in the living room where she is wearing a large blue corsage; at my aunt's dining room table behind a double-layered birthday cake that dribbles white icing, her hands covering her eyes and face as though over-whelmed.

But this raises the question: if men take the pictures, why haven't they turned the camera on their own "space"? Where are Andrew's cronies, his horse and wagon, his poses wielding an axe at the woodpile?

The Barton family lived next door to the Maksymiuks and figure frequently in Mum's recollections. Even seven, eight decades distant from her childhood in a working-class neighbourhood during the Depression, Mum thought of the Bartons as well off, well-to-do, for all their neighbourliness and Baba's friendship with Mrs. Barton. They were "English," which explained much: Mr. Barton's (unspecified) employment with the CNR elevated the entire family to the status "practically of the ruling class," according to Mum, in a neighbourhood of Ukrainian households on relief and "one Chinese group on the other side of 83rd Street."

You knew the Bartons were well off because they had a telephone, subscribed to the *Edmonton Journal*, went to the Presbyterian church where Santa Claus himself gave every child an orange in a paper bag after the Christmas concert (the Barton sisters invited Mum and her sister). And it was Mrs. Barton who made a gift of the marshmallows for the kids around the bonfire. It is impossible for me to gauge Baba's own perspective separate from Mum's on the class stratification among her neighbours: had she too noticed that the postman with the bum leg, who had the job because he was a war veteran, was "English" too? Did Baba care one way or another that the Bartons left their newspapers, once read, between the slats of the fence they shared, knowing or guessing that Dido was often without work and those smart girls of his, Mary and Annie, should not be deprived? Unlike my mother's enduring sense of class humiliation (even when embedded most of her life in the middle class as a teacher), I do not sense that, once settled into or resigned to her life as an urban lumpen proletarian, Baba was ever uncomfortable in her own skin.

In *Great Grand Mother*, we hear a voice-over narration about the joy of women's friendship: "so much we could teach each other, so much to be done.... The government wasn't meeting those needs so we women got together and did something about it ourselves." Baba's voice returns but the first phrases are unintelligible until "so we go to Salvation Army and we buy lots of clothes cheap, we make clothes for the children, and next week another lady, another lady, we help each other, English lady, Ukrainian lady, Black lady, we help" (Wheeler and Rasmussen).

Women who rummage together through a jumble of used clothing, donations from the well and warmly dressed to those "less fortunate," the threadbare but oh-so-resourceful ones at their treadle sewing machines, transforming frayed trousers into a winter coat, its lining from a lady's peignoir. A kind of sisterhood at the Sally Ann.

There was another sisterhood, Baba's own comrades, as I surmise from a photograph of five women lined up in a row in front of the house's back door, all, except Baba, wearing thick sheared-fur coats (otter? beaver?) with broad collars, simple cloth hats and gloves. Not a smile to be seen. It's a winter day but Baba wears only a sweater over her dress and, to me, a rather ridiculous hat, broader at the crown than at her brow, resembling a dented stovepipe, and black as coal. She stands cross-armed, stout but not yet stooped. Dido is anchoring the group, smart in a dark suit, white shirt, and tie. Rather formal. What is the occasion? Mum has written on the back of the photo: "Dido in his glory." What — the only man among women a kind of glory? The women visitors look like nothing so much as the cheerless delegates from a women's organization, Ukrainian to be sure and not fancy, but checking on the management of Palahna Maksymiuk's household nevertheless.

Although the oval portraits of the Bolshevik household gods, Lenin and Stalin, had long been packed away or even discarded, I grew up hearing, repeatedly, that they had once adorned the living room wall but had been taken down after the incident of the boy from Mum's high-school class who came calling. He took one look at the Commies on the wall and bolted right back out the still open door.

But Soviet Ukrainian magazines were always around the house, mailed from Ukraine all through the years of the Cold War (1946–1979). I couldn't make much of the text, but I very much enjoyed looking at pages of informative photographs of ranks of smiling textile workers at their mechanized spools and spindles, youths flashing smiles as they rode their bright red "Belarus" tractors around the collectivized fields while girls in "traditional" costumes handed over bouquets with a curtsy to visiting Communist Party dignitaries from abroad. But one was never quite sure of Baba's own atheistic-communistic sympathies; yes, she loyally read the pro-Soviet Ukrainian Canadian press, or at least the one subscription they could afford. Dido read *Ukrainske Zhyttia* (*Ukrainian Life*) not only in ideological sympathy but also out of sheer, stubborn bitterness at the hand fate had dealt him: his long illiteracy.

They were not a happy couple, by any evidence. I never saw them exchange an affectionate look or touch; to the contrary, they seemed perpetually cross and fed up with each other (one didn't need to understand much Ukrainian to read the situation), and, with a surfeit of womanly solidarity with Baba, I hoped that Dido would die first and leave her some years of peace. (She outlived him by two years.) Long after their deaths I would begin to revisit this judgement — how marriage yokes a couple together for reasons of mutual need; how they must labour together and together provide as best they can for their children; how, when I look at their formal portraits, I see in their faces something other than the disappointment and spite and weariness I had always read there. But this was later.

The play's the thing

In the meantime, they shared membership in the Ukrainian Labour-Farmer Temple Association (renamed Association of United Ukrainian Canadians in 1946) and, on her own, Baba joined the ranks of the "oppositional femininity" of its women's group (where "they designated their female work within the Women's Section ... as fundamentally political terrain, rejecting men's opinions to the contrary" [Hinther 73]). I know this because my mother has helpfully pasted a sticky note to a large studio photo mounted on a cardboard frame: "Mother, 3rd left, Back row, Communist Group." And there she is in the back row, a big woman but still unbowed, still dark-haired in a blunt cut and no-nonsense expression to match.

She would live the rest of her days in the company of these women. They would be the comrades who would bury her, "beloved mother and grandmother," pioneer, and member of the Ukrainian Community Seniors' Club.

So off they went, Baba and Dido and sometimes their girls, to the "hall," the ULFTA Temple on 96th Street, later named the Ukrainian Cultural Centre. I understood it as the "Communist Hall," but that was untrue. The Temple did not belong to the Communist Party of Canada nor were my grandparents communists. They went to the Centre to play bingo. And there were always mandolin concerts. And plays, lots of plays.

For every outing to the Hall on Saturdays to see the Ukrainian plays with her parents and sister, Mum would receive a nickel from Dido to buy a chocolate bar. She once used the chocolate bar to entice the Barton sisters to come to the play with her, warning them, however, that they wouldn't understand a word, but it would be worth it! In fact, Eva Barton did understand a word: "organizatsiia." And there was a shooting, of course. "At the end there was always a shooting." So, Mum went because it was fun. I see them in a row — the Maksymiuk family, a Barton girl or two, one chocolate bar among them as they thrill to the adventures of "Always a Revolutionist." Here is the synopsis of the play in the SECRET Report submitted by a Ukrainian-speaking RCMP informant at the 24 July 1926 production at the Hall, one of an audience of "about sixty."

"In the first act, a revolutionist was going amongst the workers telling them they should not work for the boss and get nothing for their work, and so the workers quit work. In the second act the revolutionist came out and called propaganda meetings amongst the workers and gave a speech, saying that if all workers would stay by him the revolution would be here any time, and the capitalist class will be put out of control." It comes to a bad end for the workers, among whom is a counter-revolutionist and stool pigeon. Police break up "the movement" and jail the leaders, who live on to fight another day ("Notes Regarding").

Not that I ever heard Baba curse or fulminate against capitalist bosses — as Dido did in a game of warring newspapers with my father, his petit-bourgeois son-in-law, the schoolteacher — nor see her stand and chant the Russian verses of the Soviet National Anthem. (It was I who learned them, from a Red Army Chorus and Band record album). As far as I know, she never joined a protest march even though the women's section of the ULFTA in Edmonton marched at the very front of the Hunger March of the Unemployed in December 1932 (Hinther 50). Perhaps she stayed behind in the Hall kitchen to cook.

But on at least some occasions she must have been in the audience for a play by the Soviet Ukrainian playwright and dramaturg, Myroslav Irchan. The comrades in Winnipeg had invited him to Canada in 1923 to help their membership build its "cultural potential." He wrote plays, performed in plays, and produced plays. Some of the communities in Canada where his work was staged, often repeatedly, from 1923 to 1959, included Timmins, Lethbridge, Sudbury, Vegreville, Montreal, Oshawa, Kamsack, Coleman, Saskatoon, Edmonton, Noranda, Port Arthur and, of course, Winnipeg, from Point Douglas to East Kildonan to Transcona. This so impressed the editor of *Saturday Night* magazine, that periodical of Anglo-Canadian cultural gatekeeping, who took note in 1929 of Irchan as "the most popular and influential author in the country" (Kolasky 77).

When Irchan returned to Soviet Ukraine in May 1929, more than two hundred people came to Winnipeg's CPR train station to say goodbye, singing "The Internationale." Eight years later he was dead, executed by firing squad in Soviet Ukraine.

He should have stayed in Canada. We loved him. When he appeared at the Toronto branch's Ukrainian Labour-Farmer Temple in 1927, the reporter rhapsodized about his "strong and musical voice," his "simple and sincere language," that befit a sensitive human being "who lived in thought and pain for the unfortunate and oppressed Ukrainian workers in Canada" (Krawchuk 1998, 62).

Back in Ukraine, by 1933 his literary life came to an abrupt end — caught up in the "executed renaissance" of a generation of Ukrainian artists and intellectuals who were arrested as enemies of the people, nationalists, spies, and agents of the Gestapo in Stalin's Great Terror or Great Purge (1936–1938). Irchan's works were banned and his name was struck from the literary lists (Krawchuk 1998, 65).

In 1934 he was arrested. It was even rumoured so among the Left in Canada at a time when mainstream foreign correspondents from the West largely failed to report on the trials and purges. The men and women and children who loved his stories of crafty workers and peasants who gave the bosses and landlords the old heave-ho demanded an explanation of Irchan's improbable (to them) fate, a demand that remained unsatisfied when the Canadian Communist Party men came back from Ukraine with their tail between their legs. Irchan, they were told, had confessed under interrogation at the hands of the secret police that he had participated in "anti-Soviet activity," perhaps even in Canada. According to ULFTA's press, which chimed right in, Irchan had come to Canada as an agent of "national fascism," and the question now was: "Do we have full faith in the party and the Soviet government, which have led the toilers of Soviet Ukraine out of … bondage?" (Kolasky 193).

Ah, Baba and Dido, you Canadian toilers, did you keep the faith? Dido kept on reading his newspapers through every ideological twist and turn, but Baba? The ULFTA itself, with whose branch in Edmonton she did keep the faith, had been accused from Moscow as "not on the path of class struggle," and its mandolin orchestras as a "right-wing deviation." I'm sure this made no impression whatsoever on her. Irchan was posthumously rehabilitated in 1957, and perhaps this did make an impression. "Where were the comrades," she might have asked, "when our Slavko needed them?" Always supposing that his beloved brothers and sisters in Canada, whom he would "never, never forget" (Sangster) were still on his mind when he met his death in Solovetsky prison, herded naked with scores of other enemies of the people to face the firing squad.

Perhaps it was the cold-hearted refusal of the Soviet Union, after the War in 1945, to allow the families in Canada and their kin in Ukraine to find each other again, reach out and write letters, that finally broke Baba's proletarian heart. Heaving a big sigh, she wept into her apron.

> "Sertsem lynu, v temnyi sadochok na Ukrainu . . ."
> (And with my heart I fly to a small, dark orchard,
> in Ukraine.)
>
> (SHEVCHENKO 352)

The Hall

Built in the 1950s just south of Park Memorial funeral home, the Ukrainian Centre (no further identifying description on its marquee sign) stands solidly, blankly, on busy 97th Street in a part of Edmonton northeast of downtown that used to be the hub of

Ukrainian Canadian communities. After the ULFTA was shut down across the country in 1940 — banned under the wartime Defence of Canada Regulations Act because of its support of the USSR — it was reborn, innocuously, in 1942 as the Association of United Ukrainian Canadians with the USSR now a wartime ally. The Edmonton branch built for itself a stucco quadrangle which, following the irreversible decline in the numbers of socialist or communist Ukrainian Canadians, became a venue for entertainments and fundraisers for those who still were socialists and communists in our midst, notably Chilean refugees, and exiles in the 1970s from the dictatorial regime of General Pinochet.

Perhaps that explains its denuded interior, its décor, the framed portraits of the unexceptionable Ivan Franko and Taras Shevchenko, Ukrainian writers claimed "for the people" equally by "progressives" and "nationalists." They hang on either side of the stage's proscenium arch while a modest bronze bust of Communist Party patriarch, Matthew Shatulsky, perches on a stand on the floor, drawing absolutely no attention to itself. Once upon a time, where the portraits hang would have hung wreaths encircling jubilant slogans like "Workers of the world unite!" and "Forward to the Victory of Communism!" along with portraits of Ukrainian Canadians' own communist tribunes, Matthew Popovich and John Weir (Ivan Vyviursky), and maybe that Anglo-Canadian Communist Party leader, Tim Buck, diminutive and nattily tailored, his oratory much admired by Dido.

———

I drive south one evening along 97th Street and look over at the Hall's marquee: "Have a Nice Day!"

We get letters

Baba never went back to Dzhuriv. But she never lost her connection
with her family still living there, working on the collective farm.
I don't remember the time before the arrival in the early 1960s
of letters and photographs to Baba's address. I found the airmail
envelopes they arrived in and the Cyrillic letters of the sender's
name and address exotic, printed as they were with a sleek Aeroflot
jet streaking toward the addressee. They told the news over the
decades that was always vaguely reassuring, bereft of detail. They
are healthy; the children are doing well in school; Katrusia's other
son-in-law, Vasyl, is in Siberia on a construction site; Katrusia's
garden is spectacular this year. In black-and-white photographs,
in studio and outdoors, we followed the development of the generations as they went to school, married, had children.

One such small photo — black-and-white with a delicately scal-
loped edge — identifies in an unschooled hand that "this is inside
the house. Petro and family guests." In the Soviet Ukrainian version of the Ukrainian Canadian family photos Baba must have
mailed to Dzhuriv, three generations are seated along one side of
a table, unsmiling in spite of the decorative bowl of sweets placed
at the centre of the tablecloth and what seems to be an oversized
transistor radio (perhaps a gift from the Canadian relatives). They
are all wearing embroidered shirts for the occasion, as will their
second cousins in Canada in the heyday of the festivals, concerts,
and heritage days of multiculturalism.

By the time I meet the Kosovans in person in 1984 in Dzhuriv,
they seem quite normal to me. When later I look again at the
photos I took of that visit, I am reminded that they looked well and
relaxed, the women in pretty cotton dresses and nylon stockings,
the men in suit jackets and white shirts. Only Katrusia, the matriarch, widow of Baba's nephew, "Blind" Petro, gives the scene away:

she wears a traditional embroidered blouse and a thick kerchief and looks wizened and worn out, and is the image I've retained of all Ukrainian women in the village since we received the first photographs.

Katrusia and I stand in front of her freshly painted white door. She holds aloft a shiny kolach (braided bread) and a salt cellar, both poised on a long, embroidered cloth that falls from her hands — the traditional gifts of greeting. I am unprepared for a ritual I have seen enacted — performed — only on a stage in Canada. But here in Dzhuriv, in Baba's village, their offering to the guest of bread and salt, ancient gifts from the earth, is being repeated in real life by real Ukrainians and handed over to me, granddaughter of the beloved young woman who left, Nikolai's prepaid steamship ticket in her pocket, and never came back. I take the bread and hold it rather uncertainly, as though afraid it may slip out of my hands, and look into the camera with a rather weepy look, the ritual significance of the moment just then sinking in. "Palahna Kosovan left and we never saw her again. In her place you have come. Welcome back."

For more than eighty years and now even five years after Baba's death in 1979, her Soviet family have kept faith with her, have passed on to a new generation — those who write the letters with an educated hand — the love they owe her for never having forgotten them despite the violent ruptures of occupations and wars.

And now I hold the last letter Baba wrote them on April 27, 1979, which she never mailed. Perhaps Baba was already too ill or simply forgot to put it in the mailbox or to give it to Mum or Aunt Anne to mail, and it was only found after her death. It is barely literate, scarcely a single phrase of which I can make out. It is only when I read a word out loud that I realize she has written an English word — groceries, fridge, rheumatism — in Cyrillic letters. Her head hurts. Snow is falling. She is deeply sorry that her blind nephew cannot see his own children. Her legs are weak — the doctor has explained that this is age-related rheumatism — but she has good children (my mother and my aunt) who visit her and drive her around (that would be my mother, the daughter with the driver's licence) to the grocery store, "for the fridge" and "for baking." There is something about "her" half of the garden and the housework, which is constant, but I think these issues are related to her "good children" who help her. They are happy that she stays mostly at home now, for she suffers terribly from the cold (the "romatose") which no number of decades in north-eastern Alberta have made tolerable. Then this: "Please don't take me seriously. You are still young." She died the following October.

> Out in the fields, down-beaten, rye lies upon its face
>
> So do I live without thee, the good Lord giving His grace.
>
> On the crest of the hill is the rye, cut high on its blooming stem:
>
> Down below is a well where the horses drink water drawn for them.
>
> With thy breath the water is blown; pray why dost thou not drink?
>
> (LIVESAY 132)

Pastorale

Sometime in the early 1960s Baba and Dido had moved back into the city from the acreage — a market garden, in fact — just outside the city limits, a property their daughters and sons-in-law helped them purchase in flight from the last ravages of the Depression. Bringing an acre of land into production — vegetables for the municipal farmers' market — was the hardest labour of their lives in Canada. Except for the winter months, it required sixteen hours a day. On cool and dusky late September afternoons, while all the grown-ups, Mum and Dad, and my aunt and uncle as well as Baba and Dido hoed and dug among the carrots, potatoes and cabbages, we cousins played in and around Dido's toolshed with its enigmatic tools and implements of a singularly masculine purpose, a world away from Baba's stove and aprons and bread dough rising under a tea towel in the house.

The Depression was the great calamity of their productive years. As with most children born to parents whose own childhood had been stunted by poverty, I had heard my mother's stories over and over again to the point of stupefaction, never having witnessed any of it. Instead, I revelled in visits to the acreage with its friendly cow and comical chickens, the cool depths of the well in which Baba suspended cream and butter in a blue pail, the glee of running through rows of corn so tall I disappeared from everyone's view. As for the farmers' market, I had not calculated the gruelling labour that had brought the cream and eggs, cabbages and beets, to my Dido's stall. This too would come later.

It has only now occurred to me that Baba and Dido were still holed up on that acreage all through my adolescence. But I do not remember it that way: my memories of the acreage are from deepest, perpetual childhood, and in that zone all is perfect innocence.

We drive along a dirt road dappled by the sunlight flickering through the trembling aspen and turn through the rudimentary gate into the long, rutted road that runs parallel to the trammelled grass paddock where there is always a horse and surely also a cow. On the left, in my child's-eye view a cornucopia, the garden, out to the horizon, of cabbages, corn, pea vines, the bushy tops of turnips and potatoes and the feathery carrot tops, but I may be imagining the fat pumpkins.

The root cellar. The wooden staved well. A few more steps sideways, the summer kitchen shed with its own wood-burning stove. Baba would set a large copper cauldron to heat to boiling point, waiting to receive the decapitated but still-feathered chickens, that, spellbound, I had just watched losing their heads on the wooden stump in the yard set there for its bloody purpose. City children we may have been but were not spared the sight of that wild flapping of the creature's wings as Dad or Uncle or Dido or even Baba gripped it by its scabby yellow legs and laid its screeching head upon the stump, then, with the axe in the other hand, Whump! And the chicken is released to make a gyrating, headless run around the yard before finally being scooped up and plunged into the copper cauldron, its wet feathers releasing a pungent aroma of burned hair that rushed up my nose in globs of steam and sent me running outside.

A low-roofed barn with two stalls, a small window on the eastern wall that shed morning light in pale streams across the rump of the cow who mooed softly at Baba's approach with pail and stool. I touched a teat once — not a grip but a tentative curl of my fingers around its sausage shape — and gave a yank before springing open my fist at the spongy palpability of animal flesh. Urine, manure, straw all mingled underfoot — I smelled whiffs of ammonia, but I don't remember minding. The barn was warm, shadowy, and snug. Outside, space opened up under the assault of the blinding prairie sun and the arch of the cobalt sky as it curved over the windrows of lilacs, hedges as tall as grown-ups. At night in starshine we would stand in the yard and marvel at the glow of Edmonton's lights arrayed along the rim of the world.

In the small front living room that opened onto a porch, I remember (all from Eaton's Catalogue?) an upholstered couch and chairs, a wooden settee, and a folding table around which we all sat, the two families of Baba's and Dido's daughters, for Easter lunch — Easter! — where I learned that this climactic Christian feast could be celebrated simply as an in-gathering of family: matriarch and patriarch, two teachers, a seamstress, a carpenter, and four girls. Dido, clean-shaven, a bit shrunken inside the collar of his immaculate white shirt, stood gravely at the large enamel basin he had himself prepared the night before so the aromas of raw garlic and horseradish root could marinate the thick slices of Baba's *paska* along with the garlic sausage and ham, boiled eggs, white cheese, beet pickles, and green onions. This must have been exactly as he remembered old man Maksymiuk's assembling of it in Dzhuriv, his stepmother intoning the prayers. With us, though, no prayers, just a long collective inhalation as Dido carefully took apart the layers and ceremonially filled our plates. I think there was a bottle of rye whisky on that table too, and ginger ale.

For all our exposure to Baba, of her Ukrainian heritage we learned very little. She cooked simple meals in the Ukrainian fashion (*holubtsi*, borshch, *nachynka* [baked cornmeal], boiled carrots) but did bake creditable braided breads for our Christmas and Easter tables. Her cross-stitching was rudimentary, and she never painted an Easter egg. I learned no songs from her, although she would sing them, tapping her foot while strumming a mouth harp between verses.

When my sister and I spent weekends with them, Dido was forever remote (we had the impression he spoke little English as we spoke only a smattering of Ukrainian), approaching us only to solemnly open his wallet and extract a dollar bill, one for each of us, for which we did have the Ukrainian words for "Thank you, Dido." Baba's treat for us, besides the glass jar with assorted candies "hidden" in the top drawer of her bedroom dresser, was the preparation of skillet-sized pancakes in the cast-iron frying pan on her wood-burning stove (we could hear and smell all this while still tucked deliciously in bed), served up in pools of Rogers Golden Syrup.

We were saturated with love.

The acreage has been turned under a suburb now, and the dappled road down which we approached the acreage is a main north-south thoroughfare that rushes by St. Michael's Cemetery and my parents' graves.

7

Who Was Uncle Nick?

Man with Cucumbers

The photo has fallen out of my mother's album, which lies on my lap. On the back of the photo there are two inscriptions: in the lower right corner, partly obscured by the little glued paper triangle that had held that corner in place on the page of the album, "1934." In a larger hand, recognizably my mother's and in pencil, "Baba's brother Nick, Lethbridge, 1941."

I turn the photo over to look again at "Uncle Nick."

The black-and-white photograph, such as taken by a Brownie box camera, shows a man, perhaps forty years old, with the sun and windburned face of a farmer, a thick hank of dark hair falling across his forehead. He wears a workman's denim bib and coveralls and kneels on one knee in the middle of a flat ploughed field, perhaps recently harvested. The edge of the field is the horizon that cuts dramatically at an angle to the sky. The man, who looks straight into the camera with a bit of a smile, holds an armful of cucumbers.

I haven't the slightest idea who he is. I do not recall seeing his likeness in any other photo in my mother's collections. But there he is, tucked into the pages of a family album as though he had every right to be there, explanations unrequired. I ask my cousins on my mother's side: who was this Nick Kosovan, our Baba's brother, uncle to our mothers? They haven't a clue either, nor has my sister, although one cousin vaguely remembers a story about a "fratricide" in the family. No one remembers a photograph. Yet I am looking at him in a field in Lethbridge, appearing every inch the immigrant homesteader at an admittedly uncertain date, excised from the family story, perhaps by sheer carelessness.

I knew all about my Baba's sister Sophie. She lived in Lethbridge and would come up by Greyhound bus to visit us all in Edmonton. Invariably someone took a picture: two elderly ladies seated at a table that is suitably draped for a visitor and set with teacups. But there was never an inkling or a whiff of a brother who might have been expected to come visit as well. We all knew the dramatic and tragic tale of a brother, Yuri, in Ukraine who had been violently wrested from the bosom of the family by the "bandits" in an atrocity vaguely associated with the immediate end of the Second World War. But a *Nick*, peaceable in a cucumber patch in Lethbridge?

Now Baba and Mum and Aunty Anne are gone, and I am on my own to crack this case.

Blessing the gods of the internet, and post-Soviet Ukrainian technological catch-up, I scanned the photo and emailed it to Petro Kosovan, a second cousin, who lives in Zabolotiv, western Ukraine. We are closely related: my Baba and his grandfather, the much-lamented Yuri, were siblings, making Nick a great-uncle to us both. Now it is our own generation born after the Second World War that is the eldest and holds the treasure trove of family stories, perhaps even secrets. This was my great hope. After all, by the time Nick popped up in Canada, Baba had already been twenty years away from Dzhuriv.

The archive from below

In Ukrainian, Petro replied, "This [photo] is Mykola, 'Nick,' one of seven children including four brothers, your Baba's siblings. At the time of the 1917 Revolution, he was an activist and participated in meetings. Then he went to Canada (where his sisters Sophie and your Baba already lived) and there he again took up revolutionary activity. He was arrested and deported back to Ukraine. Myrna, I don't know anything more exact but this is what I remember from my father's conversations. If I learn anything more, I'll write you." (He never did.)

December 23, 2012, I wrote back: "Nothing about what then happened to him?"

"Nothing I recall."

(This was to become a theme.)

A young man from a western Ukrainian village near the Romanian border somehow becomes radicalized by a Bolshevik revolution miles and borders away in Czarist Russia. But, wait, if he is going "to meetings," there must have been a Bolshevizing organization near Dzhuriv. Years pass. He leaves for Canada, perhaps invited by his sisters. A photo is taken, whether in the 1930s or 1940s (c'mon, Mum, which is it?), in which he seems to be a man of the land (those cucumbers). Instead, he *resumes* "revolutionary activity" (in Lethbridge! Where did he find the revolution?). Unsurprisingly, he is arrested and deported. End of story. How could such a fantastical tale have slipped out of the family yarns told in Canada?

I had once been shown how to glean clues from Soviet-era gazetteers, and out of curiosity I had looked up the entry for Dzhuriv, Baba's and Dido's home village. Now I went back to re-read the photocopied entry. Bingo! Dzhuriv had incubated an active centre of the (illegal) Communist Party West Ukraine in the 1920s, and Nick's brother, "Yu. Kosovan," had been a member. Perhaps he invited Nick to the meetings. The next mention of political activity — village delegates are sent to the People's Elections of West Ukraine (1939–1941) — covers a period when Nick may still have been in Canada or, alternatively, deported. He's not mentioned as a delegate. Next comes the fascist occupation (1941–1944); villager S.G. Gordyi is named as "active in the Zabolotiv underground communist organization," but again Nick is not mentioned. He seems not to have amounted to much from the point of view of Soviet gazetteers.

> The archive has to be read from below, from a position
> of solidarity with those displaced, deformed, silenced, or
> made invisible by the machineries of profit and progress.
> (Sekula 451)

I suppose that's what I've been assembling, an archive, whether of photos and letters or of items snatched from the sticky world wide web of the digitized. But with Nick, I have an artefact I can handle and the opportunity (as Sekula invites) to keep solidarity with Nick as I construct a possible story for him, the class-conscious proletarian abroad among displaced and silenced countrymen.

Next, the internet, prodded by search words, tosses up a long narrative full of incident about a Yuri Vyrostok who "tells the story of his immigration to Canada and first experiences in a new country." His story had first been told in the socialist *The Ukrainian Canadian* magazine. "Socialist": this was promising. I went back to the site and searched for "Lethbridge" and "radicals" and "Ukrainians." Here is Vyrostok in Lethbridge in the 1900s (too early for Nick's dates, but still):

"Having settled into this job [as a blacksmith's assistant on track repairs for the CPR], I started looking around for our people so as to form a Ukrainian organization. In time, I became acquainted with a progressive worker, Tom Semak, from the village of Zavalya by the Cheremosh River, and through him with a number of like-minded men from Bukovyna: I. Trofanenko. A. Tomacky, and others. We held our first general meeting in the mine union hall and through the efforts of Tom Tomashevsky we established the 'Fighters for Freedom' society and elected an executive. So began our organizational activity in Lethbridge in 1910" (Vyrostok).

All went rather well for a while. Coal miners joined in impressive numbers, including even three grocers (who then competed among the membership for customers). I find no traces of the Freedom Fighters after 1911 or so. "New forces came and went," Vyrostok recalled, "depending on available jobs and where one could get them." Vyrostok moved on to Fernie, British Columbia, where his story continues:

Sometime in the 1920s a group of men sit around a campfire in the Crowsnest Pass and reminisce. They are Galician immigrants, labourers from Sniatyn district in (now) western Ukraine, from Zabolotiv and Illintsi, and they break stones all day long that will be hauled to the coke ovens in Hosmer, BC. They reminisce about "how our peasants once rebelled in the neighbouring villages, initiated by those in Illintsi." This was more than nostalgia; this was a collective dreaming of a peasantry that would throw off the landlord's yoke forever and "become free citizens in their own land." There had been peasant strikes. So, another clue has dropped as to Nick's "radicalization." Perhaps he didn't need a Bolshevik revolution, just a peasant strike close to home.

I put the question to the online Encyclopedia of Ukraine: what is a peasant strike?

Inspired by the Irish Land War of the mid-1890s, wave upon wave of work stoppages broke over landlords' estates in Galicia — 400 villages in Eastern Galicia alone in 1900 and 1902. On 2 June 1902, a mass of Lviv's proletarians gathered in Striletsky Square and demanded higher wages and a shorter working day. There's a sketch, in the collection of Lviv's Historical Museum (at least it was there in 1988), of the scene on that square when soldiers got down off their horses to shoot point-blank at the demonstrators.

In Galicia the paltry wages, physical abuse, constraints on access to forests and pastures, pushed the tenant farmers and labourers beyond endurance. They occupied the land they worked, fought off strikebreakers, and brought the wrath of soldiers down upon their heads. Ukrainian Radicals and Ukrainian Social Democrats — parties already planting branches in Canada — supported them ("Peasant strikes").

Was Nick already dreaming? Perhaps he had heard these stories too, as a lad in one of those 400 Galician villages. If his father, employed hauling casks of beer from village tavern to village tavern, had joined the strikes, no such story has come down to us. Had Nick read the newspaper *Hromads'kyi Holos* (*Community Voice*) or one like it? There he would learn that, failing all else in the way of revolution in Galicia, "a free community of our countrymen will arise in Canada."

His sister Palahna made the journey to Canada in 1911, followed a few years later by her sister Sophie who settled in Lethbridge.

It would take Nick another twenty years to join Sophie in Lethbridge, and by then he was already radicalized by village socialist intellectuals, the ones with the newspapers and pamphlets in their satchels, who wrote that property was theft.

In 2013, while visiting Petro and Maria Kosovan in Zabolotiv, Ukraine, I strolled with them along a tree-lined street toward an unassuming block of rough granite that nevertheless had caught my attention. We stopped so I could take a picture. The inscription affixed to a square of white marble was: *Here on May 1 in 1924 There Took Place a Mass Demonstration of Workers of Zabolotiv with the Participation of Villagers from Surrounding Villages.* There is no Soviet marking, no Red Star, nor Hammer and Sickle — I assume effaced by post-Soviet popular demand — as though liberated Ukrainians wanted no remembrance of uprising toilers in Galicia, inspired by socialism. Perhaps in 1924 Nick had been among them.

———

Yet "the Ukrainian peasants ... knew the hopelessness of working a grudging, shrinking patch of land ... They found intolerable a system in which most of what they earned seemed to accrue to the nobles, the innkeepers, the mine owners, the priests — to everyone but themselves" (Himka 1982, 23).

I am left to imagine or construct how Nick managed entry into Canada with such a background, and how, once settled after a fashion in Lethbridge with Sophie and her husband, he found circles of "revolutionary activity" which, inevitably, this being the Depression years, led to his arrest and deportation. But what had he done?

Nick in Lethbridge

I now resorted to reading the Indexes and Bibliographies in books about Lethbridge in the Local History section of the Edmonton Public Library and continued my internet searches with keywords. This is how I decide that Nick Kosovan had arrived in Lethbridge in the middle of a brutal Depression, a working man seeking his fortune when municipal budgets could ill afford public works and services, let alone relief for the unemployed. By late 1929, Lethbridge city council had met in emergency session to consider how to meet the escalating demands for relief. An emboldened Ku Klux Klan of Canada was protesting the employment of "Orientals" and Slavs when red-blooded white men themselves had become public charges. Perhaps Nick found grunt work in the mines — the KKK didn't think much of the United Mine Workers either — in Diamond City, Shaughnessy, or Taber.

I look again at the photograph. Nick has arrived in Lethbridge, is living with sister Sophie and her husband, and this is their land where he kneels with his armful of cucumbers, behind him the cabbage patch, and on the far horizon stooks of hay. Let's say he then goes to the beet fields, one of the lucky immigrants to get a job. Only a few years later, during the Second World War, more than a thousand Japanese Canadian internees — detained under the War Measures Act — were relocated as indentured labour to these same beet fields to fill a local labour shortage (Thompson and Seager 173).

Not so lucky, in the view of the Farm Workers Industrial Union. The search engine has taken me straight to the indispensable work of two labour historians — John Herd Thompson and Allen Seager — and their 1978 article "Workers, Growers and Monopolists: the 'Labour Problem' on the Alberta Beet Sugar Industry During the 1930s." They reproduce an undated pamphlet, its title handwritten in block letters: "FASCIST MOB ATTEMTS [*sic*] TO TERRORIZE

BEET WORKERS." It opens with a flourish: "We Beet Workers of Southern Alberta, after being driven to a starvation level through cut after cut in the price of our labor, have organized, as the only means of resisting further depths of misery, and regaining some measure of a decent standard of living" (Thompson and Seager 152).

I elaborate a formula: Radical Workers + anti-fascists + depths of misery = Uncle Nick. If Nick had been looking for work, perhaps he'd found it here: planting, thinning, weeding, and hand-harvesting sugar beets. "Most farm hands would do almost anything else before they would accept beet work" (Thompson and Seager 154–155). But immigrants from the "non-preferred nationalities" — from east, central and southern Europe (Ukrainians, Czechs, Italians) — would, and beet farmers were being pressed to hire them: the unthinkable alternative was the "little yellow fellows" now excluded from even this menial labour (Thompson and Seager 157).

"Beet cultivation was tedious, back-aching, stoop labour" (Thompson and Seager 154). Except for seeding, there was nothing mechanized about it, and beet workers crawled on their knees along the rows of plantings to do it: 115 hours of their hand labour to work an acre of beets, ten times what an acre of wheat required. Nevertheless, until the Depression cancelled all expectation of a living wage, beet workers could earn at least $200 a month and were provided a "habitable house" and a garden plot (Thompson and Seager 158).

It was downhill from there, as the glut of jobless, urban women and men and the new immigrants all competed for the same scraps of contract labour, ever decreasing its value: beet workers saw their contract rate slide from $21.00 an acre to $17.00 despite steady productivity. Perhaps inspired by communist union action in the coalfields, the beet workers organized as the Beet Workers Industrial Union, then persuaded Peter Meronik, a blacklisted Ukrainian coal miner now eking out his living as a music teacher, to be their president, and issued their demand for the 1935 growing season — $20.00 per acre cash contract, all contracts to be signed in the presence of a field committee elected by the workers — and stuck to their guns. Inevitably, the Beet Growers' Association yelled "Communism!" and appealed to the provincial government to protect them from the Reds. For Nick to be in this scenario, in spite of his inability to speak English (I assume), all he needed was to be fired up by the manifest violence visited upon the weak (and the unorganized) by the local strongmen, just as in the peasant land strikes he may have witnessed or even taken part in at home in Galicia.

I see him rolling up his sleeves. He's a big guy.

May 4, 1935: The *Worker* newspaper reports evictions and vandalism in sugar beet country. Supported by their Industrial Union, many hundreds of beet workers, having refused to sign contracts, were tramping around the countryside encouraging (intimidating?) other workers to join their strike. Premier William Aberhart himself received accounts from a Taber grower that unruly "Roumanians, Bulgarians, Slaves [*sic*]" were harassing and interfering with "scabs" trying to get to work on the fields. Then, *Worker* reports, "fascist gangs of 150" retaliated, "made up of storekeepers, school teachers, preachers, elevator men, reactionary, exploiting farmers, and two RCMP men" (Thompson and Seager 162, 163).

The Beet Workers Industrial Union's own pamphlet described how the mob had ransacked the shacks of the workers' families while its members were at a meeting. The gang seized their property — meagre enough furnishings and personal effects, suitcases and bedding — and then, having "legalized" this act of housebreaking and theft "by obtaining the assistance of two members of the RCMP," they duly dumped everything in the road (Thompson and Seager 163).

This may have been the moment of Nick's story that second cousin Petro's little narrative remembers: his arrest and deportation.

The fear

On September 29, 1931, the strikes and protests in and around the coalfields of Estevan, Saskatchewan, had culminated in Black Tuesday's riot and the killing of three miners at the hands of the RCMP. By the fall of 1931, intensified political deportation had become federal policy — in that year alone, Canada deported 7,000 immigrants (Weisbord 30) — among them the loathed and feared labour organizers of the left, easily deported under charges of "vagrancy" or "taking part in an unlawful assembly." "During the 1930s, the Department of Immigration processed tens of thousands of deportations without any interference whatsoever" (Roberts 94, 97–98).

By spring 1931, seeing their opportunity to decontaminate their communities of "communistic elements," over seventy city councils in Canada had sent resolutions to the federal government to demand increased deportations, as the cost of relief was now beyond their means (Roberts 89). Not to mention the cost of police operations launched against the unemployed who had a habit of marching around town squares, shouting revolutionary slogans — or at least shouts for bread.

Kicked off the beet fields, unemployable and lined up with the others for relief, Nick was about to be deported. Between 1930 and 1935, some 28,000 immigrants were deported from Canada for having become a "public charge" (Roberts 107). Or had he been among those accused of "seditious conspiracy" or of vagrancy — plodding around the countryside, pamphleteering among his low-born countrymen who seethed with resentment with every weed they yanked out of the stubborn clods of Canadian earth? If they were deported to Poland (Eastern Galicia), they may have survived whatever prosecution the Polish authorities meted out. But Nick has simply vanished.

Baba and Dido in Canada were ardent Soviet sympathizers: why hadn't they told and retold a family legend of Nick Kosovan, working-class hero booted out of Canada by the stooges of capital?

They hadn't because they were frightened. Let Party leaders and union organizers take the risks and consequences of defying law and order. Baba and Dido, with their tenuous claim to Canada's rights and privileges, would keep their heads down. Celebrate a Bolshevik agitator on the family tree? Naturalization would not have protected them. Protest a deportation of a relative? Shame and stigma. "Red scares" rolled through Canadian society on a regular basis, an emotional reality my grandparents never outlived. There was a back alley that ran behind the houses on our block in inner city Edmonton and that's where I was in my own bad dreams, being pursued, never outrunning, down the alley by two or three men in long, black coats: *Russians*. I suppose I had seen black-and-white photos in magazines of just such sinister men, coat collars up, wide-brimmed hats pulled down, "shot" in Red Square. In Dido's bad dreams, he was being run to ground by the RCMP.

There are other photographs

Beginning in the 1960s, over the years we received many photos of Kosovan relatives in Ukraine, an entire gallery of them posed stiffly and unsmiling in studios, as they grew up and grew old, and another generation arrived, in front of modern cameras, on school trips, at weddings, at reunions. These, too, I had inherited at my mother's death. They were overly familiar to me: Baba, Mum, and Aunty Anne had pored over them, setting them aside from the square envelopes in which they had been sent, the Canadian address with its Latin letters inscribed by unsure hands. I go back now to this stash of Ukrainian photographs and lo and behold!

There is a photo of Nick, which is to say of Nikolai/Mykola Kosovan, in a studio with four other adults and one child.

I can't place him. As with all other group photographs of our families, in Ukraine and in Canada, from one generation to the next, there is no context. For nostalgic reasons, the Kostash farm becomes the preferred setting, out in the large front yard, the elders on chairs, but it's only a backdrop. In Galician studios the family members arrange themselves, squeezed shoulder to shoulder in front of a simple dark drape, squares of carpeting under their boots. Preserved in the family albums in Canada, they are displayed as a "sealed unit" (Edwards 123), with contexts resolutely outside the frame. Outside the frame are the revolutions and collectivizations, the strikes, the rallies, and the parades with banners. The American filmmaker Errol Morris, in considering the life and death of *one* soldier in the Civil War, argues that it offers "the recovery of a *unique* individual from a myriad complexities of history" (267). But I've been in search of the reverse: the recovery of those complexities from which the unique man, Nick Kosovan, has been subtracted. I have assembled entire bibliographies of sources that have helped me recover the whirl and swirl of history's complexities that spin around a young man sealed inside the family unit. His singularity in this group of six is undeniable as he and I make unblinking eye contact through the surface of the photo, but I owe him the complexity of the rest of his life.

Two young men in suits stand behind two women in embroidered blouses and kerchiefs; between them is the patriarch, a white-haired, white-mustachioed elder in a sheepskin vest, his white pants tucked into knee-high boots. A girl-child dressed in her own embroidered blouse and jacket stands on a stool between her mother and (I'm guessing) her grandfather. She is in no obvious relationship with either of the young men. This is a postcard-style photo in which my mother has written: "My uncles, my aunts, my cousin and my grandfather."

I have no recollection of seeing this photograph before, much less of having its subjects identified. As far as I was aware, my mother had no relatives except the handful accumulated in Canada. But here they are, close kin in a picture. She writes: "Uncle Nick visited us in Canada and returned some ten years later."

Returned? Not deported, not "disappeared"? I am feeling stubborn if not outright obsessed by these lacunae in a narrative I am trying to construct with all the wiles of the nonfiction writer denied evidence, testimony, eyewitness. I want to push back against this recurring absent-present as though I've become the eyewitness to an album of ghosts.

Stuck to the back of the postcard-photo is a yellow Post-it Note in my own hand, although I have no recollection of writing it: "Nikolai," I've written in Cyrillic, meaning the man with a moustache and the same shock of lank, dark hair across his forehead as the man with the cucumbers in a field in Lethbridge. Here he looks some ten years younger, so the 1920s. I have identified the others: Yuri Kosovan, Nikolai's brother; Nastunia, Nikolai's wife; Maria, his daughter; Palahna, Yuri's wife. And also, Petro, my mother's grandfather and my great-grandfather, he who rolled beer casks off his wagon into the village pubs.

On the back of another photo, I read a who's who of the assembled group some thirty years later. Baba has written in a semi-literate hand: "Brother Nikolai's daughter Maria and children, Marika and Mykola." Maria sits in an embroidered blouse and kerchief (village fashions don't seem to change), her skinny legs in heavy shoes, frowning, as is Marika. Is she a widow? In a good hand (the fruit of a Soviet education) Maria has written in Ukrainian: "This is me and my children, Kolya [Mykola] and Marusia [Marika]. Kolya is in eighth class and Marusia in fourth. But Kolya has Dido

Kosovan's character." This would be the radical Nikolai/Mykola/
Nick. "It seems (unintelligible) drops of tears." And indeed, it does
seem that Kolya is on the verge of tears.

Now I am perturbed by the possibility that, on my visit to
Dzhuriv in 1984, and my presentation to all the relatives, I may have
met Maria but had no questions for her. Would she not have had
stories about her father, however absent or exiled or deceased?
Wouldn't Petro have remembered hearing some, especially once
I had asked? They all lived in the same village, they were famil-
iars, and some other Kosovan, if not Petro, must have kept track of
genealogies, as I was to learn. But now I am stumped.

It seems, though, that all along, I have known more myself.

In 1984, on my visit to the Kosovan ancestral village, Dzhuriv,
second cousin Pavlina transcribed into a small notebook the
names and relationships of everyone I had met, namely the children of my Baba's siblings, which is to say my mother's cousins,
and their children, my second cousins: a plethora of Marias, Petros,
and Marusias, of Elena and Paraska and Olya in the plural. Pavlina
has included their (Soviet-era) occupations: accountant in a sugar
factory, trucker for a juice-extraction factory, tradeswoman in a
factory, bus driver, locksmith in a furniture factory, a shop assistant. They worked at the heart of the collectivized Soviet economy,
having putatively won the class struggle that Nick had failed utterly
to advance in Lethbridge. His (and my) Soviet Ukrainian relatives
were proletarians, skilled labourers with a secondary education,
who may be said to have made the equivalent progress through
their society as Baba's progeny had made in Canada. An education,
steady work, social benefits, healthy children.

In 1988 I met Pavlina again, this time in Kyiv, in Ukraine of the
perebudova (*perestroika* in Russian) years, and now able to speak
intelligibly in Ukrainian, I flesh out Baba's siblings and their kin
with Pavlina's voluble help one more time. So I hear again of Baba's

father Petro and of her mother Paraska, who died young, leaving seven children. Of how two of them, Baba and Sophie, got away to Canada. The other two daughters, Maria and Elena, continued to live in the village. Brother Yuri was killed by bandits in 1945, while brother Stefan and his wife Dotsia lived high above the village in the woods.

And brother Nikolai/Mykola/Nick? He lived eight years in Canada and then returned to Dzhuriv. No deportation then? No revolutionary aspirations? End of story.

Months later, however, in the middle of this research, I excitedly emailed Petro again. I wrote him with new information I had completely forgotten from thirty years ago. Although I have no recollection of writing this, alongside the notes from 1988, but in different ink, I have added: "Nikolai hanged himself."

Petro: "I know nothing of this."

He's not talking. Nobody's talking.

So then I have done the talking, here in Canada: about Uncle Nick, the radical from Dzhuriv, with his armful of cucumbers, outside agitator in Lethbridge, arrestee, deportee, suicide swinging from a rope in the village barn, vanished from recall, who I am not supposed to know.

8

Andrew Maksymiuk
1891 – 1977

There once was a horse

This is how we, his several granddaughters, remember Dido Andrew, although we have different feelings about him: skinny, bug-eyed, with grey-stubbled cheeks, often in long johns under his work pants with suspenders hoisted over his shoulders, no shirt. We also remember his good suit. It was the one he wore for the studio photographs, shoulder to shoulder with Baba, dark grey with a pale, thin stripe running through the weave. He stares straight at you. If you cover the bottom of his face, he stares at you through a pair of stricken eyes, blue.

I close my eyes and I'm in the middle of the kitchen

What were Dido's things? When I think about the things that belonged to Baba Palahna's world, I see chipped enamel basins of several sizes in which she baked the *holubtsi* or raised the dough under bleached towels from flour sacks. I see the crock of fermenting cabbage, her homemade aprons, the deck of cards in the linen closet, the little jam jars now glasses into which she poured cream soda when we sat down to a card game of *hola*.

But what were Dido's things? A razor strap, a round bowl of shaving soap, a little mirror hanging on the wall beside the cast-iron stove. A Cyrillic-alphabet newspaper. A pair of spectacles. My cousins, but neither my sister nor I, remember also a large and ornamental ring that he wore with evident pleasure on the occasions when he donned his good suit, a small vanity that my mother and Baba, the cousins recall, derided as an affectation. *Who did he think he was?*

Dido's things were *outside* the house, in a shed. A sickle and scythe, spade, hoe and rake, twine and ropes, old harnesses. Nobody took a picture.

Once there was a horse outside.

I once listened to an immigrant remembering ... *the richness of the soil, the beauty of the linden trees ... soldiers stole food, all the potatoes, but the poor would bring in their Easter baskets laden with food to be blessed and as gifts for the priest, who would toss it as slop to his pigs ... a neighbour who was punished for taking wood from the landlord ... having enough to eat was always an issue, in Canada you discard nothing from your dinner plate.*

In 1897, Dido Andrew was six years old in a village in Galicia, a subject of Austria-Hungary. Men of working age were flowing out of Galicia — in 1889 a terrible drought had shrivelled the crops to their roots, and peasants slaughtered their own horses for want of feed; for want of horses, they could neither plow nor draught

and began to starve. So there was little to hold Andrew on the pitifully small farm in Dzhuriv. In 1900, the vast majority of Galician
land was held by twenty-one landowners each owning more than
10,000 hectares (Martynowych 25) — the Maksymiuks owned 2 hectares — and, in spite of Emperor Joseph II's prohibition of displays
of servility, Galician peasants doffed their caps within 300 paces of
the manor house. There was one tavern for every 220 inhabitants,
one hospital for every 1,200 and one elementary school for every
1,500 (Subtelny 310). In 1880 only about half of Galicia's school-aged
children actually attended their village school; in Austria itself,
attendance was 95% (Himka 1988, 60).

Squeezed between the tavern keeper and the priest, what
was a peasant family to do? To the first, the household owed the
accumulating "bar tab" of the family patriarch; to the second, pay-
ment for sacramental rites held in the church. When I read of their
quarrels — over berries and plums to which the peasants helped
themselves on the priest's property, over "gleaning rights" to the
stubble left over from the priest's harvest, and over paths through
the priest's property — I began to have an inkling of Dido's hatred
of the church. "People have long walked to church and to get water,
but now the priest's servants do not allow people to pass through
and if anyone goes for water, the servants break that person's
buckets" (Himka 1988, 133–34).

Andrew would not bear it. Following his older brother, Nikolai,
Andrew left Dzhuriv at fifteen to seek work somewhere out there,
beyond the village, and found it in the Silesian coal mines that were
expanding production and required all sorts of brute labour. He
worked in the mine for four years.

Mum has kept his *Inspection Card for Immigration Officer at
Port of Arrival in Canada* (*Steerage*) and this is how I know (I never
asked during Dido's or Mum's lifetime) the name of the ship on
which he had sailed, the *Lake Michigan*, and that it had sailed from

Antwerp on the 8th May 1912 and arrived at Quebec Immigration Office on May 23. The ship's surgeon did not initial "Vaccination protected," but Dido was admitted to Canada nevertheless. *Medical examination stamp: Port of Quebec.*

He was not naturalized as a British subject of Canada until September 16, 1938. On that day he was accounted, by Trade or Occupation, to be a Labourer. Age: 47 years; Height: 5 feet 6 inches; Colour: White; Complexion: Fair; Colour of eyes: Grey; Colour of Hair: dark grey; Visible Distinguishing Marks: None.

Prayer to St. Barbara, patron of miners: *As I now descend into the dark bowels of the earth, I beseech thee, sweet Barbara, that I be kept from harm, for it liketh me not that I rush unbidden into God's presence.*
Although I have no recall of the story, my cousins remember, from what Baba told them, that after ditch-digging work in Edmonton had dried up and he had lost a job at the packing plant, Andrew was recruited from Edmonton to work in the Pennsylvania coal mines. "He went for a year and came back a changed man. Baba used to say that he left Edmonton as a young man but returned home a fearful man. We would now call it traumatized, from being underground. A terrible experience." That's all my cousin remembers.

What had happened in Pennsylvania? Cruel pit bosses? A strike savagely broken up? Men on horseback herding the bohunks out of town? Or just ten hours a day of labour in a coal seam, boots in two feet of filthy water, not enough room under the rotting timbers to straighten up. Ten hours and what do you get? $1.60. And the stink of smoke from the explosives that blasted fractures in the rock but, this time at least, left you standing upright in the fog.

Still he was lured. I place him there in 1913, still a single man but stuck in Edmonton's collapsing economy, its unemployment among men, reported by the *Labour Gazette* in 1914, higher "than at any previous time in the history of the city" (Schulze 52).

What happened in Pennsylvania?

From 1870 to 1913, 32,000 miners in northeast Pennsylvania had lost their lives. April 7, 1911, Throop, PA, seventy-three by fire. May 27, 1911 Shamokin, PA, five by explosion. January 9, 1912, Plymouth, PA, six by explosion. August 2, 1913, Tower City, PA, twenty by explosion. Say, Dido arrived on these coalfields in one of those years. He must have heard the stories of these martyrs. Stood in line as day broke, lunch pail and lantern, pick and shovel, waiting to go down into the pit, speaking with countrymen, how the dead had died, blown up, incinerated, their wives and children destitute. Hot as Hades at the coal face.

Is it to these bloodied sites that Andrew was recruited? In Edmonton, he had heard and knew nothing, but in the camps of the miners, among countrymen and countrywomen who spoke his language, I'm sure the tale was told, perhaps the graves visited, or even a militant denunciation surreptitiously repeated at a camp-fire. He returned to Edmonton a changed man, fearful thereafter of authority he had no resources on his own to defy.

In 2011, I drove the scenic and historical route through the Crowsnest Pass in southwestern Alberta, via Highway 3, which took me through the old coal mining towns of Bellevue, Hillcrest, Blairmore, and Coleman. I was doing this as both an homage to and research into the mind, heart, and spirit of a man I barely knew but who now had my full attention: my maternal step-grandfather, Andrew Maksymiuk.

Dido was a socialist, never a communist, although he passionately defended the achievements of the Soviet Union made in the name of the working class. He never homesteaded; he was a day labourer in Edmonton when he could get work, literally a ditch-digger, while Baba worked ceaselessly selling milk and cream and eggs and taking in laundry. As for his life before coming to Canada,

I know almost nothing except that he worked alongside his older brother, Nikolai, in Silesian coal mines.

Bingo! Coal mines + Socialism + Galicians = Crowsnest Pass. As I drove slowly around each community, I looked for signs of the society that had once embraced these elements. The abandoned coke ovens and collapsed collieries, the museum photographs of once-bustling main streets, a Workers Hall, a union hall. The communities of Michel and Natal have been bulldozed into the ground. A real bulldozer ran through a picket line of striking miners' wives in 1935 where now only a grassy hillside says this was Corbin.

But in the federal elections of 1908, 1911, and 1921, the socialist vote in Blairmore, AKA "Red" Blairmore, "Communist Capital of Canada," had taken 10%, then 29%, and finally 36% of the total (Seager 2022, 55). In February 1932, mine union representatives were swept into office: mayor, councillors, school board. May Day was declared a civic holiday. The town's main street, Victoria Avenue, was renamed Tim Buck Boulevard for the imprisoned leader of the Communist Party of Canada.

The street sign *Tim Buck Boulevard,* tilted sideways, sits under a sift of dust on the floor of The Crowsnest Museum.

There is a mass grave in Hillcrest, the coal town where on June 19, 1914, Canada's most lethal mining disaster took 189 lives. At 9:30 a.m., a huge underground gas explosion had ignited thickening coal dust that blew up in second and third explosions, the ghastly force of them all raging through the labyrinth of tunnels and blowing so much debris at the mine entrances that no one could get out.

I spent a long time in the cemetery, imagining Dido Andrew hovering alongside, in sympathetic solidarity, during the final hours of terror of men dying under the horrid weight of the very mineral they had been sent down to shovel out for the profit of mining companies. I imagined the despair of those gasping at the last thin streams of air before the black damp took them. And I imagined the grief of the women and children on the surface as each scorched, broken, maimed, and mutilated body was brought up from the deep. And, thanks to the small plaques fastened on the low rail of the fence encircling the mass grave, I could also imagine these young Italians, Croats, Slovaks, Irish, Galicians, in the ultimate brotherhood of workers: as the memorial says, *As they laboured together, so they are buried together.*

> Dig, dig,
> For the fatted pig.
> Coal in their blood as they paid the toll
> Give the owner blood in his coal.
> Dig, dig,
> For the fatted pig.

(DENNIS COOLEY, "ESTEVAN")

To be a communist was to be free

Rose Popeniuk talks to me about the 1930s, an era of labour radicalism in the coal towns of the southern Rockies, when she was a little girl, daughter of immigrants from Rybno, a village in southwestern Ukraine, practically in Romania, who settled in Coleman, Alberta. "I think of the people of the Crowsnest Pass." She sits, a widow, in the dream home her husband built in Fernie, BC — the big kitchen with lots of cupboards for her, the fieldstone fireplace for him — and she weaves small wool tapestries that hang on all the walls in orderly profusion, as in a gallery. I look for one with a communist theme, but what I see are landscapes of the Canadian Rockies, Ukrainian village folk scenes, and a Ukrainian Orthodox church rising up triumphantly into the light from the dark wool along the bottom edge. Yet she tells me, "Coleman never did have a Ukrainian church. Nor any movement for Ukrainian Orthodoxy. Our heroes were the miners."

A large tapestry hanging in the stairwell to the second floor shows Rose's father in three aspects: as a coal miner, dancing the *hopak*, and in a three-piece suit. "Every immigrant I ever knew had a three-piece suit." Her father was in charge of the "garderoba," the costumes and make-up for the actors, in the Workers' Hall.

Did any of the cultural activities at the hall have "socialist content"? I know for a fact that choirs in such halls had a repertoire spanning African American spirituals to "The Internationale," and that amateur theatre groups presented socialist plays by Myroslav Irchan, but Rose replies vehemently that the activities were about "being Ukrainian," and she bursts into folk song.

But in one very important sense, the Workers' Hall *was* a socialist hall. From this Hall, the coal miners would never scab. Were the Union to call a strike, the men would put down their lunch pail and lantern, the pick and shovel, and walk home, filing their way quietly from the pithead to Bushtown where their families waited to greet them with the same resolution.

In Bushtown there was no power, no running water, no sewage system. "In Coleman there was only one kind of Ukrainian — socialist," Rose tells me. "We were coal miners who had to stick together to create a union. We had Polish friends but they didn't have a cultural centre except in the Roman Catholic church hall. Poles weren't union people; I suppose because of the church's attitudes. During strikes, as a child I could see from our house, one street over from the railway tracks, the trucks that carried the scabs to the mine — our Polish neighbours."

The Ukrainian Labor Temple was at 1417–82nd Street. Built in 1927, it has been torn down and a trailer home rests on the empty lot. The Polish Hall, I make a note, is still standing.

For this Dido came to Canada?

I have no evidence for this, only a tenaciously held memory of having been told that Dido once worked digging ditches, a story that aligned neatly with the slur of being a "ditchdigger." I assume these were the ditches for the sewage pipes being laid in Edmonton in 1912, when the ditchdiggers went on strike for a thirty-five-cent hourly wage. Even at that accelerated rate, it would take three hours to earn back the one dollar they had paid to the "boss" to get the damn job.

Anarchists found him. They had him in mind when One Big Union, Canada's syndicalist union whose one big idea was the general strike, summoned "all those who by useful work of hand or brain, feed, clothe or shelter, or contribute towards the health, comfort and education of the human race" ("Revolutionary Industrial Unionism").

International Workers of the World — Wobblies — from Butte, Montana, among whom One Big Union had found support, rushed up to Edmonton in solidarity with the ditchdiggers, and to the bewilderment of city councillors and police who prepared for mayhem, staged roving and singing pickets from one ditch to another. "When you stop singing, the revolution has ended," was immortalized in 1909 in their Little Red Songbook (Rieder).

Baba had a mouth harp tucked between linens in a small cupboard and would strum away, breaking off to warble what I took to be songs from her village childhood. But I do not recall any occasion when I heard Dido sing. Did he even know the words to "The Internationale"? I did, in Russian.

> Arise, ye prisoners of starvation!
> Arise, ye wretched of the earth!
> For justice thunders condemnation:
> A better world's in birth!

August 8, 1908: J.H. Burrough of Ladysmith, Vancouver Island, writes a commentary in the *Western Clarion*, a socialist newspaper, about the recent visit of "Organizer A. Susnar," a Czech from the Crowsnest Pass, from the Slavic Socialist Union. Susnar addressed a handful of Slavs "in their own language" (all Slavic languages being mutually intelligible apparently). "Speaking very little English as a rule," Burrough goes on, "they have but an uncertain idea of the political and economic situation in Canada today. More attention must be paid in the future to the foreign element. Comrade Susnar, I believe, was the first to address the Slavs in his recent visit" (from my handwritten notes at Nanaimo Community Archives).

This would be women and men like my grandparents. At sea in a torrent of the English language and Latin alphabet, their bewilderment, confusion, and indignation inexpressible as one setback or disappointment after another washed over them from the "English" world until, finally, someone from the world of Ukrainian socialist revolutionaries speaks.

"This cohort of socialists [at the *Western Clarion*] loved to dissect the hypocrisies, shallowness, and misrepresentations of the capitalists and their liberal apologists ... Capitalism is depicted as a cunning confidence game. The people deceived by it are often mocked as wet behind the ears innocents and dumb as a doorpost know-nothings" (McKay 31).

Baba and Dido: dumb as fenceposts in English. In Ukrainian, however, when Dido made the arguments of the socialist writers in *Chervonyi Prapor* (*Red Flag*) and *Robochyi Narod* (*The Working People*), I could see, later, that he was articulate, passionate, and nobody's fool. He was being educated, in his own language, into the mighty ideas of socialism.

But Dido had his heroes among the Anglos nevertheless: Tim Buck, for example, the communist from Beccles, England, and the long-time general secretary of the Communist Party of Canada.

In the small photo I am looking at on the internet, he is short, dapper in a fedora, tie, white shirt, and high-buttoned coat that wraps his trim form if not stylishly at least suitably for the press photographer. He's smiling slightly and looks as mild as a bank teller. A machinist by trade and a fearless union organizer — looks are deceiving — he was a founder of the Communist Party of Canada in 1921 and its leader from 1930 until his death in 1973 at age eighty-two. He was almost exactly Dido's contemporary.

It was as the Party leader that Buck commanded Dido's attention and admiration, charismatic even when quiet-spoken, unbowed by what the State and Capitalist Bosses threw at him and the comrades — surveillance, beatings, police riots, raids, and arrests — during the long agony of the Depression.

In Edmonton, sympathetic Ukrainian Canadian members of the Labour and Farm Temple Association such as my grandparents convened in their hall to marvel that here was an Englishman who had offered himself up as a sacrifice for the *foreign-born* working class, even when they could not understand his words. But they understood the language of faith, as American sociologist Todd Gitlin draws out, "a faith in humanity, and a comfort in believing the future belonged to them" (Gitlin). The Galician village may have had its timeless rituals, whether folkloric or religious and some-times intertwined, performed in song and dance, hung on the wall as icons and embroidered cloths, commemorated in prayer and salt and braided bread. But now in Canada the future seemed to move forward to meet them, in charismatic leaders, theatrical revels, newspapers and magazines galore, banners and red flags, and, writes Gitlin, "you could sing 'The Internationale' and — for a moment — find refuge in an imagined future."

Yet by any standard of city life, the Maksymiuks — Andrew, Palahna, Mary, and Anne — were poor. Alberta passed its Unemploy-ment Relief Act in 1930, when 13% of Edmonton's population was on relief (Dempsey). Asking or even qualifying for relief was an additional humiliation. Who should qualify? Perhaps only the utterly destitute ("no work, no money, no food"), though the Maksymiuks had a garden. But first they had to register with the Employment Bureau in case there was work to be had: ditch-digging, anyone? Snow shovelling, laying streetcar tracks, delivering coal, washing dishes, anything at all?

How did you look? How were you dressed? In "uncouth trousers and coat with old-land fastenings, unshaven face — with the dull resentment of the hard-heel showing from eyes, joyless-looking and suspicious.... In hasty moment or as term of reproach they are locally dubbed Russians, Bohunks, Galicians, Douks maybe, and occasionally Hunkies" (Baldwin 101). How were you to be fed on a budget?

In his account of the administration of relief in Alberta, historian Hugh Dempsey cites the meal plans drawn up by dieticians at the University of Alberta: meat pie with biscuit crust, pot roast with vegetables, macaroni and tomatoes, rice pudding, gingerbread. Had these dieticians ever met a member of the immigrant working class? Fortunately, the "typical four-week supply of food for four city people" included basic peasant provisions: potatoes, cabbage, turnips, beets, lard, eggs, and — a luxury — "2 lbs. of liver, and meat depending on price and cut." And a jar of corn syrup, of all things (Dempsey).

Finally, an explanation, if one were needed, for the large can of corn syrup always proffered at breakfast with Baba: she had found a way to use corn syrup. She cooked giant pancakes and we poured on the syrup until it flooded the plate.

Then when my mother went teaching in 1934, Baba and Dido sold their house and bought an acreage outside the city where they planted a market garden. Mum was sending them money from the $600 salary meted out annually by the school trustees in Hairy Hill.

With her contribution, Dido could buy a pig, a bicycle. The market garden was not always remunerative: every spring all the unsold potatoes that he had kept in the root cellar over the winter had to be taken out by wheelbarrow and thrown over the fields.

Fruits of the earth

The acreage was the closest Dido came to being a "settler" in the sense we deploy the word now: "the colonial usurpation of Indigenous lands and the dispossession and disappearance of Indigenous peoples" (Lowman and Barker 47). His few acres had been carved out of land (whether private or Crown) covered by Treaty Six, although it is certain this was not made clear when he acquired them — and they never made him rich, unlike the large-scale farmers out in the Ukrainian bloc settlement who, well into the second generation after immigration, were buying ever more land and bigger tractors. But that is beside the point: we are all settlers now just by being challenged by some basic questions: "How do you come to be here? How do you claim belonging here?" (Lowman and Barker 19).

There is no evidence that the anti-capitalist groups Dido belonged to or the socialist press he read in Ukrainian wondered about such matters. It was sufficient for his identity that he lived in a working-class part of town and eked out a living as an unskilled labourer, dispossessed from the meagre surplus he produced for the capitalist boss(es). And, if such matters had been raised, he might have looked enquiringly around at the evidence of his family's urban-based poverty and asked how *this* constituted privilege. Relative to Indigenous poverty, the Maksymiuks were privileged (they owned a house, the children went to school, and the family stayed intact) but absolutely they were poor. Not all settlers were created equal. Not any one theory can account for people's experience (Dumitrescu 21).

Roger Epp, political scientist and of Mennonite heritage, nevertheless suggests a convergence of the "two working cultures," rural settler and Indigenous (and I would add urban poor), at the point where both have been "dispatched to the dustbin of history" by neoliberal economies (127). It may have been true in some now-distant pre-revolutionary past (before neoliberalism) that the business of farming a market garden was predicated on access to — but not always owning — property; or for a labourer, on the dignity of a fair wage. Baba and Dido briefly joined the "working culture" of rural settlers with their acquisition of a few hectares of land on the edge of town. They would never be so (relatively) wealthy again, but this was still a far cry from any likely "convergence" with the straitened working culture on a Canadian reserve.

There had been a city market in downtown Edmonton since 1916, but the one I remember, faintly, is from the 1950s, when I would weave among the vendors' stalls on hard dirt "floors," among piles of cabbages, sacks of onions, crates of eggs, jars of honey and farm cream until I found Dido at the scale behind his own pile of cabbages.

The white horse and wagon were left parked among the other rigs somewhere alongside the buildings. But there were fewer and fewer of them — to judge from archival photos — until, by the time I was a young teenager, there were none at all, and the city turned the sod and horse manure over and paved the square as a parking lot for cars and trucks. Out on the acreages just beyond city limits, urban neighbourhoods crept north, root cellars caved in, and farmers were becoming gardeners, grubbing in greenhouses to raise, unthinkably for Dido's generation, tomatoes, leeks, and peppers. Still, squeezed between stalls of bedding plants, he offered his cornucopia of cabbages, carrots, turnips, and beets.

How do you make a living selling cabbages that are no better and no worse than the ones laid out on the other stalls? How, in the Depression, do you extract your living from your neighbour?

The accidental rioter

"Hundreds of spectators had taken refuge in the fish market while hundreds more had repaired to the roof of the market building for a better view."

(MERRETT 81)

This was Andrew's one good story of political "resistance," though I cannot say I heard him tell it. But there it is, circulating among family members, that Dido had been swept up — pressed into a crowd of Hunger Marchers in Market Square — in a "Communist" parade that set off from the Square and ended for him in a cell in Fort Saskatchewan's provincial jail. As the story went, Baba got him out: he was an innocent bystander, huddled in a doorway of the fish market, they pleaded to the authorities.

This was December 20, 1932, but unemployed men had been gathering, marching around, hoisting placards, and speechifying since the Depression had first hit them hard in 1929. They wanted some relief for their families, they threatened to organize, they were hungry, so why does Dido's little story carry a whiff of a nudge and a wink of Dido the accidental rioter?

In Andrew Maksymiuk's character there was not a trace of brawny heroism — he was fearful, tentative, dour — but behind him stood his heroes, the unemployed who wore their poverty and bitterness like shields against police batons — as on that December day in 1932. The police pummelled their clubs against the backs of men and women, "hunger marchers" whom they then arrested under Section 87 of the Criminal Code on charges of unlawful assembly. There were twenty-nine defendants but some were released because of poor health or for lack of evidence. Perhaps that was Dido's case, or perhaps Baba was able to

187 ◢

get him released before he was booked, but at any rate, his name is not listed among those recollected by Helen Potrebenko in *No Streets of Gold:* Pawlyk, Nowakowsky, Mohr, Poole, Woytyshyn.... (212–213). Heroes and heroines of the Canadian Labour Defense League, heroes and heroines of the Communist Party of Canada: the "mob," according to the *Edmonton Bulletin* (qtd. in Potrebenko 208), trampled underfoot as the police broke up their unlawful parade, Dido's back bone.

Although Dido Andrew lived a long life, dying in Edmonton sixty-some years after immigrating to Canada, he was to me mainly inscrutable. I understood little Ukrainian and spoke less, and my grandfather spoke almost no English. Thus I think of him as dour and mirthless, and I was always uncomfortable, speechlessly so, in his presence, and then abashed when, with considerable ceremony, he would extract a dollar bill from his wallet for me, and another for my sister. Only now, revisiting the little scene, I sense the great pride he took in being able to distribute such largesse, the same man who had not a coin in his pockets for my mother's schoolbook. He was also proud — and this I could see and hear at the time — of his ability to hold his own in the spirited debates he'd engage with my father, about the merits and demerits of capitalism and communism, of education and labour, church and atheism. I say "held his own," but the fact is that I never heard him, the elder man, address my father other than in the formal *Vy* (you), as though deferring to the younger man, his petit-bourgeois son-in-law, William Kostash, M.Ed. B.Comm.

This is the household we visited regularly, and here the socialists' "master narrative" of the Ukrainian Canadian experience was explicitly subversive: immigrants were enticed to come to Canada to be exploited pitilessly by capitalist bosses as cheap, unskilled workers, a permanent underclass of the humiliated and hopeless to prop up the privileges of the bourgeoisie; its puppets, the politicians; and its apologists, the intellectuals and the church. The Ukrainian Canadian middle class — that would be us, the Kostashes — was a sellout to this system. But there had arisen a powerful challenger, the Soviet Union, whose people had made a revolution to put the working man and woman in power, restore them their dignity and purpose, and dethrone the fat cats (big cigars, a top hat, with dollar signs for eyeballs). The Generalissimo Joseph Stalin guided all of this with wise and paternal benevolence and defended it with fists of steel (*stal'* in Russian) against its mortal enemies in the capitalist world. *Long live great Stalin! Long live beloved Steel!*

I can see how this world view consoled and emboldened a Galician immigrant like Andrew, struck down by unemployment, obliged to accept charity (sending the children to get the food vouchers), terrified of getting sick, shamed by Anglo-Canadian racism, infuriated by the overweening power of police in Canada and the jackboot advance of fascism in Europe. (He read the papers.) I can see how the mighty effort of the Generalissimo and the Red Army to push back the Nazi juggernaut cheered the Soviet Union's sympathizers. I can see why Dido would have taken pride, if not the courage, in the sacrifices of coal miners, packing house workers, and tracklayers in Alberta who were standing up to the bosses to organize. By 1940, Alberta was second only to Ontario of the Canadian provinces that hosted centres of pro-communist activity.

While the grown-ups chatted and held forth and argued in Ukrainian, I took a great interest in the smudgy-coloured magazines strewn around the little living room. Later I understood the propagandistic naiveté of such imagery — Boy Meets Tractor, Romance Ensues — and would adopt a sneering attitude, mocking the smiling, the *euphoric*, tractor drivers and milkmaids of the collective farms and the *pulsating* cement workers and coal miners of the mammoth industrial projects of the post-war Soviet Union. But at the time they were simply part of the atmosphere of my grandparents' home. In my childhood they fascinated me, like demigods of heroic proportion in an exaggerated landscape that nevertheless bore some resemblance to the world I was beginning to pay attention to.

————

In 1992 I spent long hours in the Guggenheim Museum in New York to look at virtually each object in the mammoth exhibit, The Great Utopia: The Russian and Soviet Avant-Garde 1915–1932. *On the cover of the June 1930 monthly magazine,* Our Achievements, *edited by Maxim Gorky, for example, a row of tractors hauling disc ploughs heads out in stately procession across fields as broad as Saskatchewan. And this: Sergei Burylin's* Tractors. *The cotton square has been stretched taut under a glass pane, its woven pattern so cunning that I had to bend very close to see how it was made. It took me a few minutes to focus on streaks and blocks, discs and circles, red cylinders and rhomboids assembled in slanting rows across the cloth, hundreds of tiny red tractors rolling from horizon to horizon, past farm buildings and standing fields of grain over which is poised the blade of a scythe.*

I did not snicker. In fact, I was in tears and stood there at the display cabinet, touched by this lingering, not-yet-perfectly Stalinist, moment of the festive, of fertility even, as the great machines of the twentieth century, alluring on the brilliant red ground of textile, move out for the spring planting on the chernozem, the black earth.

————

It's the Depression, the proletariat of Edmonton is standing in patient lines at soup kitchens, treading with grave circumspection, hat in hand, from back alleys, up the sidewalks, and to the screened and latched back doors of modest homes, where a kindly housewife might be moved to wrap up in a clean rag some bread and a boiled egg. The proletariat is pulling out both trouser pockets and saying, here is all I have, lint and a rubber band.

Meanwhile, over there, where the East is Red, one-sixth of the planet — a vast, curved land under heaven and the dominion of Slavs — workers and peasants are enthusiastically constructing a new homeland in Baba's and Dido's names. I can imagine Dido learning to stand with his back straightened, shoulders pulled back, hands snapping his suspenders.

———

Dido never returned to his birthplace and so he never put himself to the test: was the Ukrainian Soviet Socialist Republic the fulfillment of what he wished for, for his people if not for himself? In a few pages of *The Ukrainian Canadian* magazine, May 1971, in a photo essay, "Ukraine Today," he would have been much reassured of his countrymen's and countrywomen's progress. Men in lab coats discuss the engineering of aircraft. A cultural club rehearses folk dances down by a river. At Victory Square in Kyiv there is a bus in view, as well as pedestrians and several Lada automobiles here and there on the broad boulevard named for the "victorious expulsion" of the German armies in 1944. A machine digs a trench for the irrigation system of a collective farm. And, although he would not have cared one way or another, the village of Tukholka has preserved its seventeenth-century wooden church, an exuberant pile of eaves, gables, drums, and domes, surmounted brazenly by crosses. Here was evidence clear as day that Soviet Ukrainians worked and played in joy and camaraderie, whether hoeing beets or hammering rivets or enjoying an impromptu concert by an accordionist down by the river.

Meanwhile

From my notebook (source unrecorded): *Only a few months ear-*
lier (in 1965), *the First Secretary of the Communist Party of Ukraine,*
Petro Shelest, in a speech entitled "On Most Urgent Measures For the
Development of Soviet Agriculture," cited the astonishing, not to say
depressing, fact that the price of a set of tires for a tractor cost almost
a quarter of the cost of the whole tractor and that, in order to be able
to afford to buy a tire for the drive wheel on a combine harvester, a
collective farm would have to sell three metric tons of wheat.

Skip forward twenty-five years and another Party leader, V.V. Shcher-
bytskyi, acknowledges that in a typical oblast of Ukraine two-thirds
of the villages have no public baths, some 160 have no hard-surfaced
roads, and less than one per cent of households are hooked up for
gas central heating. Many state shops have neither flour nor milk, oil,
fish products or even salt. Twenty-seven per cent of the designated
shipment of potatoes also fails, unaccountably, to be delivered to
the shops.

With their daughters and sons-in-law, Dido and Baba went to
Hawaii instead.

———

My mother did not like her stepfather. She knew he was a communist sympathizer from the picture of Lenin on the living room wall,
and by the time she was in grade seven or eight, she knew there
was "something not right" about that. She'd get into arguments
with him when he'd ask her what she had learned about history in
school. She would tell him, and he'd tell her that it was crazy, lies,
not to believe it. She would try to argue, but he would get so angry
he frightened her.

On the other hand: "My stepfather — and I must give him credit for this — did go to the States, I think it was to Minneapolis, to try to get work there, because someone told him you could make money in America. And I guess he must have. And he must have had a soft spot for me, which I never thought he had, when he came back home with a canary, which he had brought all the way from America. They let him on the train with this canary in a cage. And he gave it to me. You could have blown me over. I loved that canary very much. And I had a soft spot in my heart for my father too after that. We didn't talk much but we didn't fight."

I pressed the Pause button: I was unfamiliar with this story. And it was a kind of bifocalism that now brought these two people into a single lens of a new relationship for me: my mother, her recorded voice relaxing, letting into her confidence the young interviewer as she draws her *father* closer; he holds out a small bird in a cage and she steps toward him. His gift is not spurned; it will be loved.

Outside there once was a horse

From my notes: *Dido's things were outside the house, in a shed. A sickle and scythe, spade, hoe, and rake, twine and ropes, old harnesses.*

My mother's voice: "My stepfather had two horses. He did try to be a go-getter but he just never could make it. His idea for making some money was to take his horses and wagon out to the surrounding towns, buy chickens, and then bring them to the city market. I would have to go with him to count the money. There was a hotel in north Edmonton with an enormous water trough for horses passing through. On one of his trips, Dad stopped at a farm and asked to water his horses, but the farmer refused, saying his well was going dry. By the time Dad got back to the north Edmonton hotel, he let the horses drink their fill, and they drank too much and died."

It was over dinner on Sundays that my mother — in the long metrical line of her nostalgic, obsessive recall of her childhood deprivation — would break the flow, as though she had suddenly remembered them, the horses. I've heard the story umpteen times. (My cousins claim not to have heard it at all.) But I'm sure there was only one horse, and his name was Prince, a creature not from her childhood at all but from a later time when she was already out teaching and Baba and Dido had their small market garden and a horse.

I swear I was listening. I do not forget nor misremember the abrupt shift in the emphasis of her conversation — from her starchy self-pity to an anguished fellow-feeling with her step-father for whom she otherwise felt, at best, the respect due the hard-working man of the house and husband of her cherished mother.

It was a hot summer day. Perhaps it was a period of drought. Dido took Prince and wagon around to the neighbouring garden-ers, offering to sell their produce — along with his — for a cut. It was very hot. Midday. Then midafternoon. On and on they plod-ded, man and beast, from one acreage to the next. Dido loaded the cabbages and potatoes. Prince nibbled on whatever was underfoot. They sweated; they thirsted. But Dido did not take his horse to water. I do remember Mother emphasizing that the neighbours refused to offer this gift of hospitality to a suffering beast of burden. But that doesn't seem right. Too mean, even in a drought, with loose earth and sand filling the troughs. You might begrudge a neighbour, but his horse? But I also remember when she would claim that Dido was too proud to ask. And so it wasn't until he and Prince were back in their own farmyard that Dido led his companion to the trough and pumped out so much water to slake the beast's desperate thirst that he killed him.

"Colic! This is a dreaded term for anyone who has had to deal with a serious bout of colic in his or her horse. This disruption of the horse's natural digestive process can range in severity from a case of simple discomfort to a truly and agonizingly life-threatening condition. [It] can be caused by … allowing a very hot horse too much water" ("Colic Emergencies").

It is at this point in the story that, through my mother's sigh, her hand over her mouth, I share her spasm of compassion for a poor man blighted enough by want and need driven now to his knees. He was helpless, while noble, patient, companionable Prince died in agony, with the wagon still full of a harvest he would not reap. A cousin remembers: "I'll never forget how Dido Maksymiuk would shake — be physically ill — if his acreage crops were ruined. How would he provide for his family?"

The wooden sidewalks in front of our house must have been constructed of two-by-fours on frames, spaced just far enough apart that you could drop things — pennies and nickels, cat's-eye marbles — between the boards and, kneeling down with your face pressed against the crack, see them in the sand a few tantalizing inches below, out of reach.

I remember how the iceman strode up the back sidewalk from the alley, a cape of thick, black rubber across his back and shoulders that scarcely bent under the mass of ice, clasped between enormous tongs, that he bore up to the screen door, through it, and to the icebox where mother stood holding the door open to the upper chamber.

I remember that Dido would bring his horse and wagon to town on market day and parked the beast and rig in the alley next to the fence at the bottom of the garden. It is difficult now to imagine how he made his way through road intersections and along traffic lanes — surely he stopped at red lights — to turn, plodding, into our back lane where kids from the block came to feed the "horsey" apples and sugar cubes. He was a very large, white, broad-rumped beast with a mane that tumbled shaggily over his forehead, who stood patiently shifting his weight among his four legs, subdued by his own willingness to be stroked, there, in the thick, short hair between his eyes. His fleshy, flabby lips that ever so gently fluttered and scooped up the treats with a delicious tickle across the palm of my hand. I remember no name.

9

Man in a Photograph

Oleksa Voropay explains, in a song played on the lyra, how painted *pysanky* (Easter eggs) came to be: Christ on his way to Golgotha could bear the cross no more, and fell. A poor man who had come along to sell eggs left his basket and took up the cross, dragging it up the hill. When he returned to retrieve his basket, it shone with gold and inside were gloriously painted eggs.

———

2013 visit to Ukraine, from my notes: *Our little tour group from Canada has been invited into the home of a musician and his wife at the highest point of the Carpathians we've been today, Kryvorivne, their homestead reached at the end of a narrow, rocky road. All his working life Vasyl was a blacksmith on the collective farm but now he makes and plays Hutsul folk instruments, and so we are gathered in his kitchen to watch him play flutes, a violin, a lyra.*

I make note of a modern stove, a big and little fridge, a bench along one wall where his wife, Maria, sits, short, stout, stumpy, head swathed in a kerchief, wearing a large, sloppy sweater, white socks, felt slippers. She sits unmoving, and I suppose she has sat through a scenario like this a hundred times since Ukrainian Canadian tourists have discovered her husband. I would guess they are in their sixties, my contemporaries. Kilims are fixed to the wall behind a narrow cot, and a mattress and pillow are laid out on the *pich* (clay oven). An electric kettle, a pail of water, no taps or sink, a radio, the image of the Holy Family. Cousin Liz tells me later she was profoundly depressed by the visit, by that very Carpathian farm kitchen that reminded her of the one she grew up in in the Kostash farm house "already decades old," not picturesque but reeking of rural poverty.

Vasyl first heard Hutsul music of the Carpathians outside a church, and the lyra during Soviet times. The musicians were never suppressed because they were war invalids, but after the last one died, none took his place. In the whole of Ukraine, no one is making the *duda* (bagpipe).

War invalids. On our way to Kryvorivne we had stopped in the village of Iavoriv, the "wool village," to admire the craft of village women whose work began with the washed and drying fleeces we saw draped in their hundreds over lines stretched in courtyards between trees. I had also asked Liz to take a picture of me standing at a memorial cross I had caught sight of behind a fence at the base of a grassy mound. I gesture toward the plastic wreath of blue and yellow flowers hung on the crosspiece and the inscription below: *Volia* (Freedom).

In June 1999, on her farm near Iavoriv, villager Hanna Kishchuk struck a glass object with her hoe, and then another. I imagine her drawing back in alarm from the half-excavated artefacts — might they explode? — then rushing over in agitation to her son's, Petro's, place. Petro carefully smoothed away dirt and lifted out two glass cylinders. They were not bombs, he reassured Hanna, but containers. Whatever had been stored in the first was now disintegrated, but the second cylinder held undeveloped camera film.

The local dentist encouraged the Kishchuks to send the film on to an amateur photographer from Iavoriv, now in Lviv, to develop. And this is how they learned that the roll of film in their glass artefact contained a collection of photographs that depicted a local unit of the Ukrainian Insurgent Army (UPA in its Ukrainian name) that had waged guerrilla warfare against the Red Army, well into the mid-1950s, from their base in the Carpathian Mountains.

Karpaty/Carpathians, land of their struggle and martyrdom. Eastern Galicia had the worst roads in Austria-Hungary and they are still deplorable here in the hills. At 7 p.m. from the hotel deck, I see the cowherd take his five cows down through the hotel's forecourt and into the bush. Is this where our breakfast milk comes from? The near-universal state of rural underdevelopment and dilapidation doesn't shock me, although it is dispiriting. At least now Ukrainian villages have gas central heating (we see the pipelines snaking along the highways a metre above ground). Trailing Lada cars on their last Soviet-made legs, we drive, as in 1984, the muddy, stone-strewn roads at ten kilometres per hour to avoid disappearing down a sinkhole. We have long since left a main road. Plaster still falls off houses exposing brick and mortar.

Chickens cluck and peck in every yard that also boasts gorgeous flower gardens of late summer (I think fleetingly of the economic "uselessness" of flowers). Families are out in the fields filling up sacks with potatoes, scores of bags per family for the winter. Dogs. Rubbish. Outhouses — still no indoor plumbing after two generations of "industrialization" and then one of "capitalism."

In 2005, the pictures developed from the Iavoriv cache were published in Lviv in a Ukrainian-language book, *Photo Archive of the Iavoriv UPA*. In 2007 a selection of these photographs with English-language text was published in Toronto as *Their Just War: Images of the Ukrainian Insurgent Army* and in due course a copy made its way to the Edmonton Public Library.

The book is a large, hardcover photo album. I skip over the text to examine the photographs, all black-and-white, of soldiers in their twos and threes, and in groups, in various coats and uniforms. The probable scene: into the clandestine forest camp of a military unit of the UPA, a photographer has arrived with unimpeded access, for no one looks the least perturbed by his presence. He may be one of them, also in uniform, but with a knack with a camera.

They are between engagements and have time to pose for photographs, even though it's summer, the best time to be launching actions beyond their forest hideout. Perhaps they have information that the "enemy," whoever it is in this case, is nowhere around, or is perhaps pinned down in an action elsewhere in their area.

In print, the photos bear captions: "Intelligence gathering," "at the campfire," "mountain crossing," "Easter, probably 1950." The photographer stands above them on a mountain ridge, looking down at their meandering line across a meadow. He follows at the rear, as they disappear into a grove of pines, and shoots close-ups, posing men with their weapons as though in a studio. He's there when they take a bath, a cask of water thrown over their shoulders.

Why are these pictures being taken? Perhaps the photographer has been making the rounds of these forest units, already thinking about an archive.

I've seen pictures of men like these — French Resistance fighters in the Maquis; the Mac-Paps (Mackenzie–Papineau Battalion brigade) in Spain, crawling out of the trenches at Fuentes de Ebro; Polish commandos in the sewers of Warsaw — but of my Ukrainian relations in uniform on the losing side of the Great War, or in interwar Poland fighting back Bolsheviks, or under German occupation 1941–1945, or, finally, under Soviet occupation, nothing. The Canadian family hasn't a single photograph taken during wars, occupations, civil wars, none of underground armies, a Red Army, Bolsheviks. Purges, pogroms, mass graves, unmarked graves: not a single image. And without images, we in Canada have been spared what Ulrich Baer calls the "spectral evidence" of traumas that we never saw, never knew (qtd. in Hirsch and Spitzer 169). Of a war that had overwhelmed our relatives in western Ukraine — of whose existence we were anyway oblivious — I knew and read and heard nothing.

Two insurgents stand side by side, behind them the woods. They are in uniform and armed, but they seem relaxed, posing; although the older man on the left, who is looking into the camera, seems wary, wearing an expression of melancholic reflection as though — compared to the younger man — he has already seen or experienced much that has unsettled him. For his part, the man on the right — with his cap tilted over his right brow, his sidelong look, his slouch, the bravado of the naked knife in his belt — is nonchalant. But even his expression, unsmiling, seems a projection of an inner feeling, and he's not so much looking sideways away from the camera as into a private reverie.

They are men of the UPA. The younger one beside him, of the village of Tulova, has my name: Stepan Fedorovych Kostashchuk.

My heart jumps a beat. In a village of some eight hundred souls, it is impossible that we are not related. What the hell is he doing here? A Kostashchuk who had taken up arms at a time when desperate, cornered guerrillas already running low on ammo might do anything to get at the throat of a man, even a neighbour, with the Red Star on his cap, and tear it out.

I scrutinize Stepan's features but of his motives they give nothing away. I'd say he's in his early twenties, clean-shaven with well-formed ears close to his head; his cap is perched at a rakish angle, and two leather straps criss-cross his jacket with its deeply wrinkled sleeves. The naked blade of the knife protrudes from his belt and his right hand lightly holds between thumb and forefinger the upright barrel of a gun. He stands at ease, right hip cocked slightly. His legs have disappeared into low-lying foliage. I can see the calf-high boots into which his pants are tucked; the boots seem to be sturdy, judging from the thick sole and bulbous toe of his right boot. He looks rather spiffy. He is not starving, likely from foraging in the countryside or receiving bread and onions direct from sympathetic peasants or stealing from them. He has been equipped with military kit and his boots are not falling apart.

Stepan has full, unsmiling lips. And it is this mouth and the rakishly tipped cap that remind me of Marlon Brando in *The Wild One*, his leathers draped over his motorcycle. The same rakish tilt of the cap, the same full lips, though on Brando they are voluptuously parted: a face I have lusted for, well past my adolescence. The jolt of aesthetic arousal, in the case of this young guerrilla in calf-high leather boots and broad-bladed knife at his hip, strikes me immediately as indecent. For one thing, he was probably long since dead; for another, he was a relative. And he belonged to an army characterized in scholarship as well as propaganda as Nazi-collaborationist-bourgeois-nationalist.

Into our know-nothingness in Canada had arrived the DPs, Displaced Persons, from Ukraine via the refugee camps in Germany, traumatized exiles with their cardboard suitcases and little else. The kids my age raised within these families were new and intimidating creatures in our midst, fluently bilingual in Ukrainian and English, deferential to their elders, and passionately committed to liberating Ukraine from Soviet captivity when they would be old enough to fight. I knew they were already marching around in drills and uniforms at their gatherings and singing in three-part harmony "Boldly we go to battle ..." I had been inoculated from birth against such nationalist pipe dreams. Their strident call to arms felt more like bullying — pushing us namby-pamby Ukrainian *Canadians* around — and I was resentful: I had a motherland, a homeplace, Canada, and the Ukrainian Soviet Socialist Republic, even as a "captive nation," was not my affair.

I turn to the text and devour the Biographical Notes, the scraps of what the surviving members of UPA in Iavoriv remember of "Stepan Kostashchuk — Born December 1928 in Tulova. County propaganda leader. Studied at Lviv Pedagogical Institute. Joined underground in 1948. Married Ivanna Iulianivna Hrankivska, a priest's daughter from Tuchapy, Sniatyn county. Betrayed, Stepan and Ivanna committed suicide Spring 1951 to avoid capture by the MGB (Ministry of State Security [formerly the NKVD])" (Luciuk 82).

"Almost every person portrayed in these pages ... fell in battle against Soviet forces, went missing in action, or was captured, interrogated then executed or exiled to the *gulag*, most not surviving their internment," wrote the book's Canadian publisher Lubomyr Luciuk in his Introduction. "While we will never know why these photographs were made, it seems certain that by the time they were buried those secreting them knew full well that their struggle was drawing to an end" (Luciuk vii). Did Stepan step out of the frame of the camera lens and back to the bunker where he would die?

This is the moment that Roland Barthes, in his reflections on photography, *Camera Lucida,* pinpointed so chillingly: "*he is going to die.*" I know this but Stepan does not, not yet. I gaze at him: he is alive and yet he is dead. The photograph is already of the "absolute past" (Barthes 96), but for Stepan the future has not yet happened. It has not yet happened to him, but it has happened for me: I know he is dead.

The photo has a caption. In its entirety it says:

Left: Ivan Melnychuk (*Halaida*); right: Stepan Kostashchuk (*Kryvonis*).

Nom de guerre: *Kryvonis*, literally crooked nose, and Stepan is not the only UPA fighter to choose it. What's in a name? "Maksym Kryvonis was one of the most effective generals of the [*Bohdan Khmelnytsky*] Uprising. He was awarded the rank of colonel of Cherkasy Regiment," one of six core regiments of registered Cossacks in the early seventeenth century. "His actions in Korsun and Pylyavtsi battles in 1648 led to crushing Cossack victories over the Polish armies. . . Kryvonis earned a reputation among the Poles and Jews for wanton cruelty as the rebels under his leadership perpetrated serious atrocities" ("Maksym Kryvonis"). Kryvonis came to a bad end himself, in a variety of versions: killed (shot) during the siege of Lviv, assassinated (poisoned) by Jesuits, killed by orders of Khmelnytsky, who loathed him, or perished of plague during the siege of Zamość in 1648. In Polish he is Maksym Krzywonos, and a character in Henryk Sienkiewicz's novel *With Fire and Sword* (1884). In the 1999 movie based on the novel he was played by Maciej Kozłowski.

I do an image search for Kozłowski and find him during the film shoot well into his role as Kryvonis. He is bare-chested, an enormous cross hanging from his neck and the fine-tooled pommel and grip of a weapon tucked into his belt, just visible in the frame. I know he is a Cossack because his head is shaved bare except for an impressive plume of hair on top, the telltale *oseledets* (Cossack haircut that leaves a lock of hair on a shaved skull), which in this case is blowing sideways in a small breeze. A female production assistant in a baseball cap is looking up at him (he is of impressive physique) in evident admiration of his figure, but Kozłowski (or is it Kryvonis?), showing his profile, is undistracted, deep in thought, and looks the other way.

I challenge myself: put Stepan in this picture.

The Ukrainian Insurgent Army was no ordinary military formation. UPA's main enemies, against whom they waged guerrilla war, were Poles, Soviet partisans and sympathizers, but as a current crop of historians recounts, UPA also committed atrocities, including pogroms against Jews; targeted assassinations of "Bolshevik" collaborators; and, most notoriously, the ethnic cleansing of between 60,000 and 100,000 ethnic Poles in Volhynia (in western Ukraine) in 1943 and 1944. UPA also died in their thousands — more than a hundred thousand in almost 40,000 Soviet operations.

By the late 1940s UPA-Iavoriv's networks of resistance to the new Soviet power had frayed utterly. So they cached the film strips, hostages against the time when a succeeding generation in a peaceful era might unearth them, print them, and pass them around the village elders, asking, "Do you know these men?"

Does Stepan even have a grave?

There is drama here, and tragedy, succinct in its few details, and suddenly I am engaged. A doomed *guerrillero* dead by his own hand at twenty-three, and a blood relative. Who was Stepan Kostashchuk? I ask a Kostash cousin in Ontario. She grew up on the Kostash farm near Vegreville, Alberta, heard all the stories, saw all the pictures. She has never heard of Stepan. (Nor of any other Kostashchuk, come to think of it.) There is no such story in Canada. "Sorry," she says.

Why does Stepan join an insurgency that is already hopeless in 1948? I wonder what a propaganda leader is doing in the middle of a forest and what that passive construction, "betrayed by," contains. I conjecture betrayal by an infiltrator from the Ministry of Security (MGB) or, back in Tulova, a vindictive neighbour reaping what may have been sown a generation earlier. Or a jealous lover, maddened by the image of Stepan and Ivanna's nuptial embrace in their forest hidey-hole. Why didn't Stepan and Ivanna shoot their tormentors instead of turning their gun on themselves? Was theirs a suicide pact in the face of existential despair? In the same villages they had enlisted to protect and defend against the Red Army, their parents were already handing over their milk cows and corn husks to the collective farm's apparatchik from Moscow. All the while, Stepan and his wife (aka "Zena" and "Olha"), a typist underground, were grinding out leaflets — *Resist!* — on the calamitous gestetner in their bunker in the hills.

In 1988 when I had first visited Tulova, my host, Hryhoryi Kostashchuk, the machinist, took me down a well-trampled dirt street leading to the house where other relatives awaited me. They were Odarka, Odarka, and Hanusia, and I have long since forgotten how we are related, though related we are. In 1988 I wasn't curious enough to enquire further. My grandfather, Fedor Kostashchuk, had left Tulova eighty-eight years earlier, and now my relatives in Tulova would be second or third cousins twice removed and beyond.

Notes prior to visit to Tulova in 2013, from conversation with tour director in Edmonton: *Villagers don't have cars although there is one paved road; there is a satellite dish and some people have two cellphones; they dress better; there is gas heating, a well in each yard, but still most houses still have outhouses; they have huge gardens and each household still keeps a cow; the kolhosp has been reactivated as a producers' co-op.*

It's fall 2013, and now Tulova seems shabby, colourless, with no one in charge; geese meander unsupervised along lanes and the green swath of village common I remember is now a windswept wasteland and all the village's structures are as though laid out on a far horizon. I see no one about. The eighteenth-century church now looks ponderous, pressed into the earth, almost squished under the exaggerated overhang of its roof. And the cemetery goes on and on and on, each grave marked by a garish plastic wreath, twenty-five years' worth of interments since I last visited.

From my notes: *At the opening of the film festival in the Fatherland cinema, during the showing of Mikhail Mamedov's film,* On Sunday Morning, *applause resounded from time to time in the hall. And at the press conference someone raised a placard: "Thanks for the film!" It was a very simple story, really, about elderly women who gather wood in a forest. Solitary women on whose shoulders fell the most terrible war and the reconstruction of the Soviet economy in its aftermath. So we see how they ploughed, sowed, reaped, grew wheat and children. But to their descendents it was a bitter bread and they were no longer starving, so off they went, abandoned the villages without prospects, turned up in the cities, for electricity and hot water, and their mothers, gone grey, left behind, are compelled once again to take up the onerous burden of post-Soviet reconstruction.*

Hryhoryi is long dead, but the two Odarkas and Hanusia are still alive and they sit waiting for me again, in their kerchiefs, oversized sweaters, and boots. They bring out snapshots taken when I was with them in 1988, in this same two-roomed house, with its framed religious pictures on the walls and enormous embroidered cushions lined up on the settee bursting at their seams. This time I have specific questions, for I have come to find out who were the other Kostashchuks my grandfather left behind, all those in the village cemetery, and who, then, was Stepan.

Odarka, Odarka, and Hanusia are anxious to be helpful. I write and scribble as best I can to transcribe their energetic babble, but I lose track of who said what.

"Well, now, there was an Ivan Kostashchuk, conscript in the Austrian army, who perished in a battle with the Russian army in 1915."

"I remember Illia Kostashchuk, conscript in the Red Army, who perished in 1944 at twenty in the Battle of Brody." This was the major operation to push the German troops from western Ukraine.

"And that other one, another kid, Hryhoryi, a cousin of Illia, maybe?"

"Yes, that one was mobilized in 1944 and was killed near Konigsberg in 1945."

"Dmytro Kostashchuk, starved to death at age fifty in a Soviet labour camp in Kazakhstan."

Wait, wait, why was he there? But they're off again.

"And Mykola Kostashchuk — we only learned this year he had died in a camp in Mordova, God knows when."

"But let's not forget venerable Vasyl Kostashchuk. He died at the age of seventy-six in 1973 — he's out there in the cemetery."

Who are these people? Where are the women? Even though I learn that one of my grandfather's brothers had three daughters — Anastasia, Anna, and Kataryna — no one tells their stories. This is all about patrilineal relationship. *Where is Stepan?* I am drawing loops and lines and boxes until something like a family tree is emerging — not an iota of it known to the Kostashes of Canada. By deduction, working back from patronymics (that essential "middle name" derived from the father's Christian name), I have found the branch where Stepan Fedorovych Kostashchuk sprouts, son of Fedor Illich, grandson of Ilia Hryhorovich — my grandfather's brother — and so my second cousin.

He is beautiful, he is lethal, and he is kin.

Suddenly, into this hubbub bursts a neighbour, Ivan Toma-schuk, excitedly waving a sheaf of papers in my direction. He's heard that I am visiting Tulova and that I want to know what happened to Stepan Fedorovich. His fistful of papers includes, I can see, a photocopy of the same photograph of Stepan that has so allured me and brought me here — Ivan has read the Ukrainian edition — but first he has a story to tell.

It's April, 1951, and Stepan and Ivanna have been betrayed by neighbours — Ivan gestures with a sweep of his arm that could mean the ones across the road or someone in the next village, or beyond all the way to Moscow — who disclosed their hiding place to the regional unit of Soviet State Security, the MGB. I am writing as fast as I can, transcribing in English (because I write Latin letters at several times the rate of speed of the Cyrillic), and cannot stop to slow him down, to ask, *which* neighbours? *why?* Were they compelled or co-operative? Ideological enemies as well as neighbours? Had this neighbour been in the woods with them, then deserted and claimed a reward? Or tortured and "turned"?

But Ivan has raced on, and now he's at the foxhole in the woods with the MGB who, pistols drawn, have surrounded Stepan and Ivanna, and shout at them to come out, there is no escape. Silence. And then two muffled gunshots from within the hole. Stepan's first bullet took Ivanna, and then, the gun aimed at his own head, the second took Stepan. The MGB drag out the bodies and convey them to their headquarters in Sniatyn's main square.

In Sniatyn they laid them out on the sidewalk and invited passersby and the curious to identify them. But first they stuck a cigarette in the corner of their mouths.

At this point, Odarka, Odarka, and Hanusia interrupt. In 1951 they were young women in this village.

"No, it wasn't like that. The NKVD had sent for Stepan's father —"

"No, his uncle —"

"— anyway, they came to Tulova and they took the boys' father, Fedir —"

"— all the way to Sniatyn —"

"— but Fedir said, 'This is not my son.'"

He said he did not recognize his son or daughter-in-law, their faces now contorted in the rictus of death. I am still writing so fast that it will occur to me only on reflection of this conversation that if the MGB men knew who the father or uncle was, then they obviously knew the identities of the dead boy and girl. In any event, there was no identification. Nor, it seems, any retribution on the family that had reared such nationalist scum.

The bodies lie on the sidewalk until night falls. Under cover of darkness, comrades from the forest creep into town to steal the bodies and bury them in an unmarked grave in the Sniatyn cemetery.

Odarka: "That's not it. The NKVD dumped them in a pit. UPA boys came at night and dug them up and reburied them in Tulova cemetery under someone else's grave marker."

One of the members of the remnant UPA unit, Natalka Fodchuk, an elderly and bed-ridden woman right here in Tulova, lived long enough to be able, at the declaration of Ukraine's independence from the USSR in 1990, to rush over to her neighbours and tell them where the bodies lay.

I have been so gripped by this unfolding, and contested, story that it is only later that I realize it has not been told by any eyewitness, not even by Natalka Fodchuk who was not there at the bunker. The NKVD were there but they have had no lines in this drama.

2013: our little tour group spills out of the van in the centre of Sniatyn and begins a stroll along the boulevard passing handsome public buildings newly scrubbed and painted, vaguely neoclassical. Walls bear plaques, which is the reason for our stroll. On one, "placed in honour of his 70th birthday," the handsome, half-smiling face of former dissident Viacheslav Chornovil, "Hero of Ukraine," hangs in bronze bas-relief above the inevitable wreath of blue and yellow flowers and ribbons. Further along, a vastly more imposing cenotaph has been fastened to the wall in the shape of a cross. Above the cross the words: "To those from Sniatyn who fought for the freedom of Ukraine, victims of communist terror." And on the cross itself, their names. Stepan's is not among them — he died for Tulova — but underneath the cross there is another plaque. My flash has obliterated some of the words, but this is what I can still make out: WE REMEMBER. At the time of the German-fascist [occupation?] from 30 June 19[43?] to 30 March 1944 almost 5 thousand peaceful residents of Sniatyn were executed, among them women and children. This is a cenotaph, a burial site is not mentioned, their bodies lie elsewhere. They are remembered not by the officially patriotic blue-and-yellow but by two bronze roses, as though laid on their elsewhere grave.

Ivan Tomaschuk has finished his story. He pulls a paper from the sheaf in its cardboard folder. It's a poem (unattributed) that I take away with me and translate later:

Forty four years have passed since the executioners took your life.
O how horribly the executioners abused your dead bodies.

He takes me back to the cemetery and Stepan's and Ivanna's are the first graves you see now as you come through the little gate. They lie under a dual granite headstone with their teenaged photo portraits imbedded in bronze plaques.

If you, Stepanka, were now with us among the living
You would not bear this, proclaimed the anonymous poet.
O sleep sweet young friends, we will lay a curse for you.

But only a simple black cross has been inscribed in the granite and someone has left a large plastic wreath of yellow flowers. Once upon a time, Stepan forsook the village for the camaraderie of the forest, but here he is simply Stepanka of Tulova, one of God's children now, and their own.

> The people of Ukraine have taken it upon themselves to honour their partisans. Those best placed to know what the OUN (Organization of Ukrainian Nationalists) and UPA was — family neighbours and descendants — have erected dozens of monuments, plaques and other memorials to hallow the victims of Nazi and Soviet oppression and to laud those who resisted foreign occupation. This reshaping of the cultural landscape has sapped Soviet-era fabrications of much of their meaning, giving strong evidence of how the people understand Ukraine's twentieth-century history. (Luciuk viii)

In 1990, on the eve of Ukrainian independence from the Soviet Union, a group of Tulova's youth began a cultural circle, "For Freedom," and proceeded to renew village monuments that had been "ruined by the totalitarian system of the Communist Party," such as a memorial cross erected for an earlier and unluckier generation of "fighters for the freedom and independence of Ukraine." Also in the works, a monument "to the Heroes of Ukraine from Tulova Village," going all the way back to the First World War, "especially the six active participants in the Ukrainian National Organization-Ukrainian Insurgent Army, who gave their young lives for the freedom and independence of Ukraine. Eternal Be Their Memory" (Kharyton and Biiovskyi 52).

Good as done. In 2013 I view them all, plaques, crosses, wreaths, national symbols, and inscribed tablets, and I make note of all the Kostashchuks, inscribing them all in my own Notebook of the Violently Dead. On the granite base of an imposing grassy *mohyla* (mound, barrow) a dedication has been inscribed: "To the fighters for the state independence of Ukraine 1939–1950." Stepan's name is there, Ivanna's is not. (Likewise, I will find Stepan's name but not hers on a Ukrainian Wikipedia page, "Martyrology of the Slain Activists of OUN and UPA.")

Ivan Tomaschuk had one more poem:

> While we still live, we will not forget you.
> Rise up, friends, look, there is a new Spring.

To the villagers of Tulova Stepan is a martyr to the cause of Ukrainian independence, an identity to which, I confess, I am gradually surrendering my political prejudices. By the time Stepan joined the UPA unit, its organization and structures had collapsed, prised loose even from the fascist ideology that had first formed the army in its heyday. Stepan's short and violent life, as I mournfully consider it now at the cemetery gate, has left me bereft of the revulsion I have nurtured about these "boys" of UPA since my childhood. I have had the luxury of being a Ukrainian Canadian whose grandfather, having emigrated from the village where such awful choices had to be confronted, freed me from taking part in that history.

Perhaps both can be true: the martyrdom and the pogroms? It's complicated: an educated youth is raised within a family of some means in a Galician village but heads for the hills as soon as he is old enough to volunteer. Surely he knows the cause is hopeless, that the ranks of UPA have been riddled by Soviet agents. But it's his only chance to act. Stepan the Pedagogical Institute student burns uselessly with anti-Polish, then anti-German, then anti-Soviet fever until finally he can pick up a gun and shoot the land's tormenters.

Does he remember the Jews? (According to national statistics, in 1939 there were no Jews in Tulova, nor any ethnic population other than Ukrainian [Kubijovic 79].) By 1943, over 1,400,000 Jews had been executed in the occupied Soviet Union, most on Ukrainian territory, by the *Einsatzgruppen,* paramilitary death squads, sometimes with the co-operation of local Ukrainian Auxiliary Police (United States Holocaust Memorial Museum). Stepan was fifteen years old when it was all over for them. But in Tulova in 2013 Jewish suffering is never mentioned, the pits into which they were driven never visited. Lives as vapour. Only Ukrainian bodies are exhumed.

I imagine his youthful foolhardiness, the idealized fervour for a fight he doesn't want to miss, a commitment he has made to his parents, his teachers, his buddies, his God. In my world, they had burst out of Cuba's Sierra Maestra; they had charged down Viet Nam's Ho Chi Minh Trail; they had thrown petrol bombs at newspapers offices in Johannesburg. My admiration of them, my doomed darlings, did not seem complicated.

I have been deceived by the "illusion of continuity over time and space" that Marianne Hirsch, in *Family Frames*, suggests family photographs provide (xi). I have the images but not the story, and I wonder: which is more essential to my memory-making, story or image? Once the image has been shorn of context, has it also lost its capacity to tell its story? Stepan's image is free-floating. It arrives abruptly, without context, all surface, seductive. He is *here* for me in a suspended moment that can never lead to the present: a chronology has been discontinued (Berger and Mohr 91). It is very easy to superimpose on it now the beautiful, dreamy boy dead by his own hand in a foxhole in a Galician forest, who I thought looked like Marlon Brando.

10

Yuri:
Versions of
a Murder

When Baba Palahna left Dzhuriv to marry Nikolai Maksymiuk in Edmonton, she left behind a sister, Sophia, who later followed her to Canada, two other sisters, Maria and Elena, who never emerged from the obscurity into which they subsided after Palahna's emigration, and two brothers, Nick — the man with the armful of cucumbers — and Yuri.

Yuri was the only one who came down to us in a story, as tragic as it was dramatic: from what I could make of it, likely through my mother's retelling, Yuri had been violently wrested from the bosom of the family in an atrocity vaguely associated with the immediate end of the Second World War and the consolidation of Soviet power in western Ukraine. Sometimes Baba would weep inconsolably, her face buried in her apron, growling her anguish yet again about the fate of "poor, poor Yurochko," murdered by "*bandyty*" (bandits) at the stoop of his parents' home in Dzhuriv. He was just a simple conscripted Red Army soldier, home for Christmas. The scenario never varied in the telling.

There was something in her mourning that I thought of as maternal, as though in his presumed innocence Yuri was a boy left to die on the threshold of the familial cottage by agents unknown. Perhaps it was the singularity of this recollection — there were no keenings over the fates of sundry other close relations in Dzhuriv who remained unstoried in Baba's kitchen — that infused it with such condensed grief, all other deaths or vanishings distilled into the fate of Yurochko.

But a Canadian cousin recalls a few twists: "'They' were soldiers he had betrayed somehow and they came for him in the middle of the night. They executed him in the woods. His body was retrieved by the villagers. Baba always told this story with great anguish. An innocent young man. She told this story as though it had happened to her, the terror, the anguish. It was very vivid. The terrible detail of finding his tortured body. I don't remember that this was her brother."

Whatever it was that happened the day Yuri Kosovan died, it was decades since Baba had left him behind in Dzhuriv, yet she wept as though his ghost lay just outside her backdoor.

"People don't live history," the poet Erìn Moure writes, citing the Spanish/Galician poet, Chus Pato, "'they live their lives. History is a catastrophe that passes over them'" (87). This is what I too have thought about the lives of my Baba's people as they survived, or not, one catastrophe after another — that these cataclysmic events left them essentially unchanged. It was the day-to-day events that constituted "history" for them: digging potatoes, nursing the sick, mourning the cow seized for the collective herd.

But not so Yuri. His history *was* the catastrophe.

I possess an undated photo-postcard, pre-Soviet, of the Kosovan family group that also includes Yuri's older brother, Nick. It is the only image I have of Yuri, identified on the back simply as one among "my uncles, aunts, cousins, grandfather" in pencil in my mother's hand. In ink she has added, "Uncle Nick visited us in Canada and returned some ten years later." When I compare the Nick of this photo and that of the one taken in Lethbridge where he looks considerably older, I would date this one to the early 1920s. Nick wears a suit jacket rather snug (he can do up only the top button) with narrow lapels, white shirt, striped tie smartly knotted under a narrow collar. (By contrast, his father, Petro Kosovan, my great-grandfather, is dressed in full-*muzhik*.) Yuri's hair is dark and straight, slicked firmly to his head with a little tuft that sticks up at the back of the part. A long, oval face, clean-shaven, unsmiling, with unfurrowed brow and a clear, open gaze.

Among the many photographs lifted out of the shoeboxes filled with photos sent with persistent regularity from Dzhuriv, I find no more of Yuri.

He had still some twenty-five years to live and he could have been anywhere, moving around for work or under military orders. Or nowhere at all except in Dzhuriv, buffeted by punitive social, economic, political, and cultural systems that masqueraded as revolution.

––––––––––

November 1922, Peter Svarich returns from a lengthy tour of European countries:

> To the Editor of Vegreville Observer, Dear Sir: — A month ago as I was leaving Galicia [Svarich had returned to Tulova to bring his widowed sister, Kateryna, back to Canada with him], three bands of well-armed and trained cavalry men called "Death Battalions" terrorised the Polish authorities by their sudden appearance and disappearance ... killing police, officials and landlords and burning down their estates.... I have met several leaders of this rebellion and they told me that this was the only way to throw off the yoke of the invaders.... I got out of this hell just in the nick of time. ("Canada best country" 10)

As a Canadian with the same exposure to the conventional account of the events collectively known as the Second World War as anyone of my generation, I have struggled to shift my gaze from ground zero on the Normandy beaches (or the liberation of the Netherlands or the first photos from Auschwitz-Birkenau) to what is now Western Ukraine and to zoom in on the Kosovans of Dzhuriv. I need to add them to the fund of pathos and condolence that I already hold as a Canadian thinking about the European victims of world war. Sometimes I will see them only within a mass of human misery but sometimes as a man here, a woman there, an orphan anywhere, or as a cottage burns, a grave pit fills, a tank rolls over a beet field. Yuri here, Yuri there.

On September 17, 1939, following on a secret treaty between Nazi Germany and the Soviet Union, a million Soviet troops roared in from the east into eastern Poland (now western Ukraine). While German troops overwhelmed the rest of Poland, the Red Army was on a campaign to liberate the Ukrainian masses from the yoke of bourgeois capitalist, not to say fascist, Poland. To bring the Ukrainians finally into the longed-for unification with Soviet Ukraine. The Kosovans wait for them to liberate Dzhuriv.

The handbook, of modest production value that served as a guidebook to Lviv's Historical Museum, was printed in 1987 by *Kameniar* (stonebreaker, quarryman) publishing house. With it in hand, I made a tour in 1988. I remember nothing of that visit, but I reread it now, interested in how that state institution, still Soviet in 1987, viewed a history whose interpretation was soon to be consigned to the curatorial dustbins. (Emigration to Canada, Brazil, and the United States is described as "forced"; in Soviet terms, forced by economic conditions in "feudal" Galicia) (Dunets).

I'm curious how certain pages of this history account as context for what Yuri may have lived through and how he himself may have told the story.

———

On a city map tucked into the back cover, the main streets and monuments of 1987 are given in Russian but written in Latin letters as though, any day now in the Ukraine of perestroika, many busloads of tourists will be arriving to see the sights and they won't be just Ukrainian Canadians who know their Cyrillic alphabet and rush off to the ancestral villages. These new tourists will want to wander along Bogdan Khmelnitskogo Ulitsa (Street), Komsomolskaya Ulitsa, Prospekt Lenina, Ulitsa Pervogo Travnya (First of May), Ulitsa Mayakovskogo.

The guidebook offers an historical overview of the city of Lviv (also known historically as Lvov, Lwow, and Lemberg). It is a veritable mishmash of dates and armies, congresses and conferences, manifestoes and decrees of the "international character of the revolutionary struggle," and of mass political actions and united fronts (Dunets). All of it under the unflappable leadership of the communists toiling in the foul precincts of "bourgeois-landowner

Poland." The extremely short-lived Galician Soviet Socialist Republic (July–September 1920) had nevertheless "left a deep imprint on the minds of working people" who then thrilled to the arrival of the Red Army onto Eastern Galician territory on September 17, 1939. A flurry of declarations was then adopted. I imagine Yuri being transfixed by one in particular as he reads it in a Party newspaper: "The Declaration on Confiscation of Landed Estates Owned by Lords, Monasteries and Government Officials." The Kosovans, it will be recalled, are land poor.

The elders had grown up in the now-defunct Austro-Hungarian Empire, the younger ones in reconstituted Poland, and now all of them would be subsumed within the UkrSSR without having moved a metre out of Dzhuriv. (Where then are they from? *Tuteshni*, they will say; we're from *here*.)

Sympathizers of the Red Army wave red flags as trucks and fuel tanks rumble in under festal arches, throwing up a dust that settles back on everyone, peasant, merchant, priest, and prole-tarian alike. And on Yuri Kosovan, who joins the crowd to read a propaganda poster already nailed to the door of the Reading Room. "We stretched our hand to our brothers so that they could straighten their backs." And true to their word, the Soviet admin-istrators began land redistribution to the peasants.

No sooner had land been redistributed, it was collectivized. The poorest of the poor of Dzhuriv voluntarily signed up for work on the new collectives, and some, with demonstrable enthusiasm, stepped up to manage the village's new business. But it proved to be the same old labour. In a Soviet photo, Ukrainian "peasants" (still not *farmers*) reap and harvest without a machine in sight. Perhaps there is a threshing machine just outside the frame, or will these peasants pound away on the threshing floor with the immemor-ial technology of the wooden flail?

The Soviets set up revolutionary committees in Kolomyia,

Sniatyn, Stanyslaviv, and Kosiv, all in the near vicinity of Dzhuriv. Backs straightened, the revolutionary masses went on a killing spree. They dragged a Polish soldier to his death behind a horse. They hacked away at Polish settlers with axes and hammers. Mobs murdered entire families, "rows of corpses lining up the Włodawsa-Kowel road" (Jan Gross 36–38). Military-age men were drafted into the Red Army, credit unions and co-operatives were shut down as well as the Greek (Ukrainian) Catholic Church, reading rooms, local newspapers, libraries, and community theatres. In February 1940 the deportations began. The deportees — the usual suspects, priests, lawyers, intellectuals — were the enemies of the people but these now included the *kulaks*, the "rich" peasants. Fifty percent of Ukrainian peasants owned less than two hectares of land per household: was Yuri among those zealots of land collectivization who "outed" neighbours who owned four?

First version

In 1984 I visited Dzhuriv. Technically, this was illegal. The oblast in which Dzhuriv was located was closed to foreigners. Westerners met their Soviet relatives in awkward groups, chatting and weeping, in and around the Intourist hotel in Chernivtsi. My Kosovan relatives did exercise a certain amount of subterfuge in getting me to and out of the village but, while I was with them, their hospitality was exuberant and unrestrained. Their beloved Palahna had left them seventy-five years earlier; I had come back in her place.

Before they would let me go, they insisted I walk with them to the top of the main street. There, on a small plaza, stood a monument that seemed to serve the same purpose as all the cenotaphs in Canadian towns dedicated to the memory of their war dead. A Soviet soldier in a helmet, a battle rifle held across his chest — stalwart, broad-shouldered, and Aryan — protectively rests an arm on the shoulder of a young girl who clutches a large circular wreath, the unending circle of life, I suppose, as laid at memorial places. Just so, here. The two figures stand on top of a large marble base on which are inscribed a red star and the words, "To Our Countrymen Who Perished on the Fronts of the Great Patriotic War and at the Hands of the Ukrainian Bourgeois Nationalists, with Gratitude from the Workers of the Village of Dzhuriv." The relatives stand around me, arms crossed over their chests, looking stern, even a little proud. It takes me a few moments to realize why I have been brought here: on a separate marble installation two columns of names have been engraved. On one, those who fought on the fronts; on the other, "These perished at the hands of Ukrainian bourgeois nationalists." I read down the list and there he is, Kosovan, Yuri P. In my ear, Baba's voice: *Poor, poor Yurochko.*

I take a couple of photos but ask no questions. I wish I had. "There are eighteen names, including Yuri's; how did they die?" In the garbled version I have from Baba I guess I do know: all of them killed by the *bandyty.* I always knew it was tragic, but I did *not* know that in Dzhuriv Yurko Kosovan was a Soviet hero. Hero! I would like to know more, but the history is a hodgepodge in my mind and I haven't got the language.

———

From my 1984 notebook: *Old Maria, planted in a chair by the big ceramic furnace, tells us the story, detail by vivid detail. My Great-Uncle Yurko was murdered by Ukrainian guerrillas of the Ukrainian Insurgent Army known as Banderites, named after their military leader, Stepan Bandera, the very "bourgeois nationalists" at whose hands Yuri perished.* But as I write this down, I correct Maria in my notes: "Actually," I wrote, with Baba's brief account in mind, "*he simply vanished after being unaccountably arrested by bandyty the night he returned to the village — a Soviet soldier — to spend Christmas.*"

———

Years later, in the treasure trove of photographs kept by my mother, I will see written on the back of a group photo: "Maria, Baba's sister." Sister! I no longer recall whether any of my hosts had made the connection for me. But there she had sat, Old Maria, the source of Baba's mangled version retold in Canada over decades.

———————

Suddenly, in June 1941, German armies rolled over the Polish border into Soviet Ukraine and unleashed Operation Barbarossa, a "lightning war" that took Western Ukraine completely by surprise. What were the Soviets to do with the thousands of political prisoners incarcerated by the Secret Police over the course of twenty-one months of occupation in Western Ukraine? Panicked, the NKVD massacred the lot, some 10,000 (accounts of which are nauseating in their detail), before fleeing east.

Their retreat was highly disorganized. Only "leading personnel" were evacuated — the Party organizers, the managers, the NKVD. The inhabitants of Dzhuriv remained where they were, and waited.

I look at a photograph in Richard Overy's *Russia's War,* presumably taken by the ubiquitous camera of the German officer on scene for every triumph. A procession of women in what seems to be a city street, possibly Lviv, bears a large, framed portrait of Hitler as though his image, replacing the processional icon of the Mother of God, were now the justified "protector of Christians." A banner reads, "Hitler, Liberator."

No sooner were they occupied by Germans goose-stepping across Galicia than grateful Ukrainians were placed into almost all positions of authority in the smaller towns and villages. These, the collaborators, were the ones to collect onerous tribute — cattle and grain — from their kith and kin and ensure a steady supply of *Ostarbeiter* (East-Workers) conscripted labour from their own youth, scooped up in shops, in the cinema, even in church, and transported to German farms, mines, and factories. By the end of the war in 1944, Ukraine had supplied four-fifths of all forced labour from the East (Overy 135). No wonder: given the "endlessly fertile Ukrainian soil," the Soviet Union was the only realistic source of calories for a Germany feeding a gluttonous war machine. "As Hitler knew," ninety percent of the food shipments from the Soviet Union came from Soviet Ukraine (Snyder 161).

It is within this furious cauldron of events that I try to imagine Yuri, to place him in the one datum I find when I begin to look, not in Ukraine or in family photos, but in a book on a shelf in Canada.

I visit retired political scientist and professor emeritus Peter Potichnyj in his home office in Hamilton. I am hoping that, as an archivist of documents and memoirs on the Ukrainian liberation struggle in the twentieth century, he can help me "decode" Yuri's story as told by Baba: dead at the hand of *bandyty* in 1945. He gestures to the shelves of volumes of the Gazetteer of the Ukrainian Soviet Socialist Republic, and suggests that we may find an entry for "Dzhuriv," and something of interest there that relates to Yuri Kosovan. To my utter amazement, there is.

Dzhuriv: From the 1920s, a centre of the Communist Party West Ukraine was active in which M. Shulepa, Yu. Kosovan, S. Gordyi, G. Shulepa, S. Tymoshuk and others participated.

There he is!

As for the Communist Party of Western Ukraine, I've never heard of it. And the Wikipedia entry leaves me cross-eyed with the effort to follow the Party's twists and turns. The Internet Encyclopedia of Ukraine is more helpful, once I understand that by this time in the 1920s the CPWU operated illegally in the newly restored republic of Poland, its main goal to carry out the revolution in Poland and to "establish the dictatorship of the proletariat." So: Yurochko, a communist sympathizer since the 1920s. This datum did some violence to the image I have carried of "poor

Yurko" who haunted Baba in Canada: Yuri Kosovan the simple villager, an army conscript, a youth cut down by assassins in a deed
of inexplicable motivation. He seems to have been a teen-aged
member of an illegal Communist Party in a Galician village when
all hell breaks loose. Another world war has arrived and he will be
drawn into its maw until he is spat out, somewhere in a forest not
so far from home. Is this the making of a Soviet hero?

In 1941 Yuri still had four years to live; with the Germans now
in control of the cities, it is likely that he was in Dzhuriv the whole
time. And with that I begin a frustrating search for stories about
what life was like in a western Ukrainian village under the Nazis.

The modestly published memoirs in English translation
that I have collected (separate from the literature documenting
the Shoah) all concerned events in central Ukraine, as did Vasilii
Grossman's war journalism for the *Red Star*, the Soviet Army's
newspaper. For all the dramatic accounts of the Soviets' scorched
earth policy, as I learned, it did not scorch Galician earth. Even a
Polish novel, Wanda Wasilewska's *Rainbow*, the story of a Ukrainian
village within the German lines, follows the eventually victorious Red Army only to the threshold of Galicia. Timothy Snyder's
Bloodlands: Europe Between Hitler and Stalin, despite its promising
subtitle, is overwhelmingly concerned with the fate of the Jewish
and Polish populations in Eastern Galicia/Western Ukraine. It is
unclear in his book whether references to "Soviet Ukraine" under
Nazi occupation includes western Ukraine in every instance.

Come to think of it, we Canadian relatives do not seem to have
passed around any stories whatsoever about any Kosovan who
suffered during the war years in Western Ukraine, 1939 to 1945,
in any army or in any famine or deportation or from a confiscation or compelled labour as an *Ostarbeiter* (Eastern Worker). Were
the Kosovans among those *Untermenschen* (subhuman), "useless
eaters," Jews and Slavs, who had no "need" to consume all that

they produced, whose "surplus" food was confiscated? No such story from them has come down to us in Canada, even after censored correspondence with the Kosovans in Dzhuriv resumed in the 1960s. Did they all survive as slave labourers who had to be fed enough to survive? Did they, even Yuri, somehow just go about their business, sowing and reaping, cooking and eating, rising and sleeping? While a war swirled around them, soldiers — and did it matter whose? — were shooting flame-throwers or blowing up tanks, or were being blown up inside tanks, or simply dying on their feet, their bodies rotting in furrows of black earth, the season's fertilizer.

While the Ukrainian *Untermenschen* starved, their Jewish neighbours were murdered, shot at the edge of pits just outside of town, just outside the averted gaze of the Kosovans.

There are war photographs — German — reproduced in magazines I have picked up in used bookshops that show villages somewhere in Ukraine (or might they have been in Romania?). From the point of view of the photographer standing near a tank, soldiers crawl in snow on their bellies while the tank's turret swivels its gun toward the target, a stand-alone thatched-roof cottage. In another, the photographer is standing with a group of soldiers in winter whites, weapons at the ready, as they creep cautiously around the corner of a cottage, one plastered wall already blown up. In a chapter of Vasilii Grossman's war journalism, "Back into the Ukraine," a black-and-white photo is captioned "Ukrainian women taking home the bodies of their menfolk." I think of them as Eternal Ukraina, in the feminine. It is women who do the burying in war, when there is decent burying to be done. Here three women in headscarves, with bare hands push at the rear of a wooden wagon, its wooden wheels churning laboriously in the frozen ruts of a field of mud. I suppose it is here in the mud that the men fell. They now lie every which way, as frozen as the violated earth itself.

Yuri still has two years to live.

Second version

In 1988 when I am again in Ukraine, this time in Kyiv for the Millennium Celebration of the conversion of Kyivan-Rus to Christianity, my second cousin Pavlina, last seen in Dzhuriv in 1984, comes to visit me in my hotel. It is the era of perestroika, of glasnost, and I feel comfortable inviting her to have a Heineken in the hotel's hard currency bar. I've learned to speak Ukrainian. Pavlina erupts in an astonishing flow of opinions, political and historical, accounts and assertions expressed with utmost confidence. Yuri was her grandfather.

From my 1988 notebook: *Yuri's story according to Pavlina. In 1934 he had joined the Party — an underground organization in then-Poland — and was at home at Christmas in 1945 when Soviet authority was reconstituting itself in western Ukraine. He was arrested at home by some members of the nationalist UPA (including some who were second cousins) who were still operating in the area and who took him together with his documents. Obviously, there was some sort of vengeance in such an event, settling scores with those communists who were guilty of deporting peasants during the 1939–1941 Soviet occupation, but Pavlina assures me her grandfather was incapable of such violence: he was a communist for the most unimpeachable of reasons, struggling for justice in the Galician countryside. He was probably taken for those documents, which would prove useful in the event of the Red Army's eventual success (UPA could see it coming), as false ID for a bandyt trying to cross the Ukrainian frontier into Slovakia. Yuri was likely shot somewhere on a forced trek out of the mountains. For two weeks after his disappearance, his wife (Pavlina's grandmother) had scoured the woods for his body but found no trace. Thirty years later Pavlina took his photo to a fortune teller who consulted her astrological charts and read there that this man was living in a faraway place with a new wife and daughter and very much wanted to return home to the village, but would die on the voyage.*

———————

Now Yuri Kosovan has emerged as something of a village Party man, victim of the desperate cutthroat insurgents, "bandits." Contrary to other versions in the family, his body was never recovered. The magical possibility that he had somehow been whisked out of the forest and over the seas to, say, Argentina, comforted his family: *the wife whom the bandits had raped,* according to Pavlina, matter-of-factly, *and the children they had hammered with their boots.* They would not dignify the murderers by their name, the UPA. Even in a humble village like Dzhuriv, Yuri would be dignified under a Red Star on a slender post.

———————

By the time I seek the stories on visits to Ukraine, the elders are already in their eighties; born in the 1930s, they were still children under the triple occupations in 1939, 1941, 1945. Soviet, Nazi, Soviet. I hear their sighs, watch their twisted hands, listen to their history-in-a-nutshell: "During the war, the German army occupied almost every village on our western lands. The Germans hated the Jews. In November 1944 they drove all the Jews uphill to Khomiv, which is behind Zabolotiv, and shot them all. Some were still alive when they were buried in the pit. So-and-so's mother spoke of how that pit 'breathed' for three days. Thus the Germans mocked the Jews."

In 2013, in Zabolotiv, I stroll with Petro and Maria who (because I asked) take me to see the remnants of a Jewish cemetery behind the town stadium. A small field of grasses gone wild, unmown for a generation (how long unvisited until we three have appeared?) and bordered by lush bushes that still anchor a wobbly row of headstones. One, upright, clearly bears the engraved Star of David and below it barely legible Hebrew script. It's a warm September evening and everything is hushed — even the streets on the other side of the bush — as though even the bones in their disintegrated shrouds are holding their breath.

In August 1941 the *Einsatzgruppen* (paramilitary death squads) began the systematic wholesale liquidation, with mass shootings at the edge of pits or in improvised gas chambers in the back of trucks (the death camps were in Poland) overwhelmingly of Jews. They also murdered Soviet political commissars when they could find them and anti-fascist Ukrainian nationalists. Somehow Yuri escaped the noose. Perhaps he slipped away into the woods eventually to meet up with Red Partisans who, in their acts of sabotage against the Nazi occupiers, unleashed a ruthless fury: for every German death between fifty and a hundred civilian hostages would be executed (Overy 144).

But there is another scenario in which Yuri might be placed.

In his *Russia's War: History of the Soviet War Effort: 1941–1945*, British military historian Richard Overy writes that "the *Einsatzgruppen* were inundated with denunciations from the *local people* of Jews, communists or political 'undesirables'" (142; my italics). Pogroms ensued: "*local* militias … killed and instigated others" to kill almost 20,000 Jews (Snyder 196; my italics). Which Jews? In the environs of Dzhuriv and Tulova alone, "all the Jews who were still left in Sniatyn were grouped together and either taken to the nearby forest and shot by Nazis and local Nazi sympathizers — or sent to the death camp at Belzec [Poland]" ("Snyatyn").

Then this: "Violence against Jews also allowed local Estonians, Latvians, Lithuanians, Ukrainians, Belorusians and Poles who had themselves co-operated with the Soviet regime to escape any such taint" (Snyder 196). *Who had themselves co-operated with the Soviet regime....* I force myself to accept the possibility that Yuri sought cover within a mob of fellow villagers on a murderous rampage against Jewish neighbours who had not already been herded into the ghettoes of Horodenka, Kolomyia, Sniatyn. "Most of Kolomyia's Jews were murdered by February 1943 in the forest outside the city.... At the end of the war, only 200 Jews from Kolomyia survived" ("Snyatyn"). Horodenka, Kolomyia, Sniatyn. Place names that in Canada are redolent only of settler nostalgia.

November 6, 1943, Kyiv is liberated nine months after the Battle of Stalingrad, marking the end of Germany's advances into the Soviet Union. By June 1944, the Red Army marching ever westward to Berlin approaches Kolomyia. The retreating Germans have been through: windows have been blown out; roofs ripped off; rooms filled with a luxurious, vital abundance of weeds. In a pile of bricks, a child rummages for a pan, a pot, a wooden toy, while loudspeakers blare forth "The Internationale" in the town square (Grossman 240). For Vasilii Grossman, journalist embedded with the Red Army, who was there, the liberation of Ukraine was an "emotional process" (248). He sees: peasants come out of hiding in the woods and marshes, too exhausted by grief to throw their caps into the air and cheer.

There has been no harvest. This is what happens in war zones, when men armed to the teeth and tanks and field artillery run amok across open fields and farmsteads: potatoes rot in the ground, apples putrefy alongside the carcass of a cow, of a blacksmith, of a soldier. Stands of corn and flax and rye have been sacrificed to the conflagration while those who planted and tended this wealth starve to death.

On the last page of Wanda Wasilewska's novel, *Rainbow*, men of the Red Army march slowly, with measured tread (themselves exhausted) westward from Stalingrad. The snow-blanketed plain lies dazzling before them, for there at the horizon lie the approaches to Galicia. "Gripping the rifles in their hands they marched towards the land of the Ukraine, trampled underfoot, suffocating under the German yoke, and yet unconquered, inflexible, still fighting back" (184).

For the novelist, the war ends here, as though in the sign of the rainbow that arcs a "radiant streak" across the western sky the triumph of the Red Army is a foregone conclusion. But the war will still go on in Galicia, for many of the Western Ukrainians do "fight back," in a protracted and hopeless guerrilla war against these units of intrepid, marching Reds on their way to Berlin.

The Reds will be back, and in 1946 western Ukraine will finally be granted membership within Soviet Ukraine in the "fraternal family of nations of the Soviet Union," whereupon almost 45,000 horses, 2,000 oxen and 72,000 cows newly liberated from the private ownership of peasant families will be distributed among the new *kolhospy* (collective farms). Yuri will be murdered before he even has the chance to pick up his own cudgel and hurry the revolutionary process along.

Version three

After my mother's death in 2010, my sister and I took up the responsibility, once shared between mother and her sister, Aunt Anne, to correspond with and send money to the relatives in Ukraine. This was now the generation of my second cousins, Pavlina and Petro: their grandfather was the luckless Yuri, their deceased father, his blind son, Petro. My correspondents were the junior Petro and his wife Maria, who had recently learned to use their daughter's computer and to send email.

I picked up the threads I had dropped in 1988 and emailed Petro, thinking he might be able to clear up some of the ambiguities in the versions of Yuri's death that I had from Baba and Pavlina. Petro went over the story again.

> Dido Yuri was more a socialist and anti-nationalist than a communist but was installed by the Soviet regime in some civic function in the village. We think he was betrayed by neighbours who supported the UPA, and who had lost family members killed by the Soviets. Dido was 'disappeared' by the *Banderivtsi* [Banderites, UPA] at Christmas. This happened in 1945. They came to the house one evening and took Dido Yurko away. To this day we don't know whether they executed him on the spot or led him away somewhere. Dad told us that in those days it was impossible to go looking for anyone because then the Banderivtsi might have shot the whole family.

The Canadian novelist, Antanas Sileika, in his novel, *Underground*, has imagined the drama of the Lithuanian anti-Soviet resistance movement. I read it as the same world in the Carpathian uplands of western Ukraine, where the Ukrainian Insurgent Army hide and shelter themselves in the forests. Feared, admired, loathed in equal measure by the rural dwellers in their field of operations, the UPA, these guerrillas, these bandits, crept out from their underground bunkers on suicidal missions: to kill when they could, or merely to capture, interrogate, and torture the "enemies of the Ukrainian people." And to raid the Soviet larder for food. Sileika's Lithuanian guerrillas go out on a mission: "Two were going out to assassinate a Red activist in the village of N, where the priest kept a hidey-hole under the altar, and six others to raid a government dairy for butter and cheese. Three squads of four went out to patrol as country rangers, looking for Red thieves who descended on the farms by night to steal food or other goods" (43).

Or to assassinate a Red activist in the village.

Yuri has only weeks or days or hours to live.

They know who he is: a Bolshevik by conviction since at least the 1920s, a collaborator twice over with the Red order (1939–1941), and now, 1945, taking up his old position in some restored Soviet village rank or other. I can't imagine the terror that coagulated in the blood running through Yuri and all his relatives in Dzhuriv as they waited for the next UPA "mission" to strike.

As luck would have it, the relatives were spared.

And here they are. On a photocopied page, undated, I find my mother's handwritten genealogical notes, likely made when Baba was still alive so there would be a record. For whose benefit I can't say as I had never seen it. Here is an extravagance of Baba's and Mum's and my relations, now into the second generation since the War and a catalogue of new family names brought by marriage into the Kosovan clan: Paraniuk, Nikiforuk, and Porokh. Mum writes that among them is a widow, a "cripple," a Petro who is in Siberia with his family, and Yuri's widow, Palahna, still living. She has jotted down: "[Baba's] Brother Yurko, murdered by Banupibmzi," Mum's spectacularly mangled combination of Latin and Cyrillic letters for "Banderivtsi."

And on the back of a large black-and-white photograph taken in 1973, the whole kit and caboodle again, at least those still living when Baba's sister Sophie visited from Lethbridge. She's planted in the middle of a row of women in floral headscarves, each identified on the back of the photo in Mum's writing. Baba's sister Maria, of grim visage, is here, as are Blind Petro and Baba's brother, Stepan, the "cripple" who does not seem crippled. And with them all still, Palahna, Yuri's widow.

She's been here all along, but no one has told me her story, except one: the bandits burst through the door and raped her. Terrorized, and silenced — I am trying to understand why so little was made of this violence when disclosed by Palahna's own grand-daughter, Pavlina. As for why Baba in Edmonton mourned only Yuri's fate, well, it is his name, not hers, that is on the village ceno-taph, under the Red Star.

By 1945, the UPA had stopped the practice of killing the families of collaborators, of gouging out their eyes and hacking their bodies to pieces with farmyard axes in front of their fellow villagers summoned to the village common. It was proving to be demoralizing for the struggle. But in the hyper-masculinized theatre of UPA's soldiering, the bodies of female civilians could be defiled with impunity, especially the "other" women — Poles, Jews, Bolsheviks — who were fair game. "Women became a part of mil-itary tactics with the aim to terrorize, demoralize and humiliate the enemy" (Havryshko).

"Other victims of the UPA included Soviet activists sent to Galicia from other parts of the Soviet Union; heads of village Soviets, those sheltering or feeding Red Army personnel, and even people turning food in to collective farms" ("Ukrainian Insurgent Army"). *Heads of village Soviets …*

Fourth version

I return to my notes from my visit in 2010 with Professor Peter Potichnyj, and now I know where to slot them. *Yuri Kosovan was not a simple Red Army boy — the insurgents would have released him because UPA didn't fight the Red Army as such. Kosovan may have been a member of the NKVD secret police [searching for UPA members] while UPA was fighting the Soviet militia or Soviet surety forces. He would have been a target especially if he was working in the territory, knew the terrain, and was bringing harm to the underground. The version you heard in Canada is the helpful one for the family in Soviet Ukraine: 'our son fought for the Soviet motherland.' This protected them.*

––––––––

Notes from a telephone conversation in 2013 with Professor Lubomyr Luciuk, editor and publisher of *Their Just War: Unless captured in actual battle, UPA tended to release conscripts if they were ethnic Ukrainians; they would give them a strong lecture and relieve them of their weapons. But if they were NKVD troops or Soviet commissars, "there was no mercy."*

––––––––

"We warn Ukrainian citizens: anyone who works with the organs of the NKVD-MGB, all those who by any means whatsoever work with the NKVD ... will be considered traitors, and we will deal with them as with our greatest enemies" (qtd. in Burds 303).

Dragged from the stoop of his house and into the woods, interrogated, then charged and found guilty of "collaboration" with the Soviet enemy by an improvised "court" of the resistance, and, who knows, perhaps on the basis of a "confession," Yuri was summarily executed minutes later. The image is universal: a body dangles from a crude tripod of unhewn timber, a balcony, a tree limb, a lamppost, the head bent sideways as though the hanged man or woman or child has snoozed off, hands tied behind their back. An explanatory placard hangs around the neck, read by a crowd of subdued witnesses. One side of an argument has prevailed and hanged the enemy, the traitor, the collaborator. Or perhaps it's the other side of the argument that has prevailed and done the deed. Or perhaps it's both: they take turns.

––––––––

In 2013 on a stroll around memorial sites in Lviv and hoping to visit the Lonsky Prison National Memorial Museum on Bandera Street, I found it closed and took a photo of the bilingual plaque instead. It informed me that at different times the building that had stood here served as a "prison of three occupational regimes: Polish, Nazi and Soviet."

I strolled across the square to take more photos of the imposing, not to say brutalist, sculpture that reared up from the massive stone slabs and pediments of a memorial. I gradually made out from its twisted mass of lumps and angles the exaggerated form of a superman who seems to be hurling himself (it's always a male body) against the thick bars of a fearsome grid. *Typically Soviet,* I thought, until I read the inscription, hefty letters partly covered by large floral bouquets and ribbons: "To the Victims of Communist Criminals."

Much later, after I have printed these photos, I also see that someone has left a black-and-white photo tucked under a ribbon and now almost faded. A young, good-looking man in a modern ski jacket and scarf, grins with pleasure at the photographer, as though he had just turned his head at her cry, "Yurochko!"

Eternal Memory
вічная пам'ять
vichnaia pamiat'

Fred Kostash's obituary has been clipped from the *Vegreville Observer* and glued to a sheet of paper, everything now yellowed. There is no date. In fact, he died, or "breathed his last," of pneumonia, December 6, 1938, aged sixty-seven.

Two days after his death, his funeral service began "from the family residence," which is to say the farmhouse, and concluded in the Ukrainian Orthodox church in Sich. The report of the funeral service includes a long list of names of those who provided "beautiful floral tributes" — forty-eight, among them from Andrew School staff and students, and Hairy Hill School staff, colleagues of my father and his brother, Lad — and I can only wonder at Baba's sinking heart as she watched them pile up.

"These were the pioneers," eulogized J.G. MacGregor in *Vilni Zemli* in 1969, "whose well-kept and revered tombstones, row on row, and file on file, fill the chuchyards — the Melnyks, Lakustas, Kostashes...." (6)

I find notecards. My father has written notes, perhaps for a "pioneer" biography of the type he was always asked to compose by family members, about Fred Kostash, 1871–1938. Even abbreviated, they present the archetypal Ukrainian pioneer saga.

Born in Tulova, Sniatyn. Parents: Hrycko and Nastia (Molofy). Related thru' aunt on father's side to a [Pleshkan] relative of [famed Galician writer] Wasyl Stefanyk. Education — Sniatyn and Kolomea — 3 classes of *gimnaziia*. Army service to age 24 — sergeant (*zugsfeuhrer*). Came to Canada via *Arcadia* from Hamburg, landed Halifax April 18, 1900. Landed in Strathcona, ferried to Edmonton, bought team and wagon, stopped at Edna, proceeded to homestead 11 miles north of Vegreville. Till CN came through in 1905, freighted goods from Edmonton. Worked on section gang, threshing outfit, sec. of threshing company; trustee; chairman; postmaster (Kolomea), brought mail from Beaver Lake. Orthodox Church member, 1921, sang bass in church choir.

And there the story of Fred Kostash ends. He will live another seventeen years but, as though his life's labours are all but done, good and faithful servant, he joins a choir.

Blessed are the meek, for they shall inherit the earth.
Matthew 5:5

There is a lovely scene in my father's memoir, of an evening during the season between Christmas (January 6) and Epiphany (January 18) when family and hired hands kept the frigid dark at bay. Fred and Anna, their children, and the hired hands — relatives from Galicia who had found no other work — gathered in the kitchen by the stove after all the day's chores were done. The hired hands missed their wives and children very much, and "Uncle" Ivan beckoned Anna's boys to come forward and sing a Christmas carol or two. So they did, with more enthusiasm than harmony, looking forward to the small coin Uncle would press into their palm. Fred hummed along, for he had a fine, deep bass voice. And Anna, at last seated with some mending, her household now calm, warm, and fed, would join in with her soft and melancholy voice, singing into the space that had opened for the Christ Child.

And so, for as long as she had her sons with her on the farm, not yet exposed to the town let alone the city, Baba would teach them the Catechism she knew by heart, the Lord's Prayer, the Credo, and the Ave Maria. The prayers and petitions were in Old Church Slavonic, and it is doubtful that she understood most of what she had memorized. But among homesteaders who might have seen a priest only every now and then, it was the basis of a godly life.

Anna Kostash née Svarich died in 1964 at the age of 83, having recently buried a teenaged grandson in a blasphemous reversal of chronology, herself to be buried in the month of December, *Hruden*. She had prayed to be taken by death in the spring, when the earth would have thawed and spared the gravediggers their burdensome labour at their shovels on her behalf. *Hruda* in Ukrainian, is the word for lumps, lumps of hard earth.

Who doesn't need a place to break her bread?
Who doesn't need a place to lay his head?
(Here's) a chance to leave old poverty behind
With a willing hand for any work you find.

(DUNN ET AL.)

Lewis Rendell, genealogist at the Canadian Museum of Immigration at Pier 21, had rolled up the photocopied pages of the ship's manifest and the Purser's page. This was 2014, four years after my mother's death.

"Is there anything else you'd like to know about your grandfather?"

"Yes. Where is his grave?"

The new databases, more and more of them, might cough up more alternatives to "Nikolai Maksymiuk," and so I suggested several of them — Nicolaus, Nicholas, Nikolay, Mykola — but I could think of no alternatives to "Maksymiuk." Scrolling around the World Wide Web, Ms. Rendell landed on Canadian Passenger List 865-1935 at Ancestry.com, and there found "Mykola Maksymick." Gender: Male. Age: 25. Estimated (estimated?) Birth Year: abt. 1886. (Facts start to line up with his Immigration Inspection Card that I have already filed away in a ziplock bag.) Date of Arrival: 20 May 1911. Vessel: *Gothland*. Port of Arrival: Quebec. Port of Departure: Rotterdam, Netherlands.

Maksymick.

Lewis fed this into a database of Canadian cemetery registries. And there he lies: Nick Maksymick, buried 08/12/1918, Block 0003, Plot 0054. Beechmount cemetery in Edmonton.

I wept.

"That happens a lot here," said Lewis, and passed a box of tissues.

With this information, I went to the cemetery. With no trouble at all, the staffer located the relevant page and printed it off — lot and row — and showed me how to pace it off. I found the row. A broken stone here, an effaced plaque there, but no obvious demarcation between one plot and the next. I paced in one direction, then back, and again paced. Finally, I stood on a smooth patch of green lawn within whose perimeter I willed myself to believe my grandfather lay, a place so long unmarked, unblessed, unvisited. In my mother's garden there were always gladioli. I was carrying a stem of pink gladiola and I laid her flower down.

From the Memorial Record at Andrew's funeral

> Relatives and Friends: Anna and Dmytro Dorosh, Steve and Nancy Belyk, Mr. and Mrs. Fred Hunka, Marie McKinlay, A. Kostyniuk, L. Wakal, Dot Barton, Hafia Janishewski, S. Kyforuk ...

The Memorial Record book for Andrew Maksymiuk, supplied by Park Memorial funeral home (who to this day bury a diversity of Ukrainian Canadians in Edmonton), has three very red roses embossed on the cover, and on the first inside page a text from St. Paul, "Death is swallowed up in victory. O death where is thy sting?" He was buried June 27, 1977 and five pages of signatures attest to the community of bereaved. Had I been there, I would have been surprised by their number. I recognize names of Baba and Dido's neighbours, a couple of my father's relatives, a girlhood friend of my aunt, one of my mother's pupils from Hairy Hill in the 1930s, and my godmother. Many names I cannot place. All other pages of the little book have been left blank, except a line where my mother has entered Andrew's birthplace: Ukraine. Nothing has been entered under Family Record, Music (Special Song Selection), Organizations, Sermon Notes. The man and the funeral service are virtually featureless. Compared to the notice given Baba's passing two years later — funeral eulogies reprinted in the comradely press — Andrew Maksymiuk seemed not to have warranted even an obituary in the *Edmonton Journal*. I have found no such clipping in my father's papers. If there had been, he would have clipped it: he would have probably written it.

But then I do find something. The original is yellowed but the photocopy is clear. A photograph of Baba and Dido in their advanced age appears to have been taken outdoors — a shadow falls over Baba's right cheek, Dido's dark suit merges into the foliage — where Baba smiles her little smile while Dido, erect as a post, unsmiling as ever, seems in my new estimation rather to be dignified than morose. In Ukrainian, on page fourteen of the uncredited newspaper, over the names of "Daughters Anna and Maria, sons-in-law and grandchildren," two columns of text have been submitted under the title "In honour of our beloved parents."

I have no doubt my father wrote this.

"Four years have passed since their father [Andrew] passed away, two years since their mother's [Pauline's] passing. Their photograph was not placed in 'Life and Word,' so now their daughters are donating $200 in their memory, $100 to go to the press fund of 'Life and Word,' and $100 for the education of children in the school at the Ukrainian Cultural Centre in Edmonton."

Better late than never, I suppose. Perhaps conscience-stricken by the failure to have honoured Andrew at the appropriate time of his passing, we now read that he belonged to that "category" of Ukrainian pioneers who lived through the "heavy trials" not only in their native country but in Canada as well. Both Palahna and Andrew were of "progressive views," joining the Ukrainian Workers' Hall as soon as it was formed, and both read the Ukrainian Canadian progressive press, "treasured it, financially supported it, learned from it." Then: "Daughters Anna and Maria will never forget their parents, nor will they ever belittle their organizational

affiliations, nor belittle their ideas." What a startling public confession this was — as it reads to me — as though at this moment of
belated eulogy these half-sisters with one voice of contrition finally
unburdened themselves of the unspent filial respect and even love
they had withheld.

Then Aunt Anne is quoted. "We, the family, bow our heads in
your honour." The image of a collective of bowed heads is striking.
I think of the times Andrew Maksymiuk would never have bowed
his head, neither, cap in hand, to the Polish landlord passing by
smartly in his barouche nor in front of an icon in the village church
nor to the Ukrainian Canadian lawyer plying his trade among the
working poor, but I like to think that with a small tilt of his head
he would have accepted ours.

———

From the obituary (in Ukrainian) in *Zhyttia I Slovo* (*Word and Life*),
12 November, 1979, by Mykhailo Holovchak:

> *In Memory of Palahna Maksymiuk*
>
> *On Oct 4 1979, after a brief, painful illness, Palahna
> Makysmiuk, pioneer, member of AUUC [Association
> of United Ukrainian Canadians] and the Ukrainian
> Community Seniors' Club, has passed away.*

The comrades buried her. (I wasn't there; I am reading the
newspaper clipping). The funeral took place October 9, 1979, at
Park Memorial funeral home, a block north of the Hall. Speaking
in Ukrainian, Mykhailo Holovchak mentioned the newspaper, *Life
and Word*, to which Baba had been a faithful subscriber (although I
never saw her read it) and to its press fund, "according to her means."
The widow's mite extracted coin by coin from a pocket in her dog-
eared handbag. Now she has gone to her "eternal rest," at the end

of a long life as an honest and hard-working "citizen of Canada." Holovchak calls Palahna Maksymiuk "our beloved mother and grandmother," evoking the new community of relations in Canada into which she had been received almost from her day of arrival.

My father also spoke, in English, and I read his Eulogy typewritten on the index cards I have found among his papers. He briefly reviews the "bare statistics" of her life, already rehearsed by Holovchak, in order to bring "Baba" into view: "I shall call her Baba Maksymiuk. When her grandchildren came, she became Baba not only to them, but to all the young and old in the neighbourhood, even to the nurses who were so kind to her in her last days in the hospital." (She was Baba even to my mother.) Mindful of whom he was addressing and among whom her memory was being evoked, my father continued his eulogy with a mention of her "humble beginnings" and her sympathy with "the working classes and the organizations that fought in their cause."

Then he narrows his perspective to zoom in on the railway tracks of the CN line near her home. "Her concern for humanity extended even to people she did not know ... and the unfortunates who rode the rods in the Depression years knew that they could always get a sandwich or a piece of bread from the kind [he has crossed out "dear" for the better chosen "kind"] lady who lived by the tracks. She made no distinction as to race, colour, or creed when she saw that they were in dire need." I did not hear this story or have forgotten I did, but I am thankful to my father, who loved Baba as his "second mother," for recalling it.

Finally, he closes with a nod in the direction of Baba's youthful, and perhaps never abandoned, religious faith. "Her philosophy of life was simple — and essentially Christian. Love thy neighbor as thyself and do unto others as you would have them do unto you."

But the funeral was not in a church. Her comrades' last words for her sent her off to "eternal rest":

May the Canadian land, which she loved and for which she laboured, lie lightly upon her.

It was the traditional, ancient even, epitaph lettered on grave markers in the Old Country: *Nekhai zemlia bude iomu lekhkoiu abo perom:* May the earth rest upon him lightly as a feather. The comrades chose well. Their people knew earth, under bare feet, in the creases of their hands, clotted around beets and potatoes, seedbed of life. We dug Baba's grave, and earth took her in.

Coda:
On the land

How do people "home" here when they're not from here?

(DAVID GARNEAU)

The story is told of a certain village neighbouring a monastery with a large estate. Unsatisfied with their allotment of property, the monks summarily incorporated a portion of the village's meadow and forest — land that had been used communally — into their estate. If your cow wandered over the meadow, you were slapped with a fine and another fine if you were caught picking berries and mushrooms from what had once been provided by the Good Lord's own larder.

On rereading Peter Svarich's *Memoirs*, I note that, from this story onward, land will only be privately held. Peter's father, Ivan, sells 15 morgs in Tulova, turning land into cash, then cash back into land title in Canada.

On September 30, 1976, the Land Titles office of North Alberta Land Registration District certified that Myrna Ann Kostash "is now the owner of an estate," of the NE Quarter of Section 31 in Township 55 at Range 12, W of the 4th Meridian" — almost six miles due north of the town of Two Hills — "containing 160 acres, more or less."

In June 1975, I had moved almost without stopping from Toronto to the Frontenac motel in Two Hills where I would live three months. I had set myself to write a book about my parents' generation, the first Ukrainian Canadians. I recorded interviews in and around the town (overwhelmingly Ukrainian Canadian) as well as writing pages of "immersive reportage," diary-like entries about visits to the priest's house, volunteering at the local rodeo selling hot dogs, listening to accordion music wafting from the verandah from the seniors' lodge across the road from the motel. And I became friends with the young family that was determined to make a go of it, farming the quarter section of mediocre land they had just bought, six miles north of town. They came from working-class roots in BC's Slocan Valley and knew from rural experience how to scrounge and retrofit and improvise until they had a habitable dwelling. A year later, defeated by the stark impossibility of wresting a living on a mere 135 arable acres, they put it up for sale: was I interested in buying it?

They had built an outhouse, dug a garden, rigged up a rain barrel, installed a magnificent wood-burning stove with oven, and already had a woodpile ready for the coming autumnal chill. My mother and I bought it for cash. I moved in for the rest of the season, and with a couple of kerosene lamps, a Coleman camping stove, and my portable typewriter, I began writing *All of Baba's Children*. By the time the book was published in January 1978, I had a name for my estate after the ancestral village of the Kostashes, and I nailed a rustic board to the outside wall by the door, inscribed in white paint: TULOVA.

To me, the name echoed the western-most point of my forebears' journey to Canada. By nailing up the board painted with the letters TULOVA, I was laying claim, two generations later, to the memory of leave-taking, uprooting, and exodus. But I was also announcing that that exodus had a terminus: it came to an end, a "somewhere," a "here," which, two generations later, would symbolically terminate in the location I called home.

I was also saying that this "here" was not an arbitrarily designated place. It didn't take shape just anywhere; it was a specific site. It was in the heart of Ukrainian Canadian settlement in Alberta. It was a place saturated with communal meaning. For the next several summers I lived out months and months of the most deeply contented life I had ever known. I chopped wood and planted peas; gathered pails of saskatoons, pin cherries and chokecherries for jam; washed myself in rain water; knew that June would bring forth the extravagantly aromatic wild roses in the ditches and that marsh marigolds flourished along the little stream in a neighbour's field. I watched for deer, jackrabbits, owls, and porcupines. I went into Two Hills to shop at the Co-op store (I was a member), pay visits, and collect my mail at General Delivery. I explored the area for miles around for old churches, cemeteries, and Narodni Domy (community halls, their faded names above the doors, still written in Cyrillic). I read, wrote, daydreamed. I was mostly alone.

I took my stewardship seriously. A farmer down the road agreed to rent the arable portion of the 135 acres and showed me how to drive a tractor. I paid for a soil test — sandy, eroded, deficient in potassium and organic matter — and took advantage of a program that provided baby trees (as I thought of them) for planting down a field as a windbreak: I chose Scotch pine, not native to North America at all but fast-growing. The renter agreed to plant forage crops — legumes — in rotation, to increase the poor soil's nitrogen, phosphate, potash, and sulphur. Apparently, this was not nearly good enough: the renter argued the soil needed fertilizer right away and with alacrity applied multiple doses of the weed-killer, Roundup. What did I know? I deferred to the expertise of a successful Ukrainian Canadian farmer, who farmed some thousand acres and owned a fleet of gigantic machines.

———

Forty-five years later, I can now appreciate what I had unknowingly done: brought into a single imagined space the two historical sources of my identity: a homestead on Treaty Six Territory and a village in Galicia circa 1900. I understood my enterprise as one of simply "settling in" on my portion of the Ukrainian bloc settlement area northeast of Edmonton, my birthplace.

Only a year into my proprietorship, still smitten by my own rusticity, my snapshots in 1977 caught a sunset when the fields had already darkened but clouds in the western sky layered themselves in brooding slashes of purple. I once planted sunflowers that grew taller than my sister who stands among them, and renter Pete grew a crop of wheat whose stalks — fully headed-out, well past July 12, Sts. Peter and Paul Day — almost engulf two children who have come to play. I stand hip-cocked, almost insolently, rake in hand at the shack's front and only door. Indoors, on the west wall a poster of Che Guevara and my Baba's washing board. At the east-facing window, on my childhood desk, my portable Olivetti red as a ripe tomato, my first typewriter, purchased in 1971 when I thought I would still write novels.

Epiphany on a mountaintop

In November 1987, on a writing retreat in Banff, I took a walk —
slowly, slowly, climbing Tunnel Mountain — the gently rising mound
behind the Banff Centre that opens up to a dramatic view of Mount
Rundle. I read my journal entry now and realize that for a decade
I had been "slouching to Galicia," travelling in Eastern Europe to
research and write books about my roots in its history and politics,
lost to North America and its experiment, the settlers from away. Its
rhetorical hubris makes me wince now, but I was onto something.

———————

From my notebooks: *November 4, 1987: I catch the view — how the
rear end of Tunnel drops, a precipice, that once sent tons of rock
plummeting — and I look around over my shoulder, the massive stri-
ated shoulder of splendid, magisterial Rundle. This is the New World
and it's ancient. Here are the rocks in the belly of the New World
and I have its dust on my shoes. This is something I have not paid
enough attention to, these last ten years, the years of my slouching
to Galicia. And in that slouching, in that sometimes reluctant shuf-
fling, sometimes passionate flight, I have forgotten this other place
that I came from. I was born here and my mother before me and
does this not root me too even if shallowly in the shallow dirt of a
mountain path? It's not long, only two generations born in Canada,
but the new-to-us world began just like this: a woman wades ashore
and plants a garden, and enters the narrative of the Americas.*

*I have not been thinking of this. All my thinking has been of the
reverse journey, the North American going back, ultimately beyond
the Carpathians, before any Galician had thought of making the trip
to North America. I do not regret my journey but for this: it has been
greedy, demanding, taxing of my loyalties. As long as I keep beating
this path to the ancestral mounds, then I am lost to the New World
and its great experiment.*

———————

A year later I wrote from "Tulova," the shack: *October 10, 1988: It's time I reconnected here. The place is falling apart. The eavestrough has fallen off the outhouse. The wooden structure that holds up the rain barrel is rotten. The woodpile is low, the bush is creeping in and the garden plot is completely overgrown. I haven't picked a pail of saskatoons in years. It's time I got reconnected.*

To reorient myself to this zone, this latitude, this quadrant of the Milky Way. To make myself available again to the ghosts of this motherland. I'm trying, with some difficulty, to remember how it felt to belong here, unclaimed by Europe. To feel bred by only two generations, circumscribed by one homestead, summoned to local tasks. Not to mention being aroused by only one language. But there's no unknowing what I know, unfeeling what I felt in the Old Country where there's a cemetery full of grave markers that bear my family name in Cyrillic.

———

Although I would not sell "Tulova" until 1996, I did not keep faith with "this zone, this latitude" until another decade had passed (one last fling among the ancestors) in the bones of Byzantium. While I was working on *Prodigal Daughter: A Journey to Byzantium* (2010), I made several road trips in 2003 and 2004 to towns and historic sites along the North Saskatchewan River. As I took the measure of its course from the Rockies to Lake Winnipeg, I was also taking measure of the history (primordial, ecological, human, cultural) associated with this waterway. This is how the stories of bison hunts and geological surveys, of the fur trade and Christian missions and NWMP posts, of piles of bleaching bison bones, of Treaties, of the Indian Act and the CPR, and of the 1885 Northwest Resistance seeped into my western Canadian consciousness and conscience until they were drenched to the roots.

———

Victoria Settlement Historic Site: a Petition from Cree and Métis at Victoria and Whitefish Lake "Some [of us] are afraid that when the white man comes our hunting grounds will be destroyed and our lands taken for nothing.... They see some settlers making gardens in our lands. The buffalo tracks are growing over with grass" (qtd. in Melnycky 29).

My research and collection of texts historical and literary came together in *Reading the River: A Traveller's Companion to the North Saskatchewan River* (2005). But I was not done with 1885, the river and the Plains Cree.

On the morning of April 2, 1885, at the settlement of Frog Lake (now Alberta), North-West Territories, Cree warriors of the band of Big Bear (Mistahi-maskwa) but under the leadership of war chief Wandering Spirit (Kapapamahchakwew) killed nine unarmed men, among them the Indian agent, farming instructor, two priests, a carpenter, a trader. This has been known popularly ever since as the Frog Lake Massacre. It was followed by the taking of hostages from Frog Lake and Fort Pitt, and increasingly desperate military engagement with Canadian militia at Frenchman Butte and Steele Narrows (now Saskatchewan). A week after the hanging in Regina of Métis leader Louis Riel, six Cree warriors, condemned for their role at Frog Lake, alongside two Assiniboine men condemned for a murder committed on March 29 near Battleford, were hanged, on November 27, 1885, at Fort Battleford, in the largest mass execution in Canadian history and the closing act of the Resistance of 1885. (Kostash 2018, 35)

A gravesite off the beaten track on the side road to the historic site of Fort Battleford in Saskatchewan proved — I see this now — an intellectual, emotional, and moral turning point for me before I knew I would write *Ghosts*. It was the grave of the Indigenous warriors who had been hanged for the slayings at Frog Lake settlement. I'm a lifelong Albertan but I knew nothing about any of it. It took almost a literal stumble along the bank of the Battle River to come across the site, now dignified by a black granite headstone, encircled by a ring of skinned and weathered tipi poles, the ribs of a tipi, open to the four directions.

It had been raining: the narrow foot-beaten track to the turnstile was a bit muddy. The fencing around the site had begun to tilt and the enclosure sheltering the grave was filling up with wolf willow shrubs and chokecherry bushes, bearing their translucent red clumps that late summer day. Yet the footpath was well-trampled and no one had left garbage behind. The sun struck the back of my neck.

I knew that, of Wandering Spirit, only his bones are here, his soul having long ago been sucked into the blue ether, but I thought about those bones: how we might see the neck of the war chief broken, there precisely where his spirit fluttered helplessly in the hempen cord. Would strands of his hair, whitened overnight in the bush when Steele's Scouts closed in on him, cling to his skull? But, no, before he hanged he had been shorn.

It is a mass grave. The names of the interred have been inscribed in English and in Cree:

Kapapamahchakwew Wandering Spirit

Paypamakeesit Round the Sky

Manachoos Bad Arrow

Kittimakegin Miserable Man

Nabpace Iron Body

Apaschiskoos Little Bear

Itka Crooked Leg

Wawanitch Man Without Blood.

Wandering Spirit, warrior, war chief and buffalo hunter had once been able to feed and protect his people according to Plains Cree culture and tradition. But the bison herds were gone and the settlers were coming. "Now he could do none of those things," in the recollection of Fred Horse, an Elder from Frog Nation. Now, humiliated and anguished by his people's hunger and raggedness, "he had to crawl after gophers where once he had raced amidst the thundering herds" (Goodwill and Sluman 50–51).

The incessant wind blowing past my ears and the raucous *caw caw* of the crows flapping among the tree tops are what remain of the world they rode through, Plains Cree warriors of the band of Chief Big Bear who hanged together. The hanged men were cut down from their nooses just over there, back up the slope and east of the parking lot, on the gallows of Fort Battleford and dumped here, in a trench hacked out of the frozen ground.

I read the names and, although there are no dates included in the inscription, I knew they had been buried in 1885, and so I stood transfixed at the granite stone. Up to that moment, I had not taken note of how narrow was the slit in time between the two events: the crushing in 1885 of the last resistance to incarceration on the reserves and the arrival in June 1900 of my paternal grandparents from Galicia. Fifteen years. The gap was fifteen years — but it may as well have been an eon between two chronologies, as though all that had gone before "our" arrival and possession of the land belonged to unrecorded time.

And so I was determined to track down every printed account, from any point of view, about the events that took place between the killings and the hangings: the siege of Fort Pitt, the Battle of Frenchman Butte, the Battle of Loon Lake, the surrenders, the trials, in order to understand it, to situate the events of 1885 within the large context of the disappearance of the buffalo on the plains, the misery of the hungry removed to newly established reserves and the disillusionment about Treaty promises already broken.

———

Altogether, the research was a chastening experience, releasing a tumult of emotions I didn't know I had — grief, anguish, outrage, shame — and an education I had not anticipated. I knew the broad outlines of First Nations/Canadian relations but to absorb them in their sequence was harrowing. From the fur trade to epidemics, from the disappearance of the bison then to famine, the Treaties and the establishment of the reserves to the completion of the CPR and the settlement of white farmers on ceded Indigenous lands, the residential schools and the Indigenous communities bereft of their children: tabulated as such a chronology, the long and multi-stranded intertwined history is embedded in violence.

It is intertwined in me, too. As a socially conscious Ukrainian Canadian writer, I had rarely said or written as much in public. (When I did speak or write it was in the context of large themes such as racism or political radicalism or the history of the fur trade in Canada.) I had gone on to write in deep sympathy with the first homesteaders who, on arrival in Edmonton, "bought some sacks of flour and a plough, loaded up a wagon and walked fifty, sixty, ninety miles to their homestead, following Indian trails" (Kostash 1992, 10).

This is the ur-narrative of my paternal forebears circa 1900 and it hinges in 1976 with my very own title to my very own home-stead (*my* saskatoon bushes, *my* Co-op shares, *my* profit when I sold it on).

Palimpsest on the land

The surveyors of the Dominion Land Survey had begun their work in 1871, a grid laid over grasslands and parklands, a fait accompli of sovereignty over some 178,000,000 acres (720,000 sq. km) undertaken in anticipation of tracks laid for a transcontinental railway and the influx of European, Canadian and American settler-passengers. But there were other sovereigns with prior claims to ancestral territories that had long been webbed together through kinship relations, trade routes, seasonal hunts, and sacred geographies. These too had been mapped — but rarely transferred to the maps drawn up by the newcomers — from oral histories and the traditional knowledge they contained (Malone and Chisholm).

"It was rumoured [in 1875] that the Indians would be asked to give up their rights to the land. None of them could understand why they should give up what had been their right to enjoy since the earliest memory of the oldest story of their tribe" (Erasmus 228).

In the library of St. Peter's College in Muenster Saskatchewan, behind the librarian's station sat a banker's box labelled in thick black marker, Treaty 6 Materials. Classes were not yet in session so I took possession of the box, grateful, away from my home library, to lay hands on sources of information precisely on this topic: Treaty 6, one of eleven Numbered Treaties negotiated from 1871 to 1921 between the Crown and Indigenous delegations. By the time Treaty 6 was negotiated in 1876 at Forts Carlton and Pitt on the North Saskatchewan River, I would learn that its terms were driven more "on economic practicality" — the need to remove an Indigenous population struck down by starvation and disease to clear the plains for agricultural settlement — "than it was on any conception of Indigenous rights" (Hall). I opened the box and settled into the story.

"I thought I knew this stuff," I murmured contritely, faced with the evidence of what I did not know or knew imperfectly or that I had never put two and two together — all within a few pages of one book, *Bounty and Benevolence: A History of Saskatchewan Treaties*. There was the stark and brute reality of Cree hunger and of the smallpox that ravaged them in the early 1870s interpreted through the language of appeal for famine relief and medicines. What was wanted was guarantees that the Crown would provide for the very basic security of people who could see what was coming.

Ahtakakup, senior Chief: "Can we stop the power of the white man from spreading over the land like the grasshoppers that cloud the sky. . . ?" (Ray et al. 132).

Earlier, in 1871, at Fort Edmonton, the need was already acute. The land of the Plains Crees could no longer support them. In a message to be sent to Ottawa, in language that made me flinch, Weekaskookeeseyin (Sweet Grass), called out from his people's poverty and helplessness and asked for pity. "We want you to pity us. We want cattle, tools, agricultural implements and assistance in everything when we come to settle" (Alexander Morris 171).

The full catastrophe: millions of acres of plains and parklands, water courses and coulees, from which the numberless herds of bison had vanished and with them food, shelter, and clothing.

At the same time, I reflected, none of these urgent needs precluded the accompanying vision of a "pact" that the Chiefs were also deliberating, a pact that would leave open the territories that lay beyond the reserves to share with settlers (Ray et al. 130), each in pursuit of their own activities; in fact, a sharing that implied a partnership of interests. But the imbalance of power between Chiefs and Crown representatives was staggering.

Iskonikan: *reserve, reservation; portion; leftover*

In 1881, five years after Treaty 6 was signed, Treaty 6 Chiefs were still asking for teachers, a Treaty promise. In 1884, the Chiefs who met with the representatives of the Department of Indian Affairs at Fort Carlton bewailed the "too wild" livestock that had been provided them, the rickety wagons too "poorly made" for purpose; and this: where was the clothing promised them by Treaty? The people were freezing to death. Meanwhile, it was obvious to the Indigenous population on their meagre reserves ("shall not exceed in all one square mile for each family of five") that the white farmers on their homesteads were marvellously equipped with threshing machines, mills, mowers, reapers, and rakes. Such confidence as had been vested in the Dominion government had collapsed to such a degree that the chiefs demanded maps of their reserves "in order that the band not be robbed of it" (Ray et al. 197, 198, 199, 200). Finally, a temporary emergency decree issued in May 1885 — during the troubles in Saskatchewan River country between Métis communities and Dominion authorities — confined First Nations on their reserves. Never rescinded, this decree became the notorious pass system: a form of "incarceration" imposed to control the movements of the Treaty population (Daschuk xxii).

That there still was nevertheless the notion that the treaties forged an alliance among brothers dumbfounded me. The Chiefs who addressed Treaty Commissioner Alexander Morris entreated friendship with the "white man," not the spilling of blood, and of their relations as "brothers," clasping hands under the gaze of the Great Father (Alexander Morris 171, 237).

As to the agreement on which the Chiefs had written their Marks, Commissioner Alexander Morris summarized as "a relinquishment, in all the great region from Lake Superior to the foot of the Rocky Mountains, of all their right and title to lands covered by the treaties saving certain reservations for their own use." Or, in the language of Treaty 6, signed by forty-six Head Chiefs, Chiefs, and Councillors, they did thereby "cede, release, surrender and yield up to the Government of Canada for Her Majesty the Queen and her successors forever, all their rights, titles and privileges whatsoever ..." (Alexander Morris 285, 352).

And it was here, reading now in its context this short, familiar piece of the text of Treaty 6, that I had a question that I raised for the first time in my thinking. "What were the Cree words, spoken by the interpreters, that were the equivalent of 'cede, release, surrender ... forever' within a discourse of negotiations between 'brothers'? What did the Chiefs believe they were agreeing to? What, for that matter is the Cree word for 'treaty'?"

––––––––

Anthony Hall, writing in *The Canadian Encyclopedia*, is succinct: from the Crown's point of view, treaties provided the legal surrender of Indigenous Rights to the land. From the Indigenous point of view, even as they were signing, treaties provided for "relationships between autonomous peoples who agree to share the lands and resources of Canada. Seen from the Indigenous perspective, treaties do not surrender rights; rather, they confirm Indigenous rights" (Hall).

Agree. Share. Rights. Relationships. Brothers.

I turned to my friend the poet Naomi McIlwraith who writes in her "second / Mother tongue" (6), Cree, as well as in English. She writes: "Listen. Can you hear the lyricism in the language / of *nêhiyawak*?" (30). We met in a neighbourhood shawarma diner. She scribbled on a piece of paper and turned the words to me:

Older brother: *ostêsimâw*

Something written: *masinahikan*

Treaty: *ostêsimâwasinahikan*

Treaty: a relationship with brothers, written and signed

Relationship, says Naomi, is kinship, understood as much more than blood; it is an alliance.

————————

At the monastery, the noon meal is taken in silence. We fill our plates quietly and take our places while one of the monks, on rotation, reads aloud to us. It is something edifying — last time I was at the monastery Br Basil read from a biography of St. Catherine of Siena. It was gripping. This time it's Br Kurt with the mellifluous voice of a host on FM radio; he takes his time, and he is pronouncing with impressive assurance a string of words in Indigenous languages. He is reading from a "guide on justice and right relationship," *Listening to Indigenous Voices*, a project of the Jesuit Forum for Social Faith and Justice. Published in 2021, it could not be more timely, and I'm listening.

We listen to the voice of writer and activist, Jeannette Armstrong, who tells us that in her Okanagan language the word for "land" lies inside the word for human bodies, as though, I am thinking, within the womb of earth I am struck by the implications, which she draws out: you speak the word for "land," and so you evoke its seamlessness with your own corporal being. It is not possible to love one and not the other, our brothers and sisters. But it is always a choice. We can destroy the land or we can love the land — and now Br Kurt's reading draws us into another voice, of writer and botanist Robin Wall Kimmerer (Citizen Potawatomi Nation, "Keepers of the Sacred Fire"). When land is understood to be sacred, she writes, "our sustainer, our pharmacy, our identity, out home, our library" — and the ground on which we fulfil our responsibility as keepers of the sacred fire, then we act as moral beings "in return for our very lives" (Jesuit Forum 29, 28, 30).

The dining room stays very quiet, cutlery has been laid down, mouths wiped, while Br Kurt presses on, to the voice of Anishinaabe writer and educator, Niigaanwewidam James Sinclair, who with the very word used by Treaty Commissioner Morris himself — *gift* — poses the challenge of choice — we always have the choice — and of the future that the treaties represent. For Alexander Morris, writing a revisionist account in 1880, the treaties were an act of benevolence extended in fellow-feeling to "this helpless [Indian] population" (295). But Sinclair speaks from an old place, "Turtle Island," and extends *his* hand to us nonindigenous populations the "opportunity" to keep the treaties' promises. "Without the gift of treaties, relationships fade, wither and decay, eventually becoming forgotten and lost" (Jesuit Forum 44).

Embodied land, landfilled bodies, sacred land and sacred fires, gift, opportunity, responsibility, relationship, promises, the future ...

From Louise Bernice Halfe — Sky Dancer's great-grandfather, her *câpân pâhpâscês* — comes this message:

> *This is beautiful land.*
> *It is wrong that we should stain the soil*
> *of the land of the Red Sun with the blood*
> *of our white brothers.*
> *We accept this and seek a new road*
> *for our people. We must find the pathway*
> *that leads to the stars.*
> *I have spoken.* (33)

"Hospitality, writes William Davies, "is the terrain of both safety and danger." It "is never without risk," for "it involves taking the outsider — the foreigner, the potential enemy — into one's home as a guest." And then he stresses that "hospitality is not truly hospitality if the host doesn't retain some authority to exclude: to be a guest is to be invited in, to cross a threshold of some kind.... The host must choose whether to treat the stranger as a guest or as an enemy."

The story is told of an old man who sits in the flap of his tent, in the shade of a tree, in the heat of the day. His gaze wanders freely over the open plain that stretches to the horizon, the plain on which his old wife, their kin and their children have pitched their home. Staring into the waves of heat that rise from the earth, the old man descries three figures that slowly approach his camp, a man, a woman, and a child. As they draw nearer, he sees that they are strangers. He rises, runs to greet them and bows low to the ground. He sees their weariness. The old woman, standing at the flap of the tent, sees their hunger. Quickly a blanket is laid in the shade of the tree, a skin of water is fetched, and a bowl of seeds and berries is prepared to comfort their hearts. Refreshed, the strangers rise and take their leave, the old woman and the old man walking with them to see them safely on their way.

Seeds, berries, and water. The common bowl and cup.

Common too was the land, the *chernozem*, its goodness and fertility, across which the strangers have made their way. Can we settlers accept the image of the good earth and its fruits that sustain us as an icon of sharing, of the hospitality of the old man and woman who welcomed three strangers from the open plain? When we came to this country, exhausted travellers, comfortless in our bewilderment, were we not once those strangers at the threshold of our new home?

WORKS CITED

Baldwin, Edmund William. "Ethnic Stratification in Railway Construction Camps." *Immigration and the Rise of Multiculturalism*, edited by Howard Palmer. Copp Clark, 1975, 97–105.

Barthes, Roland. *Camera Lucida: Reflections on Photography*. Translated by Richard Howard. Vintage Books, 2000.

Berger, John and Jean Mohr. *Another Way of Telling*. Pantheon, 1982.

"Bohunk." *Canadian Oxford Dictionary*. 1st ed. 2002.

Burds, Jeffrey. "Gender and Policing in Soviet West Ukraine 1944–1948." *Cahiers du monde russe, 42, 2001, 279–320. ResearchGate,* www.researchgate.net/publication/30447892_Gender_and_policing_in_Soviet_West_Ukraine_1944-1948. Accessed 5 Jan. 2022.

Chambers, Allan. *On the Line: The Struggles of Alberta's Packing Plant Workers*. AFL & Alberta Labour History Institute, 2012.

"Charworman." *Concise Oxford Dictionary*. 5th ed. 1964.

"Chautauqua." *The Canadian Encyclopedia*, 7 Feb. 2006, www.thecanadian encyclopedia.ca/en/article/chautauqua-emc. Accessed 7 Jan. 2022.

"Colic Emergencies." *KBR Horse Health Information,* www.kbrhorse.net/hea/colic01.html. Accessed 7 Jan. 2022.

Cooley, Dennis. "Estevan." *NeWest Review,* June/July 1989, 22.

"Copy of Treaty No. 6." www.rcaanc-cirnac.gc.ca/eng/1100100028710/158 1292569426 Accessed 7 Jan. 2022.

Daschuk, James. *Clearing the Plains: Disease, Politics of Starvation, and the Loss of Aboriginal Life*. U of Regina P, 2013.

Davies, William. "Friend or Threat." *The London Review of Books,* 43, 12, 17 June 2021, www.lrb.co.uk/the-paper/v43/n12/william-davies/short-cuts. Accessed 5 Jan. 2022.

Dempsey, Hugh. "Alberta's Unemployment Relief 1930–1934." *Alberta History,* Summer 2018. *The Free Library,* www.thefreelibrary.com/ALBERTA%27S+UNEMPLOYMENT+RELIEF+1930-1934.-a0549582585. Accessed 17 Feb. 2022.

Dumitrescu, Irina. "Don't Get Too Comfortable." *The New York Review of Books,* 27 May 2021, 20–22.

Dunets, V.O., et al. *Lvivskyi Istorychnyi Muzei* (Lviv Historical Museum). Kameniar, 1987.

Dunn, Maria, Don Bouzek and Catherine C. Cole. *Packingtown Video Ballad.* Unpublished script obtained from the authors, 2019.

Edwards, Steve. *Photography: A Very Short Introduction.* Oxford UP, 2006.

Enright Anne. "We always speak of women's safety. Let's talk about male violence instead." *The Guardian,* 20 Mar. 2021, www.theguardian.com/books/2021/mar/20/we-always-speak-of-womens-safety-lets-talk-about-male-violence-instead. Accessed 5 Jan. 2022.

Epp, Roger. *We Are All Treaty People: Prairie Essays.* U of Alberta P, 2008.

Erasmus, Peter. *Buffalo Days and Nights.* Fifth House, 1999,

"Extermination of the Jews of Kolomyja and District." Translated by *JewishGen,* 2005. www.jewishgen.org/Yizkor/galicia/gal005.html. Accessed 7 Jan. 2022.

Fodchuk, Roman. *Zhorna: Material Culture of the Ukrainian Pioneers.* U of Calgary P, 2006.

Fowler, H.W. and F.G. Fowler, editors. *Concise Oxford Dictionary.* OUP, 1964.

Garneau, David. "Art Collaborations as Creative Care." YouTube, uploaded by Kule Folk Centre, 27 Apr. 2021. www.youtube.com/watch?v=lqpoq28eUWo. Accessed 16 Jan. 2022.

Gitlin, Todd. "The Missing Music of the Left." *The New York Review of Books,* 28 May 2018. www.nybooks.com/daily/2018/05/28/the-missing-music-of-the-left. Accessed 7 Jan. 2022.

Goodwill, Jean and Norma Sluman. *John Tootoosis: A Biography of a Cree Leader.* Golden Dog, 1982.

"Gothland." Caledonian Maritime Research Trust. www.clydeships.co.uk/view.php?year_built=&builder=&ref=22303&vessel=GOTHLAND. Accessed 7 Jan. 2022.

The Great Utopia: The Russian and Soviet Avant-Garde, 1915–1932. Guggenheim Museum, 1992.

Griffiths, Linda and Maria Campbell. *The Book of Jessica: A Theatrical Transformation.* Coach House P, 1989.

Gross, Jan T. *Revolution from Abroad: The Soviet Conquest of Poland's Western Ukraine and Western Belorussia.* Princeton UP, 2002.

Gross, Philippe L. *The Tao of Photography: Seeing Beyond Seeing.* Ten Speed P, 2001.

Grossman, Vasilii. *A Writer at War: A Soviet Journalist with the Red Army, 1941–1945,* edited and translated by Antony Beevor and Luba Vinogradova. Vintage Books, 2013.

Halfe, Louise Bernice. (Sky Dancer.) *Burning in This Midnight Dream.* Brick Books, 2021.

Hall, Anthony J. "Treaties with Indigenous Peoples in Canada." *The Canadian Encyclopedia,* 11 Sept. 2017. www.thecanadianencyclopedia. ca/en/article/aboriginal-treaties. Accessed 7 Jan. 2022.

Havryshko, Marta. "Illegitimate sexual practices in the OUN underground and UPA in Western Ukraine in the 1940s and 1950s." *The Journal of Power Institutions in Post-Soviet Societies,* 17, 2016. www.journals.openedition.org/pipss/4214. Accessed 7 Jan. 2022.

Highmore, Ben. "Common People review – family history as a new genre of non-fiction." *The Guardian,* 19 Oct. 2014. www.theguardian.com/ books/2014/oct/19/alison-light-common-people-review-geneaology-social-history. Accessed 5 Jan. 2022.

Himka, John-Paul. "The Background to Emigration: Ukrainians of Galicia and Bukovyna." *A Heritage in Transition: Essays in the History of Ukrainians in Canada,* edited by Manoly Lupul, McClelland & Stewart, 1982, 11–31.

———. *Galician Villagers and the Ukrainian National Movement in the Nineteenth Century.* CIUS P, 1988.

Hinther, Rhonda L. *Perogies and Politics: Canada's Ukrainian Left, 1891–1991.* U of Toronto P, 2018.

Hirsch, Marianne. *Family Frames: Photography, Narrative and Postmemory.* Harvard UP, 1997.

Hirsch, Marianne. "Interview with Marianne Hirsch: Author of "The Generation of Postmemory." https://cupblog.org/2012/10/10/ interview-with-marianne-hirsch-author-of-the-generation-of-postmemory/. Accessed 21 May 2022.

Hirsch, Marianne and Leo Spitzer. *"What's Wrong with This Picture?" Truth in Nonfiction: Essays,* edited by David Lazar. U of Iowa P, 2008, 163–188.

Hoerder, Dirk. *Creating Societies: Immigrant Lives in Canada.* McGill-Queens UP, 1999.

Hromadskyi Holos (Ukrainian Voice). Winnipeg, 15 Apr. 1900.

Hryniuk, Stella. *Peasants with Promise: Ukrainians in Southeastern Galicia 1880–1900.* CIUS P, 1991.

Jesuit Forum for Social Faith and Justice. *Listening to Indigenous Voices: A Dialogue Guide on Justice and Right Relationships,* edited by Mark Hathaway, Victoria Blanco, Jayce Chiblow, and Anne-Marie Jackson. Novalis, 2021.

Kharyton, Vasyl. *Pokutiany (People of Pokuttia).* PrutPrynt, 2010.

Kharyton, Vasyl and Mykola Biiovskyi. *Tam, De Dobri Lovy: Narysy Istorii Tulovy (There Where the Hunting is Good: Sketches of the History of Tulova).* PrutPrynt, 2002.

Kishkan, Theresa. "Museum of the Multitude Village." *Blue Portugal and Other Essays.* University of Alberta P, 2022, 157–170.

Kolasky, John. *Prophets & Proletarians: Documents on the History of the Rise and Decline of Ukrainian Communism in Canada.* Canadian Institute of Ukrainian Studies, 1990.

Kostash, Myrna. "A White Man's View of Big Bear." *Saturday Night,* Feb. 1974, 32–33.

——. "Baba Was a Bohunk." *Saturday Night,* Oct. 1976, 34–38.

——. *All of Baba's Children.* 1977. NeWest P, 1992.

——. "Ghosts That Walk the Parkland." *This Country Canada,* Summer 1992, 65–69.

——. *Bloodlines: A Journey into Eastern Europe.* Douglas & McIntyre, 1993.

——. *The Frog Lake Reader.* NeWest P, 2009.

——. "Wandering Spirit." *Let's Keep Doing This: Writings in Honour of Stan Persky,* edited by Thomas Marquard and Brian Fawcett. Dooneys, 2018, 35–65.

Kostash, William. *A Gift to Last.* Unpublished. 1980.

Kostashchuk, Vasyl. *Volodar Dum Selianskykh (Ruler of Peasant Dreams).* Karpaty P, 1968.

Krawchuk, Peter. *The Unforgettable Myroslav Irchan: Pages from a Valiant Life.* Kobzar P, 1998.

———. "Ukrainian Socialists in Canada, 1900–1918." *Socialist History Project.* www.socialisthistory.ca/Docs/History/Krawchuk-OurHistory.htm. Accessed 7 Jan. 2022.

Kubijovyč, Volodymyr. *Ethnic Groups of the South-Western Ukraine (Halyčyna-Galicia) 1.1.1939.* National Statistics of Halyčyna-Galicia. Otto Harrassowitz, 1983.

Laboucan, Amei-lee. "How To Be a Better Treaty Person." *New Trail,* 23 July 2021. www.ualberta.ca/newtrail/how-to/how-to-be-a-better-treaty-person.html. Accessed 7 Jan. 2022.

Livesay, Florence H. R., translator. *Songs of Ukrania: With Ruthenian Poems.* Dent, 1916.

Lowman, Emma Battell and Adam J. Barker. *Settler: Identity and Colonialism in 21st Century Canada.* Fernwood, 2015.

Luciuk, Lubomyr Y. *Their Just War: Images of the Ukrainian Insurgent Army.* Kashtan P, 2007.

Luckyj, George S. N. *Literary Politics in the Soviet Ukraine, 1917–1934.* Rev. ed. Duke UP, 1990.

MacGregor, J. G. *Vilni Zemli: Free Lands; The Ukrainian Settlement of Alberta.* McClelland & Stewart, 1969.

"Maksym Kryvonis." *Wikipedia,* 27 Dec. 2020. www.en.wikipedia.org/wiki/Maksym_Kryvonis#Khmelnytsky_Uprising. Accessed 9 Jan. 2022.

Malone, Molly and Libby Chisholm. "Indigenous Territory." *The Canadian Encyclopedia,* 5 July 2016, www.thecanadianencyclopedia.ca/en/article/indigenous-territory. Accessed 7 Jan. 2022.

Martynowych, Orest. *Ukrainians in Canada: The Formative Years 1891–1924.* CIUS P, 1991.

McCue, Harvey. "Reserves." *The Canadian Encyclopedia,* 12 July 2018. www.thecanadianencyclopedia.ca/en/article/aboriginal-reserves. Accessed 7 Jan. 2022.

McIlwraith Naomi. *kiyâm.* AU P, 2012.

McKay, Ian. *Reasoning Otherwise: Leftists and the People's Enlightenment in Canada, 1890–1920.* Between the Lines, 2008.

Melnycky, Peter. *A Veritable Canaan: Alberta's Victoria Settlement.* Friends of Fort Victoria Historical Society, 1997.

Merrett, Kathryn Chase. *A History of the Edmonton City Market, 1900–2000: Urban Values and Urban Culture.* U of Calgary P, 2001.

Morris, Alexander. *The Treaties of Canada with the Indians of Manitoba and the North-West Territories Including the Negotiations on Which They Were Based.* Fifth House, 1991.

Morris, Errol. *Believing is Seeing: Observations on the Mysteries of Photography.* Penguin, 2011.

Morris, Wright. "In Our Image." *The Photography Reader,* edited by Liz Wells. Routledge, 2003, 67–75.

Moure, Erìn. "Tuteshni." *Unbound: Ukrainian Canadians Writing Home,* edited by Lisa Grekul and Lindy Ledohowski. U of Toronto P, 2016, 86–99.

Mucz, Michael. *Baba's Kitchen Medicines: Folk Remedies of Ukrainian Settlers in Western Canada.* U of Alberta P, 2012.

"The North-West Rebellion. (North-West Resistance)." *Library and Archives Canada Blog,* 18 Mar. 2015. www.thediscoverblog.com/2015/03/18/the-north-west-rebellion-north-west-resistance. Accessed 7 Jan. 2022.

"Notes Regarding Revolutionary Organizations and Agitators In Canada." Royal Canadian Mounted Police Headquarters. No. 334, Weekly Summary. Ottawa, 9 Sep. 1926. www.journals.lib.unb.ca. Accessed 7 Jan. 2022.

Overy, Richard. *Russia's War: A History of the Soviet War Effort: 1941–1945.* Penguin, 1997.

"Peasant strikes in Galicia and Bukovyna." *Internet Encyclopedia of Ukraine,* 1993. www.encyclopediaofukraine.com/display.asp?link path=pages% 5CP%5CE%5CPeasantstrikesinGaliciaandBukovyna. htm. Accessed 17 Feb. 2022.

Petryshyn, Jaroslav. *Peasants in the Promised Land: Canada and the Ukrainians 1891–1914.* James Lorimer & Co, 1985.

Potrebenko, Helen. *No Streets of Gold: A Social History of Ukrainians in Alberta.* New Star Books, 1977.

Ray, Arthur J., Jim Miller and Frank Tough. *Bounty and Benevolence: A History of Saskatchewan Treaties.* McGill-Queens UP, 2000.

Regan Paulette. *Unsettling the Settler Within: Indian Residential Schools, Truth Telling, and Reconciliation in Canada.* UBC P, 2011.

Rieder, Ross. "Industrial Workers of the World (IWW)." *History Link,* 12 Aug. 1999, www.historylink.org/File/2016. Accessed 8 Jan. 2022.

Roberts, Barbara. "Shovelling Out the 'Mutinous:' Political Deportation from Canada Before 1936." *Labour / Le Travail,* 18, 1986. 77–110. www.lltjournal.ca/index.php/llt/issue/view/298. Accessed 7 Jan. 2022.

Sangster, Joan. "Robitnytsia, Ukrainian Communists, and the 'Porcupinism' Debate: Reassessing Ethnicity, Gender, and Class in Early Canadian Communism, 1922–1930." *Labour / Le Travail,* 50, 2005, 51–89. www.lltjournal.ca/index.php/llt/article/download/5381/6250/0. Accessed 7 Jan. 2022.

Schulze, D. "The Industrial Workers of the World and the Unemployed in Edmonton and Calgary in the Depression of 1913–1915." *Labour / Le Travail,* 25, 1990, 47–75. www.lltjournal.ca/index.php/llt/article/view/4756. Accessed 7 Jan. 2022.

Seager, Allen. "Socialists and Workers: The Western Canadian Coal Miners, 1900–21." *Labour / Le Travail,* 16, 1985, 23–59. www.lltjournal.ca/index.php/llt/article/view/2471. Accessed 7 Jan. 2022.

———."Revolutionary industrial unionism." *The Canadian Encyclopedia,* 14 Dec. 2013. www.thecanadianencyclopedia.ca/en/article/revolutionary-industrial-unionism. Accessed 8 Jan. 2022.

Sekula, Allan. "Photography between Labour and Capital." *The Photography Reader,* edited by Liz Wells. Routledge, 2003, 443–451.

Shevchenko, Taras. *Kobzar.* Dnipro, 1982.

Sifton, Sir Clifford. "Only Farmers Need Apply." *Immigration and the Rise of Multiculturalism,* edited by Howard Palmer. Copp Clark, 1975, 34–37.

Sileika, Antanas. *Underground: A Novel.* Thomas Allen, 2011.

"Snyatyn (Sniatyn): A Jewish shtetl from the mid 1500s through the mid 1940s." *JewishGen.* www.kehilalinks.jewishgen.org/sniatyn/. Accessed 16 Jan. 2022.

Snyder, Timothy. *Bloodlands: Europe between Hitler and Stalin.* Basic Books, 2010.

Subtelny, Orest. *Ukraine: A History.* U of Toronto P, 1988.

Svarich, Peter. *Memoirs 1877–1904.* Translated by William Kostash. Ukrainian Pioneers' Association of Alberta and the Huculak Chair of Ukrainian Culture and Ethnography, 1999.

———. "Canada best country in the world." *Vegreville Observer,* 22 Nov. 1922, 10.

Swyripa, Frances. "Ukrainian Edmonton: Ethnicity, Space, and Identity in a Canadian Cityscape." *Tentorium Honorum: Essays Presented to Frank E. Sysyn on His Sixtieth Birthday,* edited by Olga A Andriewsky, et al. CIUS P, 2010, 429–440.

Szarkowski, John. "Introduction to the Photographer's Eye." *The Photography Reader,* edited by Liz Wells. Routledge, 2003, 97–103.

Thompson, John Herd and Allen Seager. "Workers, Growers and Monopolists: The 'Labour Problem' in the Alberta Beet Sugar Industry during the 1930s." *Labour / Le Travail*, 3, 1978, 153–174.

"Ukrainian Canadians." *Wikipedia*, 12 Feb. 2022. www.en.wikipedia.org/wiki/Ukrainian_Canadians#cite_ref-10. Accessed 17 Feb. 2022.

"Ukrainian Insurgent Army." *Wikipedia*, 5 Jan. 2022. www.en.wikipedia.org/wiki/Ukrainian_Insurgent_Army. Accessed 12 Jan. 2022.

The Ukrainian Pioneers in Alberta, Canada. Ukrainian Pioneers Association, 1970.

United States Holocaust Memorial Museum. "Einsatzgruppen and Other SS and Police Units in the Soviet Union." *Holocaust Encyclopedia*. www.encyclopedia.ushmm.org/content/en/article/einsatzgruppen-and-other-ss-and-police-units-in-the-soviet-union. Accessed 17 Feb. 2022.

Van Tighem, Kevin. "Treaty People, Treaty Place." *Alberta Views,* May 2021, 53.

Voropay. Oleksa, "Pysanka Legends." *Pysanka*. www.pysanky.info/Pysanka_Legends/Legends_Home.html. Accessed 16 Jan. 2022.

Vyrostok, Yuri. "Yuri Vyrostok tells the story of his immigration to Canada and first experiences in a new country." *Taras Shevchenko Museum*. www.communitystories.ca/v1/pm_v2.php?id=story_line&lg=English&fl=0&ex=00000464&sl=5509. Accessed 7 Jan. 2022.

Wagner, Anne. "At Tate Britain: Salt and Silver." *London Review of Books*, 37, 10, 21 May 2015. www.lrb.co.uk/the-paper/v37/n10/anne-wagner/at-tate-britain. Accessed 7 Jan. 2022.

Wasilewska, Wanda. *Rainbow*. Translated by Edith Bone. Hutchinson and Co., 1944.

Weisbord, Merrily. *The Strangest Dream: Canadian Communists, the Spy Trials and the Cold War*. Lester, Orpen and Dennys, 1983.

Wheeler, Anne and Lorna Rasmussen. *Great Grand Mother*. National Film Board, 1975. www.nfb.ca/film/great_grand_mother. Accessed 7 Jan. 2022.

Wolfe, Morris. "Tim Buck, Too." *The Canadian Forum*, Dec. 1991. www.grubstreetbooks.ca/essays/timbuck.html. Accessed 7 Jan. 2022.

Woodsworth, J.S. "Immigrant Churches." *Immigration and the Rise of Multiculturalism*, edited by Howard Palmer. Copp Clark, 1975, 170–176.

———. *Strangers Within Our Gates*. Toronto, UTP, 1972.

ACKNOWLEDGEMENTS

The discovery of the photograph of Stepan Fedorovych Kostash-chuk in Lubomyr Luciuk's book, *Their Just War*, was the moment when the germ of an idea for this book was planted. I was already familiar with the story on my mother's side of Yuri Kosovan, who had been "disappeared" in Soviet Ukraine, and so the germ that was planted was of the story of how two family lines, on opposing sides of fratricidal conflict in Ukraine, merged when my parents married in Canada in 1939. It was the consideration of that merger that displaced the original idea with that of the chronicle that is *Ghosts in a Photograph.*

There is always another draft and so there are many people on whom I relied and turned to as I wrestled with imperfect recall and ambiguous memorabilia, or with structure and tone and point of view (those literary bedevillments), or questions of historical or archival fact, or where to look for a specific datum.

My first readers were, naturally enough, close members of my family, patient and encouraging without surcease, my sister Janice Kostash and her husband John Hannigan, and my cousins Elizabeth Kostash and Verna Semotuk. The deeper I burrowed into my grandparents' prehistories in Galicia, the more I relied on the recollections (and their hospitality in Zabolotiv) of my second cousins in Ukraine, Petro and Maria Kosovan. For the opportunity in 2013 to visit the ancestral village, Tulova, I thank Vince Rees of Cobblestone Freeway Tours.

Crucial to the evolution of first drafts was the critical reading by writer friends George Melnyk and Eve Zaremba, whose blunt feedback rescued my project from certain embarrassment had it been published.

For their scholarly expertise that I called on as questions arose, especially related to the fraught history of western Ukraine, I am grateful to Serge Cipko, John-Paul Himka, Iaroslav Kovalchuk, Lubomyr Luciuk, the late Andrij Makuch, David Marples, Orest Martynowych, Andriy Nahachewsky, Peter Potichnyj, Frank Sysyn, and Oksana Vynnyk.

Thanks to Peter Melnycky for alerting me to the fact that the Edmonton Public Library held a copy of *Their Just War* and to the late Bernard Bloom for showing me how to "read" a photograph. For their assistance in translating archival documents and family letters I thank Sergei Chikalov, Serge Havrylov, and Tom Szostek. For her willingness to walk me through some very basic instruction in how the Cree language forms words, I am grateful to Naomi McIlwraith.

Without the gift of hospitality alongside silence and a shared life of worship offered me by Guestmaster Fr Demetrius Wasylyniuk OSB of the Abbey of St. Peter's in Muenster, SK, and by Fr Glenn Zimmer OMI and the late Sr Margaret Dick SNJM, hosts of the Qu'Appelle Valley House of Prayer, I would have gone mad somewhere between drafts. For their fellowship around their dinner table and among mutual friends, Jan Stoody and Jim Harding of Ft Qu'Appelle. Likewise, without the bliss of uninterrupted time, every March for a decade, while house-sitting in Qualicum Beach, BC, the home of Elizabeth Smythe and Jay Smith, deeper madness.

By the same token, I am grateful, for their camaraderie and exuberant conversation about our respective literary and artistic projects: the late Erna Paris of Toronto for decades of what became an indissoluble solidarity, long-time compañera of nonfiction Susan

Crean of Toronto, the late, indomitable, Brian Fawcett of Toronto, Laurie Graham of Peterborough Ontario, David Carpenter and Honor Kever of Saskatoon, Tom Radford of Edmonton, Caterina Edwards of Edmonton, and Kathryn and Jim Woodward of Vancouver. For their deep and abiding friendship and faith in my determination to get this book done, I am indebted to Marko and Olya Pavlyshyn of Melbourne, Australia, to Eugenia Sojka of Leśna, Poland, and to Irene Zabytko of Apopka, Florida.

As a lifelong Edmontonian, I am blessed with a circle of friends who cheer me on: Chrystia Chomiak, Jean Crozier, Liz Grieve, Alice Major, Sheila Pratt, Eva Radford, Jacqueline Tait, Lida Somchynsky, Audrey Whitson, and that former Edmontonian now in Calgary, Julia Berry Melnyk, and former Edmontonians, Miki Andrejevic and Nena Jocic of St. Ives, BC, and Nancy Mattson of London, UK.

Also cheering me on from Vancouver were cousin Bo Fodchuk and second cousin Lisa Fodchuk Gardner, with thanks for generous hospitality of Shiella Fodchuk and Mike Arthur.

Thanks to Maryna Chernyavska, Larisa Hayduk, Leah Hrycun, Kalyna Somchynsky, and Chelsea Vowel, AKA The Sistahs, who have helped me deepen and complicate my thinking about Indigenous and Ukrainian Canadian relations.

Perpetual thankfulness for the friendship of Smaro Kamboureli, and the gifts of collaboration with her as editor and co-reader nonpareil.

Finally, I owe more than I can say to the Board of NeWest Press and its staff, Matt Bowes and Claire Kelly, for having kept *All of Baba's Children* in print all these years and for offering me a contract for *Ghosts in a Photograph*.

I was supported in the writing of this book by a grant from the Canada Council for the Arts.

Portions of *Ghosts in a Photograph: A Chronicle* have appeared in various versions in *18 Bridges, Prairie Fire*, ACUA *Vitae, Alberta Views*, ALHI (Alberta Labour History Institute) online, *Let's Keep Doing This: Writings in Honour of Stan Persky*, and *Don't Tell: What Families Hide* (forthcoming).

Born and raised in Edmonton, Myrna Kostash is the author of the classic *All of Baba's Children, No Kidding: Inside the World of Teenage Girls*, winner of the Alberta Culture and Writers' Guild of Alberta prize for Best Non-Fiction, and *Prodigal Daughter: A Journey to Byzantium*, which received the 2010 City of Edmonton Book Prize, the Writers' Guild of Alberta Wilfred Eggleston Award for Best Nonfiction, and was shortlisted for the 2011 Runcimann Award (UK). Her other titles include *The Doomed Bridegroom: A Memoir, Bloodlines: A Journey into Eastern Europe*, and her edited collections *Reading the River: A Traveller's Companion to the North Saskatchewan River, The Frog Lake Reader*, and *The Seven Oaks Reader*. Kostash, who served as Chair of The Writers' Union of Canada, has published widely in numerous magazines and lectured across Canada and Europe. In 2010, she was awarded the Writers Trust Matt Cohen Award for a Life of Writing.